WELSH COMMUNITIES

NEW ETHNOGRAPHIC PERSPECTIVES

WELSH COMMUNITIES

NEW ETHNOGRAPHIC PERSPECTIVES

Edited by
Charlotte Aull Davies
Stephanie Jones

*Published on behalf of the Social Science Committee of
the Board of Celtic Studies of the University of Wales*

UNIVERSITY OF WALES PRESS
CARDIFF
2003

British Library Cataloguing-in-Publication Data.
A catalogue record for this book is available from the British Library.

ISBN 0–7083–1782–0

Cover image: *Llwch Maesgwyn* (detail) by Tim Davies
Cover design by Andy Dark
Typeset by Mark Heslington
Printed in Great Britain by Dinefwr Press, Llandybïe

Dedicated to the memory of
Charles M. Aull and
Dorothy E. Jones

Contents

Foreword

Ronald Frankenberg

'Suddenly England, bourgeois England, wasn't my point of reference
any more. I was a Welsh European, and both levels felt different.'
                    (Raymond Williams in an interview in 1979, speaking of
                    the time after he had, for the first time, joined and worked
                    with a group of other Welsh intellectuals)*

'Your book impressed me very much, Dr Price. I believe I wrote and
told you.'
. . .
'It took a long time, I expect?'
'Yes, very long. I keep being reminded it's the only thing I've done.'
'It took a long time because it had to be lived.'
                    (From Raymond Williams's 1979 novel *The Fight for Manod*)*

Anthropology becomes us

When I went to Wales as a researcher in 1953, I lived on a tiny farm,
Talygarth Ucha(f) outside Glyn Ceiriog, with the Hugheses, a Welsh-
speaking family, accustomed, even in those days, to entertaining
paying guests in the summer. They had been recommended by the
Church in Wales vicar, a farmer himself at heart but forced by his
father's family pride to enter the church. He was happiest at the
annual sheepdog trials and cheering on the village soccer team.
(Rugby, *pace* Stephanie Jones, was not always, everywhere, the Welsh
National Game!) The farmer's son, Gwyn, just in his teens, was at
Llangollen Grammar School where he, reluctantly, studied in English.
His mother asked me to help him with the language, literature and
especially poetry and he himself volunteered to reciprocate with gifts

*Cited in J. P. Ward, *Raymond Williams*, Writers of Wales series (Cardiff: University
of Wales Press, 1981)

of fresh rabbit, which he shot and skinned for me, immediately after each lesson. After a week or two, we studied T. S. Eliot's *Old Possum's Book of Practical Cats*, not yet made famous by Andrew Lloyd Webber, and he found it hilariously funny. Our shared laughter would have rocked the house had it been less solidly built and it was to prove the end of Gwyn's lessons and my rabbit pies. Gwyn's mother felt that study should be a more serious occupation. As agreed, once summer came with its paying guests not only able and willing to pay more but also regular customers of several years' standing, my wife and I moved to a builder's bungalow just on the edge of the village to 'do' for ourselves in shared kitchen and bathroom. The son of the house was doing his Ph.D. in Physics at Aberystwyth and away from home; the grammar-school daughter did not occupy a lot of space. The Evans family, Derlwyn, were pillars of the community and of the Closed Baptist majority, the wife and daughter, as in most families, more openly committed than the males. They were also related to at least half the villagers and became staunch friends and allies, to the extent that Mrs Evans, after my book *Village on the Border* was published in 1957, said on screen that every word was true. The 'German' gentleman/spy (as some thought I was) who was staying with the Evanses, Derlwyn, had by then been threatened with a libel action by the county councillor, attacked by the *Liverpool Daily Post*, called the new Caradoc Evans, and abridged – by Harry Green – and serialized over a fortnight in the *Western Mail*. The book was the subject of one of Granada TV's very first outside broadcasts (the presenter was Welsh in origin but lived in Manchester and was not able to speak the language). By this time I was living in Pontrhydyfen, near Aberavon, studying the impact of the then new steelworks on village life and teaching 'The unimportance of class' to Robin Huws-Jones's UN Social Workers' course at Swansea. Professor Brynley Thomas, at University College, Cardiff (by which I was formally employed), who, like Richard Burton, was born in Pontrhydyfen, wrote to the *Western Mail* to protest (unsurprisingly to me) that my account was nothing like Pontrhydyfen but merely an outsider's view.

This is just a partial account of my standard anthropological transition, from an apprentice who is educated by talking *about* texts; to one who is acknowledged in the Craft which is to translate, usually but not now always embodied, talk *into* texts of his or her own; and finally to a supposed Master or even Dame Craftsperson, fully incorporated into the Guild, who is empowered as I am now to produce metatexts – reviews, advice to publish or to deny publication and ultimately prefaces, forewords and dust-wrapper quotes. *Village on the Border*, which remained in print into the twenty-first century, gave me a doctorate, the right to call full professors by their given names, to be referred to orally as Doctor and in print just by my surname and the year. It gave me a meal ticket and, with a second study in south Wales and political activity, credentials to be invited to write a Penguin book, *Communities in Britain* (which sold at least fifty times as many copies as did *Village on the Border*), and to work for the South Wales Area of the National Union of Mineworkers, notwithstanding that some of their officials, occasionally themselves with Masters degrees and later Honorary Doctorates, felt with some justice that up to that time degreed people had done little for the working class.

Like Judith Okely's book on Roma my book was described as like a novel but, in my case, Gluckman intended that as praise; her reviewer intended it to be dismissive. Good novels, like good anthropological texts whether collections like this or single-author works, help us to understand society. I do not believe it possible for human behaviour in society ever to be fully and definitively explained by writers of either. Gluckman's Zulu Bridge article, an example of self-conscious Anthropology at Home, was also an intervention into the politics of both South African and anthropological identity. It was not, however, this aspect of the work which tempted me across the borders of clinical natural science into anthropology. This was rather because his demonstration of unity in and through diversity helped to lay the foundations of understanding society in general by analysing what it meant to be (and not to be) a Zulu in January 1938; in a similar way, James Joyce's *Ulysses* (and even his earlier and later books) allowed the reader to explore the imagined but nevertheless real reality of being Irish in Dublin in June 1906. Novels, however steeped they are in the cultural values and taboos of the invisible college of litterateurs, are supposed to be produced single-handedly. Novelists are not obliged to, they are even discouraged from, revealing the way they arrive at their effects and conclusions. Newspaper critics have been invented to do that for them in the weeks after publication, and literary academics to do so years or centuries after the event. (The novels of Raymond Williams are partial exceptions to both these generalizations and some literary critics for this reason dismiss him as a mere sociologist.)

Of my two main teachers on Welsh life in Glyn Ceiriog in 1952/3, Mrs Hughes, Talygarth, literally *had* no time for fiction, she worked from dawn to dusk on the pragmatics of small-farm life. Mrs Evans, Derlwyn, would *give* no time to fiction which she regarded as dangerous lies; each week she carefully removed or covered over the stories in *Woman* and *Women's Own* in order equally assiduously but critically to read the non-fiction which had at least a chance of being real and true. Her praise of my book as being true gave me as much or more pleasure than Gluckman's literary praise, although I recognized that about half the village who either did not acknowledge, or who did not in fact have, a kin relationship with her, felt otherwise. The most acceptable, because most stimulating, anthropologists, like those who wrote and edited this book, write in some sense as a collective from which they derive their strength and their authority. The very diversity – of their field sites, their dramatis personae, their topics and, especially, their individual approaches and personal life-histories – marks their authenticity for those who read them. They present, as the introduction points out, an investment for the future, the living and still growing legacy of a Welsh School, centred on, but not overwhelmed by, the colleges of the University of Wales and, at different times, Aberystwyth and Swansea within it. I like to feel, perhaps presumptuously, that my teaching and researching in Wales helped me to make at least as perceptible a contribution to this tradition as did many temporarily resident scholars, like other 1950s staff members including the classicist, Ben Farrington, and the Africanist, Paul Baxter, and those others over the years until the present day, who by teaching about social life in general, provide an additional cosmopolitan context of understanding for those who choose primarily, and to all our benefit, to focus on their own specifically Welsh milieu.

The people and the book

Any book has the potential to empower not only its writers but also its readers. There was the following *Goon Show* exchange on radio:

> 'There's a letter for you, Min!'
> 'What does it say?'
> 'It doesn't say anything, Min; you have to read it!'

My foreword must not be an attempt to say what the book says since that would be doubly redundant. It merely, as the envelope does for a letter, suggests why it needs to be read and not only by those with a specialist interest in Wales and the study of community. As a teacher of anthropology and sociology, which also implies conducting and marking examinations, I was not obliged to explain to students why I thought they should read something, although as a good, but over-didactic, teacher I often did just that. I could have just put it on the reading list and left the examination timetable and syllabus to do the rest. Unlike me, the students were often exhorted to give reasons why they chose to read it as I have to do here! As a teacher I had an old-fashioned coercive power, from which a more Foucauldian subjective resistance sometimes arose and was accepted. (In Keele, at one stage we, staff and students, including some who later pursued their careers in Swansea, even dispensed with a formal syllabus and allowed small groups of students to devise their own. We also co-marked essays with the writers themselves.) Here and now, with subjectivities already born, to adapt Marx's words, those whom one seeks to persuade are in control of the situation.

My first real teacher in anthropology was Max Gluckman and, often, after he had moved from guiding the research of colleagues to teaching beginners, he told them, with kind intentions, what books they need not read. Eventually I realized that he himself must proba-bly have read them to be so firm in not commending them to us, and that we needed to read the 'forbidden' to understand why he was approving of the texts he did set. To understand an assertion you need to identify what it is simultaneously denying. This was rein-forced for me at one point, while I was living in Wales, when the victory of a German choir singing in their own language was unsuc-cessfully challenged at an eisteddfodd by the Welsh runners-up, on the grounds that they should have sung in Welsh. The appeal committee argued that the aim of the so-called all-Welsh rule was intended to encourage (compel?) Welsh choirs entering to sing in the Welsh language and to discourage (prohibit?) mass entries by choirs singing in English; the German choir's performance threatened neither of these aims. The loss of their appeal reinforced both aims by revealing the underlying rationality of the rule. An academic discipline is defined by the questions it does not choose to ask, in addition to those that it does. Neither qualitative nor quantitative methodology is mandatory for the study of social process; what is needed, but not necessarily from the outset, is to define questions. When the questions are defined, the methods and second-level theory will define themselves. The rare wisdom of the editors of this book partly consists in their recognition that encouraging a number of scholars to show how Welshness and commonality of interest is understood does not, in itself, imply dragooning them all into asking the same questions in the same way in defiance of the fact that they are doing it at different places and times in their own lives and in the lives of those they are studying. I have always defined community as an abbreviated form of community of interest, and many chapters of this book recognize that shared interest is not limited to, or confined within, traditional views of locality (most notably by Sue Philpin, John Hutson, Janice Williams and Jeremy Segrott).

Class, status and network and the greatest of these is network?

The relationship between network and local group, which the second part of the book explores, hinges on this. What all the authors of both parts have in common is, first, the determination to engage over a period of time with people in action – people seeking both to create and to understand themselves and almost always to help others to understand them too. The book makes clear that neither Welshness nor community are essentialized and fixed entities, things. They are both not merely processes but sets of interacting processes. The persons and the situations may spring from the same sources and share some cultural similarities but they are all simultaneously both unique and shared. Over the past fifty years social anthropologists, and many sociologists, have learned to live without fixed boundaries but rather, as Goffman suggested with semi-permeable membranes, which to some extent, separate ill-defined and shifting difference and diversity, contradiction and irony. They have come, especially, to recognize that it is precisely from these that agreement and unity are constructed. It is not just the empirical content of each separate article in the book that brings this home. The diverse internal organization of each one and the organization of the book as a whole lead the reader to see how it transcends its specific subject matter and teaches lessons of more universal method and understanding. Furthermore, the questions asked engender in the reader verificatory and intellectual questions of their own, which the presentation of the articles side-by-side in one volume facilitates. They can exchange theoretical approaches between articles – Bourdieu in one, Foucault in another, for example – and ask themselves and the absent authors through their texts, which sorts of emphasis on which different areas of experience would be changed and whether for better, for worse or just different. In Manchester in the early 1950s the Masters course was, in fact, based on such a revisiting of masterworks and the analysis of its implications.

The inevitability of serendipity

The Russian philosophical writer and political activist, Plekhanov memorably defined an accident as the intersection of two or more chains of inevitability. The rules of mechanics determine that a car driven in a particular way at a particular place would fall on to a railway line; the rules of mass that a train that hit a car would be derailed; the design of the train that if it was derailed people would be injured. An unpredictable accident arose from these chains of inevitability. Many social scientists, wedded to a positivist misunderstanding of science, mistrust the understanding power of anthropologists because they cannot say with precision, and in advance, what specific events they are going to study. (Some natural scientists also make this mistake; compare Sir Alexander Fleming's failure to recognize the significance of his laboratory accident with Marie Curie's immediate reaction to hers.)

Stephanie Jones did not know that Blaengwyn was going to win the championship or that she would be able to overcome gender limits in the club's coach seating-plan; Martin O'Neill was, by chance, a paramedic before he was an anthropologist and did not know he would have to help a beaten-up gay man, the victim of family discord, in his urban neighbourhood. Dé Murphy did not know a property company was going to upset her living plan. Emma James did not know that incomers would engage in redecorating the 'local' and destroying its 'normalized' plain brown wallpaper. Each of them was able to apply Plekhanov in reverse. They discovered and analysed the chains of cultural inevitability that lay behind the specific accidentals of their lives as observers. We are entitled to hypothesize, from long experience, that other accidents which might have happened, would have led them along similar lines, because

they had trained themselves not to take any process of social reproduction for granted.

Community: love-in or fall-out

The findings of the authors on whether communities in Wales or elsewhere are cosy or conflictual may seem at first sight paradoxical,
even inconsistent with either a draw or a one- or two-goal lead in
favour of the romantic cosy against the cynically oppositional. The
book as a whole demonstrates this to be a false dichotomy.
Morriston, Swansea, in its golden years, was united by its love of
singing but torn asunder by the *cythraul canu* (lit. 'the devil of
singing', i.e. extreme rivalry in singing competitions) to which this
love gave rise. There is more loyalty and there are more murders
within families than in other social categories. Indifference, unshared
values and neutral silence are the enemies of community. Love,
hatred and gossip are its raw material.

Et in Arcadia, Ego?

In my brief period as a Welsh celebrity in the late 1950s and early
1960s, I was asked, on the BBC's *Welsh Woman's Hour*, from which
community I myself came; I answered that I did not come from a
community at all but from Cricklewood. Zadie Smith's recent novel
White Teeth explores, in its first few pages, the nature of its multicultural community as it was 'At 0627 hours on 1 January 1975' – an
even more precise temporality than even James Joyce or Max
Gluckman could achieve. She soon exhausts even Cricklewood's
cosmopolitan complexity and moves on to Willesden and other
districts. North, South, East and West. Reading this alongside Jeremy
Segrott's article, I verbalized for the first time how the chain of
inevitabilities preceding the accident of my arriving in Wales as a
researcher developed. For Cricklewood was a centre of the creation
of the Welsh dairy-industry in London and, as a baby in 1929/30
before I could speak any language at all, each day dawned for me
with the sound of milk churns being rolled along the alley behind the
shops on Cricklewood Broadway and the loud cries of 'Megan' being
called to count them off, in what was later described to me as Welsh,
into the back of Long Marston dairy. As a toddler I was taken to
watch bottles being filled automatically in the Express Dairy Plant
near the Welsh Harp reservoir in Cricklewood Lane. I thought the
reservoir, named for its shape, was called after the Welsh dairymen,

not realizing that the mass production was going to spell their eventual demise. In the 1940s I saw *The Corn is Green* at the Queen's cinema and attacked my family for not caring about the conditions of the south Wales miners and wrote to the Minister of Labour Ernest Bevin, volunteering to do my National Service in the mines. He wisely turned me down and I ended up not doing it at all. I saw *The Proud Valley* and met Paul Robeson first in Stepney Baths. Later, I encountered him again when I was well established as education officer of the SWMF/NUM South Wales Area. My Cambridge college awarded closed Rhondda Scholarships in Medicine and Law, and I was knocked flat in my first week for saying I liked Welshmen because they spoke quaintly. (The only other time I have been knocked out as an adult was by a Welsh miner in Brussels for my middle-class presumption, six months before, in referring to him in class by an obscene appellation, acceptable only from fellow miners. My successful intention had been to gain silence, but I realized immediately I had gone too far. Learning when and when not to use or accept gendered obscenity is one of the major skills of fieldwork, as others hint in this book.) As a member of the Socialist and Labour Clubs in college and university I had many Welsh friends. I studied the *Gododdin* of Aneirin with an archaeologist friend and, later, my first academic publication appeared (translated into Welsh) in *Y Genhinen* and was a comparison of Welsh and Tutsi heroic verse. I initially married a woman from Wales, and learned Welsh ways from her teacher-mother, who lived and taught in a tiny hamlet in Breconshire, and from her aunt, headmistress of a south Wales grammar school, both born in Brynmawr (subject of one of the first locality studies in Wales by Hilda Jennings) to a father whose own father had migrated from Dorset, first building, and then working on, the railway and, after sustaining an industrial accident, becoming a shopkeeper.

Is that the verdict of you all?

Like the contributors to this volume, I did not come to Wales in the same way that pioneer anthropologists approached the highlands of New Guinea, as what Nigel Barley has called 'the innocent anthropologist'. This enabled me, as it enabled them, to adopt the role of an observing 'stranger within the gates', armed with a sympathetic, basic but superficial, foreknowledge of what to expect. Perhaps we need a new category of ethnographer, added to those enumerated in the introduction, to describe those similar to us – neither innocent nor touched with (colonialist) guilt, we and our currency are 'not proven'. A complex metonym which is at once analogous in the eyes of other anthropological scholars of an older school with those subject to Scottish judicial indecision and to those (like courtly squires and damsels?) engaged in a quest in which we are helped by others to understand ourselves while we help them in turn. It is 'proved' through and by a research process, shared by its subjects in both active and passive senses, and by the published reports in which their common experience of changing identities and self-awareness are finally minted for wider circulation.

Acknowledgements

The editors would like to thank the Social Science Committee of the University of Wales Board of Celtic Studies for supporting the publication of this book, along with the Committee's anonymous readers for their many helpful comments and suggestions to improve both individual chapters and the volume's overall cohesion. We are also grateful to Ruth Dennis-Jones of the University of Wales Press, whose editorial efficiency has kept us on track throughout the publication process.

All the contributors to this volume have shown considerable patience with our requests for additions and amendments over quite a lengthy journey to final publication, while managing to maintain their enthusiasm and commitment to the project, and for this we are most appreciative. Special thanks go to Ronnie Frankenberg, to whom we all owe so much for his seminal work on community studies and reflexive ethnography, and who has also kindly provided us with an insightful and entertaining Foreword.

We are also especially grateful to Welsh artist Tim Davies, who generously gave permission to reproduce a detail of his work *Llwch Maesgwyn* for the cover. The work captures for us the fragmentary, yet palpable nature of Welsh communities, inspired as it was by a visit to an open-cast site in a former mining village in south Wales.

Members of Anthropoleg Cymru / Anthropology Wales provided a stimulating audience for many of the chapters which were presented in an embryonic stage to the society's annual conferences. The contributions have benefited from the constructive discussion and questions raised during these events, and we are grateful for the opportunities they provided to encourage and advance anthropological studies of Welsh society and culture.

Charlotte Aull Davies
Stephanie Jones

List of contributors

Charlotte Aull Davies is Senior Lecturer in Sociology and Anthropology in the School of Social Sciences and International Development, University of Wales Swansea. She has conducted research in the areas of ethnic nationalism, gender and national identities, learning disabilities and community care, minority languages and equal opportunities. She is currently contributing to a major restudy of the classic 1960s research on families, households and community in Swansea (Rosser and Harris, *Family and Social Change*, 1962).

John Hutson was Lecturer in Social Anthropology at the University of Wales Swansea. He has conducted research on farming households and tourism in France and west Wales. He is now retired and lives on Gower.

Emma James completed her Ph.D. on the effects of in-migration in Welsh rural communities at the University of Wales Swansea in 1998. Since then, as Research Officer in the Sociology Department at Swansea, she has been involved in a project investigating the gender dimensions of job insecurity, and is now Research Fellow in the National Centre for Public Policy, University of Wales Swansea.

Stephanie Jones, since completing her Ph.D. at the University of Wales Swansea, has worked as a Research Fellow at the University of Wales College of Medicine and as an Associate Lecturer at the Open University. She also teaches on the M.Sc. in Social Research at Swansea, and her own research interests include gender, disability and participatory research.

Dé Murphy completed an M.Sc. in Social Research Methods at the University of Wales, Cardiff and has worked as a researcher on various projects, ranging from care for stroke patients to mining communities and supported employment for people with learning difficulties. She is currently practising as a homeopath but retains a research interest in women's health.

Martin O'Neill carried out research on the ambulance service in Wales, towards his Ph.D. at the University of Wales Swansea. Since then, he has worked in the School of Social Sciences at the University of Wales, Cardiff where he has conducted ethnographic research in various communities mainly in the south Wales area.

Susan Philpin is Senior Lecturer in the School of Health Science, University of Wales Swansea. Her research interests include anthropological approaches to health, illness and health-care relationships. Currently she is using ethnographic research to explore the meaning and purpose of nursing rituals.

Jeremy Segrott is currently a Senior Research Assistant in the Department of Geography, University of Wales Swansea. He completed his Ph.D. on London Welsh life in 2001. His main research interests include the connections between migration and identity, and the geographies of health (with particular reference to complementary medicine).

Janice Williams completed her doctorate at the University of Sussex and has worked in television and the health service. She has conducted anthropological research in Israel and in Wales and has published work on ethnic identity, religion and food. Between 1994 and 1996, she was a Research Associate at Goldsmiths' College on the 'Concepts of Healthy Eating' Project, and later was a Tutor at the University of Wales Swansea, where she is currently an Honorary Lecturer in the School of Social Sciences and International Development.

1 Conceptualizing community

Charlotte Aull Davies

The salience of the concept of community in social theory and research has tended to ebb and flow, with each cycle exploring old ideas and developing new approaches. For anthropologists, whose research methods were developed for small-scale, comparatively homogeneous village and tribal societies, community studies provided a way into research on large-scale heterogeneous Western societies (e.g. Arensberg 1968). Rural sociologists too developed a tradition of community studies based on the idea of a rural unit that was spatially delineated and usually comparatively isolated from the broader society (e.g. Stacey 1960; Williams 1956). Both of these research traditions were heavily influenced by Tönnies's (1955) concept of *Gemeinschaft*, which depicted community as built upon face-to-face and multi-stranded personal relationships that supported a homogeneous collectivity with a cohesive social structure. Both the rationale behind rural community studies and their theoretical assumptions were reproduced subsequently in studies of urban communities, which again tended to concentrate on spatially demarcated units like ethnic neighbourhoods (e.g. Gans 1962; Whyte 1955) or the working-class communities that had grown up in association with heavy industries like coalmining and metallurgy (e.g. Dennis et al. 1969).

By the early 1970s such community studies were coming under increasing criticism (see Bell and Newby 1974). Critics maintained that the concept of community was inadequately defined and as a consequence had no analytical utility. In spite of the richness of their empirical data, community studies did not provide any basis for generalizing from their findings. Furthermore, the functionalist orientation that characterized these studies meant that they were ineffective in their handling of social change, with most such studies depicting change – if they considered it at all – as the result of disruptive forces from outside the community. Nor were they equipped to recognize internal divisions or conflict, much less analyse them. This latter criticism was subsequently expanded upon by feminists (e.g. Frazer and Lacey 1993; Young 1990) who called attention to a darker side of intolerance and suppression of difference implicit in the homogeneity and consensus of presumed close-knit communities. Their critique was directed primarily at communitarianism with its idealization of community as the most desirable basis of social life (e.g. Benhabib 1992), but much of this idealization is in accord with the representations of community found in the community studies tradition. (However, see Day 1998 for a critical evaluation of the validity of this critique based on his examination of Welsh community studies.)

Nevertheless the concept of community, while falling out of fashion with social theorists from the 1970s onwards, did not disappear entirely. Although the goal of a holistic ethnography of a community was no longer considered feasible, anthropologists continued to take communities as the locus for much of their research, even though their research questions were more tightly focused (e.g. Cohen 1987; Jones 1997; Parman 1990). Furthermore, since the 1980s the concept of community has occupied a position of prominence in social policy where it is central to a variety of initiatives, from the provision of care in the community for individuals with disabilities to neighbourhood watch as a means of crime control. Thus the concept has displayed considerable resilience in spite of the widely accepted criticisms of it. And attempts to replace it altogether by adopting the more analytically precise concept of 'locality' were ultimately unsuccessful: 'over time the term "locality" has come to correspond more and more closely to some of the earlier meanings of community, suggesting that, although badly wounded, "community" is a concept that just will not lie down' (Day and Murdoch 1993, 85).

Communities: localities, networks, identities

The main reason for this resilience – as well as for the effectiveness of the term 'community' in political discourse – is that the concept of community encapsulates several interrelated elements central to people's experience of social life. The most obvious of these elements is the significance of particular places and people's locations within them. However, in spite of the centrality of place in the definition of community for classic community studies, locality is only one aspect of the concept, and on its own, without links to social and cultural elements, lacks significance. More recent approaches recognize that community may be based on shared interests – occupational or ethnic, for example – reflected in social networks, which may be localized but are not necessarily so. Another important aspect of community is the sense of shared identity which it both promotes and depends upon; this aspect of community is constructed around cultural symbols and is closely tied to people's personal identities and sense of belonging. These three ways of understanding communities – as localities, networks and identities – are clearly not mutually exclusive but instead overlap and affect one another. They are not all of equal significance in understanding specific communities, but their relative importance and the nature of their contributions are central to such understanding and to the analysis of community more generally. This recognition has allowed researchers to consider communities in new ways and to problematize other aspects of community (Crow and Allan 1994; Wellman 1999).

Community understood primarily in terms of a network or over-lapping networks of social relationships may still refer to a circumscribed locality, such as the 'local social system' originally suggested by Stacey (1969) in her attempt to bring greater analytical precision to the definition of community. However, such networks need not be so closely tied to place, thus allowing us to consider other forms of community. For example, in this volume, occupation (as in Hutson's study of the farming community in west Wales) and lifestyle (as in Williams's discussion of vegetarians and alternatives in Newport) provide the bases for different forms of network-based communities. This orientation encourages analysis of the degree of connectedness of individuals to the network as well as to other cross-cutting networks, rather than accepting a gloss of closeness and inclusivity as inherent to all communities. A network perspective also calls attention to the role of new forms of communication in community definition and maintenance (e.g. Wellman and Gulia 1999). Thus Segrott (this volume) describes a newly emerging form for the Welsh community in London, which is itself best described as a social network and is sustained primarily by means of electronic networks.

The other aspect of community noted above directs attention to the symbolic processes by which people represent their community both to themselves and to others. This approach focuses on boundaries, which can have a territorial expression but are primarily marked by the ongoing interactions and interpretations through which belonging and not belonging are defined (Cohen 1982, 1985). This perspective problematizes the degree of permeability of such boundaries for individuals; thus James (this volume) looks at the way in which constructions of community by both locals and incomers to three west Wales villages are used not strictly to exclude but rather to regulate incomers' entry to and effect on village culture. This symbolic constructionist perspective also entails recognition of the interdependence of communities with the broader society. Instead of viewing communities as isolated, and effects from outside as simply disruptive, this approach perceives the relationship of communities with external factors as dynamic and problematic. Both Jones and Murphy (this volume) report creative but divergent responses from the communities they study to external forces, which in one case threatened to destroy the community's identity along with its economic base but in the other provided the primary stimulus and the means for a localized collectivity's construction of itself as a community. A different approach to this focus on belonging emphasizes the meanings of community – for they are found to be multiple – and how such meanings are constructed. This orientation draws attention to the relationship of community to personal identities, investigating the ways in which individuals may belong to communities and the meanings of these associations (e.g. Charles and Davies 1997). Philpin (this volume) investigates a very close relationship between community and personal well-being, and shows how this relationship is expressed through personal networks of local healers.

The perception of communities either as networks or as symbolic constructions encourages us to view community boundaries as permeable for individuals, overlapping with other communities and comparatively indistinct. This contrasts with the precisely defined boundaries of traditional community studies and allows us to problematize the significance of place rather than taking proximity as determinative of community. Thus, locality and the relationship of community to place re-enters the area of community studies as one of the questions to be answered rather than defining the object of study. O'Neill (this volume) looks at a locality, the urban neighbourhood, that for urban researchers 'has been almost synonymous with "community"' (Wellman 1999, 13) and investigates both its claims for community status in the recent past, uncovering major internal tensions, and the basis for current disquiet about community break-down.

The contributors to this volume come to the study of community from these new perspectives, looking at communities in terms of networks, identities and symbolic constructions, investigating their spatial expressions and asking how (or whether) they relate to specific places. Based on these new perspectives, individual chapters address a variety of questions about community: the relationship between socio-economic and cultural factors in the construction of community (Jones); the significance of migration, both inward and outward, for individual communities (James); the significance of place and locality, especially under conditions of globalization (O'Neill; Williams); the effects of external perceptions, often media-directed, of specific communities and of community (Hutson; Murphy); the potential role of new forms of communication in community definition and mainte-nance (Segrott); and various manifestations of the links between personal identities and community (Philpin).

All of the chapters are based on studies of particular Welsh communities undertaken using ethnographic methods, which involve a long-term and comparatively intimate relationship between researchers and their research subjects and locales. This introductory chapter thus looks briefly at two other underlying themes found in the volume: the significance of taking Wales and Welsh communities as the basis for these studies; and questions of belonging, particularly salient in ethnographic research, that pertain to the ethnographers' relationship to the communities they study.

An anthropology of Wales

The majority of the contributions to this volume were originally presented to the annual conference of Anthropology Wales/Anthro-poleg Cymru. This comparatively new organization was established in 1997 with the twofold mission of encouraging the anthropological study of Welsh society and culture and the development of anthro-pology as a discipline in Wales. It welcomes participation from cognate disciplines whose research questions and methods overlap with the ethnographic approach of anthropology – and indeed two of the contributors to this volume are geographers. However, in considering the significance of 'place' (as Wales) and 'identity' (as

Welsh communities) as the basis for the studies of community included in this volume, I want to ask some more fundamental questions about the units on which social research tends to focus, an issue to which we return briefly in the concluding chapter.

What do we mean by an anthropology of Wales? Is there an identifiable body of work that might be said to constitute such an entity? That this question has not been widely considered may be due partly to the nature of the anthropological enterprise as the study of 'other' societies and cultures – the 'stranger' the better – an orientation that has only recently come to be challenged. However, once the question is posed, the difficulties in answering are similar to those addressed by sociologists who began asking about a sociology of Wales over twenty-five years ago. The first collection of social research findings explicitly intended to establish the foundations for a sociology of Wales appeared at the end of the 1970s (Williams 1978b), the fruit of a conference sponsored by the Social Science Research Council held in Gregynog in 1976. In his introduction to the volume, the editor and prime mover behind the conference suggested that the virtual invisibility of Wales in British social research was due to 'the tendency to neglect the concept of culture as a relevant tool of analysis and to regard Wales as merely a region within a homogeneous Britain' (Williams 1978a, 1). While acknowledging the contribution of this collection of essays as a first step towards a sociology of Wales, another major proponent of its development (Day 1979) criticized the volume's haphazard array of topics and lack of theoretical unity, resulting in a focus on those aspects of Welsh society and culture that were unarguably distinctive within Britain, an orientation that mitigated against research on industrial Wales and Welsh social stratification. 'By taking as our object of interest an entity which is empirically defined, in terms of administration, political decision, and certain historical events, we are uncertain of its sociological unity' (1979, 453). The development of an anthropology of Wales faces a similar dilemma, but one that is compounded by the disciplinary emphasis on the study of 'others', particularly exotic others. In this respect it is perhaps unsurprising that much of the anthropological work on Wales since the 1970s has been produced by anthropologists from outside, for whom Wales represents an acceptably foreign, even exotic field site (e.g. Aull 1978; Bowie 1993; Khleif 1975; Trosset 1993).

The other factor affecting the development of either a sociology or

an anthropology of Wales is the institutional base for such an enterprise. Williams recognized that the ethnocentricity of British
sociology was only part of the explanation for the neglect of Wales in
sociological studies; of at least equal importance was 'the absence of
a long-standing social science tradition within the centres of higher
education in Wales' (1978a, 1). Indeed the two disciplines have to
share the story of their institutional origins within the University of
Wales, with anthropology having perhaps the prior claim to an official home there. Thus the first institutional basis for the development
of social science perspectives on Wales was in the department of
geography and anthropology at Aberystwyth where the anthropologist C. Daryll Forde, who was Gregynog Professor and head of
department in the 1930s, encouraged one of his students, Alwyn D.
Rees, to inaugurate systematic social research on Welsh rural society,
resulting in the classic community study *Life in a Welsh Countryside*.
Even after Forde was succeeded as chair by E. G. Bowen, whose
primary disciplinary orientation was to geography, the tradition of
rural community studies continued under Rees's guidance, and a
series of other community studies were carried out in the 1940s and
1950s. Nevertheless anthropology had virtually disappeared from
the department of geography by the 1960s (Carter and Davies 1976).
It continued to have a disciplinary presence in Aberystwyth in the
1970s with the department of sociology providing a home to several
anthropologists (including Janet Bujra and Van Velsen). Furthermore
the interest in rural communities in Wales, along with a developing
analytical concern with the nature of community, continued as a
theme in work in the area of rural sociology led by Graham Day (e.g.
Day and Fitton 1975; Day 1989; Day and Murdoch 1993).

Anthropology's subsequent institutional home in Wales – and its
only such home until the creation in 1998 of a department at
Lampeter – was in the University College of Swansea where a joint
chair in sociology and anthropology was established in 1963
(Williams 1990). Swansea was a centre for the promotion of social
research on Wales, particularly on urban industrial Wales, from the
early 1960s. Of central importance to the establishment of this
research tradition was the study by Rosser and Harris (1965) of
family and kinship in Swansea. This work was not primarily aimed
at developing social research on Wales but rather was inspired by a
theoretical interest in the effect on the family, particularly the
extended family, of social and economic change in an industrial

society. It was undertaken as a comparison with a similar study in London's East End (Young and Wilmott 1957), and Swansea was selected because its 'different traditions, different industries and a different social history' provided 'a suitably contrasting urban area [to Bethnal Green] for this comparative investigation' (Rosser and Harris 1965, 33). Nevertheless the research did much to illuminate the specificity of Welsh society and culture, and the resultant study is a model for those who would unite general theoretical concerns with a particular focus on Wales. The work also has considerable anthropological input – Rosser was trained as an anthropologist – methodologically, in its combination of intensive ethnographic study of each one of a sample of communities within Swansea (1965, 36) with a large-scale survey; and theoretically, in its use of the concept of culture to analyse social differentiation (1965, 112–13). Another contribution from Swansea to social research on Wales, beginning in the 1980s, came from the anthropological side of the department and, through a cooperative programme with the geography department at Aberystwyth, revived an anthropological presence in research on rural Wales (Hutson 1987; Hutson, this volume).

The tradition of Welsh community studies

To return to the earliest anthropological studies of Wales, as found in the work of Alwyn Rees and the Aberystwyth School, it is worth considering why they took the form of rural community studies. As anthropologists began to study the societies that they have variously labelled as 'complex', 'industrial' or 'Western', they tried to replicate the research conditions that they had found – or believed they had found – in their studies of 'simple', 'primitive' societies. Thus they sought out relatively isolated, apparently self-contained and geographically circumscribed units as the object of their study. These requirements appeared to be filled most adequately by rural village communities. Probably the first and certainly one of the most influential of such studies was Arensberg's *The Irish Countryman*, which was carried out in rural Ireland in the 1930s. The community studies of the Aberystwyth School were very much in this tradition. Furthermore they were in anthropology's theoretical mainstream at the time in their structural-functionalist orientation which emphasized the fundamentally harmonious, integrated and static nature of village institutions. The potential for disharmony, disintegration and fundamental change was acknowledged only in terms of external social and economic factors in the wider society that were seen as a threat to the traditional way of life of the rural community. It was this traditional way of life that the researcher investigated, trying to disentangle it from the corrupting influences of the outside world.

Certainly Alwyn Rees's (1950) pioneering study of Llanfihangel-yng-Ngwynfa, *Life in a Welsh Countryside*, adopted this perspective. Fieldwork for the study was carried out in 1939–40, with subsequent intermittent visits through 1943. Rees describes the community as a

> relatively secluded and entirely Welsh-speaking area which could be expected to have retained many features of the traditional way of life . . . [I]n spite of its proximity to the English Border, the social organisation of the area remains fairly representative of the Welsh uplands generally, but in many other respects the culture has probably been further modified by English influence than is the case in the rural areas of the neighbouring counties of Merioneth and Cardigan (Rees 1950, v).

Thus Rees makes clear both his belief in the representativeness of the community, what he regarded as its adherence to *the* 'traditional way of life', and his concern to eliminate from his enquiry those elements that may have been altered by influences from outside, particularly from England. The contents – as suggested by the chapter headings, which move from the economy and various aspects of material culture through family and kinship to religion, social control and political organization – are essentially the same as are found in most classic ethnographic studies, whether of the Nuer, the Trobriand Islanders or the Welsh. On the other hand, Rees was concerned to situate customs in a historical and comparative context, which is not generally characteristic of structural-functionalist treatments. Thus he argued that the roots of customs regarding inheritance of tenancy and illegitimacy were to be perceived in the twelfth-century laws of Hywel Dda, and he contrasted these customs and others, such as the diffuse settlement pattern of the parish, with English rural society.

After the Second World War, Rees, from his institutional base in the department of geography in Aberystwyth, was able to encourage a number of follow-up studies, in particular the four found in the volume *Welsh Rural Communities*, which was published in 1960, although based on fieldwork in the late 1940s. While each of these is a study of a particular community, they do not adopt the holistic approach of Rees's original work but instead focus on particular aspects of rural society. The most influential for subsequent analyses of Welsh society has undoubtedly been Jenkins's (1960) study of the south Cardiganshire coastal village of Aber-porth in which he argued that the important social division was not class, as defined by occupation and income, but rather *bucheddau* (ways of life), defined by differences in patterns of expenditure and behaviour between 'chapel people' and 'pub people'. While his conclusions have been contested (e.g. Day and Fitton 1975), this work did nevertheless challenge the assumption that Welsh rural communities were so close-knit as to lack systematic social divisions, while at the same time arguing that such divisions were not simply economic but also involved cultural factors and lifestyle decisions (cf. Williams 1983), an approach that was developed by Rosser and Harris (1965) in their determination of social class.

This community studies tradition, which was to all intents and purposes the sole carrier of anthropological work on Wales, was enriched by two other major research monographs on Welsh rural communities, both produced by anthropologists from outside Wales and based on fieldwork undertaken in the 1950s. While they may be regarded superficially as an extension of this tradition, each in their own way challenged the conventional community studies approach (cf. Owen 1986). Emmett's (1964) study of Llanfrothen, *A North Wales Village*, rejected the *buchedd* structure developed by Jenkins and proposed, for this locality which was an early recipient of significant English settlement, a division based on Welsh/English opposition. The other earlier study, Frankenberg's (1990) *Village on the Border*, represented an even more fundamental challenge to the underlying assumptions of the community studies tradition in that it transformed ideas about the nature of communities, and about how anthropologists should study them.

Village on the Border was based on fieldwork during 1953–4 in Glyn Ceiriog ('Pentrediwaith') in Denbighshire, a largely Welsh-speaking community where employment had been mainly in extractive industry; however, with the decline of slate and granite quarrying, many of the men were unemployed while others had found work across the border in England. These economic changes were threatening the traditional character of the community, but Frankenberg's study did not simply document community breakdown in the face of external social and economic forces, an approach that would have been very much in the older tradition of community studies. Perhaps one reason for this ability to break new theoretical (and methodological) ground in such community studies was that Frankenberg did not come to Glyn Ceiriog with a particular interest in Wales but rather by a series of circumstances, outlined in his methodological postscript ('Village on the border: a text revisited') to the 1990 edition of the book, in which access was denied to his origally selected field-site in the Caribbean. He thus brought a theoretical interest in unemployment and the family, and practical restraints requiring that he find a field-site within a day's journey of Manchester where, preferably, people spoke another language. 'Arming myself with the census returns and Ordnance Survey maps, I sought a Welsh-speaking parish with extensive unemployment and not more than 2,000 inhabitants' (1990, 172). The study he produced, while it might superficially appear to be one of the last examples of the older tradition of rural community studies, in fact breaks with that tradition in quite significant ways and in the process develops two themes, one theoretical, the other methodological, that are highly relevant for the practice of contemporary anthropology and that are pursued by the contributors to this volume.

First, Frankenberg does not simply equate a spatially defined village with community but problematizes the nature of community and investigates internal tensions, centrifugal forces and, most significantly, the mechanisms devised by villagers to construct community. Thus, rather than treating external socio-economic forces in the wider society simply as causative of the decline of a traditional way of life and attempting to reconstruct that way of life as accurately as possible prior to such external influences, Frankenberg sees them as central to his analysis and focuses on villagers' responses to them. One of these responses is villagers' attempts to construct community through the creation of a series of organizations – the brass band, the football club, the village carnival. He analyses these processes and the way in which relative outsiders are manoeuvred into positions of authority in the organizations in order that they can absorb conflicts between villagers, allowing the sense of community to survive the inevitable failure of its various organizational carriers. Certainly this perspective on community as constructed, with its focus on how such constructions are accomplished, provided a theoretical direction that has been reflected in much subsequent work on community (e.g. Cohen 1985).

Second, Frankenberg's methodology is highly original, in that it provides a very early example of the reflexive approach to research that many anthropologists have come to argue is an inherent characteristic and a strength of ethnographic research (Davies 1999; Hastrup and Hervik 1994; Okely 1996). Frankenberg indeed was one of the comparative outsiders ('strangers') who was induced to play a leading role in the community football club and then to act as a lightning rod to absorb the tensions and eventually to carry the blame for its failure. His explicit incorporation of this experience in his ethnography and his reflexive analysis of its meaning is an innovative approach to both ethnographic practice and the reporting of it.

The eight contributions to this volume, each of which is based on recent original ethnographic research, pursue these two themes. In the first place, they look at different kinds of communities in Wales and one Welsh community in England and consider a variety of ways of belonging to them. They treat the concept of community as itself problematic, examining critically a broad spectrum of collectivities that have assumed this characterization for themselves or had it applied to them from outside. Among the themes they address are: the social bases of such a characterization (Jones; O'Neill); its transformation under changing social circumstances (Hutson; James; Jones; Segrott); the processes through which it may be acquired (Murphy); the uses made of it (James; Philpin); and its meaning within the collectivity (Philpin; Williams) or outside it (Hutson). And second, all eight contributors examine reflexively their own relationship to the communities they study, asking how this relationship affects their research methodologically and thematically and also raising more general questions about the nature of anthropology 'at home', sometimes called 'native' or 'insider' anthropology.

Categorizing the studies

Locality, network and identity are interrelated aspects of all communities, but their nature and significance for individual communities have to be investigated empirically. Questions of identity figure prominently in all the studies of communities in this volume, but some are concerned primarily with the identity of a collectivity as community per se, while others are more interested in the relationship between community and personal identities. Those contributors who examine the relationship between community and locality have tended also to focus on the community's collective identity and hence to be concerned with its symbolic construction. Those contributors whose communities are better understood in terms of social networks have tended to concentrate on personal identities and belonging. Thus the chapters that follow are arranged so as to begin with those that look at the relationship between community and locality: a village in a south Wales valley; three villages in rural west Wales; a street in an urban neighbourhood; and a collection of holiday chalets turned into permanent homes. These four chapters all consider the ways in which a locality may be claimed by its residents to constitute a community and the processes of constructing community identities. They examine how such claims and the reasons for making them are affected, positively as well as adversely, by external circumstances and how internal divisions relate to community constructions. The subsequent four chapters look at community primarily in terms of social network rather than circumscribed locality. In the first of these, the study is still centred on a locality and one that could be described as very much a traditional community, but the research is primarily concerned with the networks centred on practitioners of a particular form of healing and with the relationship of those healing beliefs and practices to personal identities and ways of belonging to the community. The subsequent two chapters relate to somewhat more spatially dispersed networks, which nevertheless may themselves make claims to being communities and, equally relevant, are popularly labelled as communities by outsiders, such claims or perceptions being based in one case on occupation and in the other on lifestyle choices. These studies look at ways in which outsiders may influence how these network-based communities are perceived and their effects on belonging and on self-perceptions of their members. The final chapter, based on research on the Welsh community in London, considers how its nature and social basis has been transformed in the past few decades and its meaning for individual members altered as a consequence.

All of the contributors also examine the relationship of their communities to external social and economic forces, a relationship that varies significantly both between and within the two categories of communities. Of the four locality-based communities, the former mining village is perhaps most fundamentally undermined, both in material and symbolic terms, by the exigencies of external economic and political forces. Yet Jones finds villagers engaged in a self-conscious symbolic reconstruction of themselves as a mining community years after the last mine has been closed; interestingly both the major vehicle for this reconstruction, the rugby club, and the gendered nature of the process, including the important role of women, echo Frankenberg's findings in Glyn Ceiriog. In contrast, O'Neill argues that the perception of community breakdown in the urban neighbourhood he studied, which was based on changing employment patterns and a purported increase in newcomers, was considerably greater than the reality, which seemed to be little more than a slight restructuring of residence patterns combined with 'an attenuation of networks of knowledge . . . relating to family history' (this volume, 92). In her study of three rural Welsh villages that have become targets for significant English in-migration in recent decades, James finds that the ideal of a 'close community', valued by villagers and incomers alike, makes 'belonging' a resource that villagers control and have developed as a basis of social status in order to offset the otherwise greater cultural and economic capital of the incomers. James further notes that 'community status and the actions deemed necessary to achieve it were not such an important issue within the minds of the locals until large-scale in-migration' (this volume, 67). The process by which external factors sometimes may strengthen community self-identity is also considered in Murphy's chapter, the fourth locality-based community. Murphy finds that the residents of The Field have a very ambiguous relationship to external forces, for while these forces threaten to end the actual physical existence of the community, they are also the principal stimulus that brings it into being as a self-conscious symbolic construction.

The four chapters that deal with communities expressed primarily as networks rather than localities show a similar variability in their relationship to the wider society. The first chapter in this section (Philpin) looks at what could be regarded as the most 'traditional Welsh' community considered in this volume. It is based on a rural locality, yet the community is largely defined, not by reference to any external perceptions of it, but by its adherence to a particular thera-peutic practice which depends on a few healers who are 'important base points or anchors in a number of networks' (this volume, 131).

The subsequent two chapters (Hutson; Williams) deal with com-munities that share with residents of The Field an identity construction that owes as much to external forces and perceptions as to internal realities. This is perhaps particularly the case for the collectivity of vegetarians in Newport in west Wales. Certainly Williams's study clearly demonstrates the internal heterogeneity of this collectivity, in spite of external perceptions of sameness, as well as revealing the ambiguities of the symbols out of which it is constructed. Yet the degree to which individuals construct their sense of self in terms of their 'belonging' to this collectivity reminds us of the intimate ties between self-identity and community that seem to lie at the heart of the resilience of community as a 'folk' concept. Williams also looks at the links between this interest community and the locality-based traditionally defined community of Newport. Hutson's chapter, which is based on research extending over twenty years on 'the farming community' in Pembrokeshire, argues that altered expectations by the wider society of what farmers should do, as well as changing economic conditions, have produced both material changes in this community, such as the reduced likelihood of intergenerational continuity, and confusion about its symbolic content, the meaning of farming. Thus, in this case external perceptions are seriously challenging the ability of individual members to construct their identities around their sense of belonging to this farming community. The final chapter in this section on communities as networks (Segrott) describes the transformation of an immigrant community, the London Welsh, from a comparatively close network organized around particular localities to a new form of virtual community, 'decentred and mobile . . . frequently operating as much in cyberspace as on the ground' (this volume, 199), yet of continuing significance for the construction of personal identities.

While these contributions do not seek nor provide agreement on the nature of community, they share several features in their outlook on the study of community. Perhaps most fundamentally, they disagree with those who would dismiss the study of community as theoretically irrelevant. In this, they are again following Frankenberg, who, noting how 'community studies fell out of fashion' in the 1960s and 1970s, commented:

> It is true that I did not foresee the way that communities of shared village experience and language or perceived ethnicity were going to shape the politics of the modern world as much as, if not more than, class. At least, however, I did not sweep them to one side as irrelevant to real life. (1990, 187)

Community is important for anthropologists to address and try to understand because it is important to our informants. People attach significance to community, attempt to define it, worry about its demise and structure their identities around it. Clearly it is not a theoretically pure concept, yet much like the related concepts of nation and national identity (Davies and Jones, this volume), it is one that social theorists cannot ignore. Anthropologists especially – with their methodological orientation to real people's lives, observations 'on the ground' and understanding others' perspectives – must continue to concern themselves with community and its related concepts of belonging and identity. Furthermore, the questions raised about belonging are also methodologically significant for anthropologists given their disciplinary bias towards ethnographic methods, particularly participant observation, in their research strategies.

Ethnographers' ways of belonging

These community studies are all based on ethnographic research, mainly participant observation augmented by semi-structured interviewing. The effectiveness of these methods rests heavily on the ethnographers' success in developing a productive relationship with their research subjects. Thus the issue of belonging, and recognition of the variety of ways of belonging, is important not simply in terms of the composition of these communities, but also in terms of research methodology. Ethnographers must cultivate a reflexive awareness of their own ways of belonging to the communities they study and how such belonging affects their findings. All of the contributors discuss their own relationship to the communities they study and how this affects their data and informs their analysis. These relationships depend on the characteristics of both ethnographers and research subjects. So it is not surprising that the ways of belonging and reflecting on it in these studies are so varied as almost to defy classification. But some patterns can be seen in the contributors' reflexive engagement with their research and how this reflexivity contributes to analysis. One common methodological theme is that all eight contributions are indisputably examples of ethnography 'at home' (Jackson 1987) – all eight contributors live and work in Wales. Whether or not they are also examples of 'native' ethnography (Lal 1996) raises the thorny issue of Welshness and how it is defined (cf. Thompson and Day 1999). Four of the contributors claim to be Welsh by virtue of being born and raised in Wales; but there their similarity ends. Of these four, Williams is a first-language Welsh speaker from rural Carmarthenshire. Also from a Carmarthenshire village (Llansteffan), James is a first-language English speaker whose schooling was through the medium of Welsh. Jones from Haverfordwest – the granddaughter of coalminers – has learned Welsh. And O'Neill, a non-Welsh speaker, hails from that melting pot, yet quintessentially Welsh town of Merthyr Tydfil. The relationships of the other four contributors to Welsh identity and its significance for their research varies. At one extreme Philpin expresses concern with her ethnic identity as English/Australian and her awareness of 'the impact my lack of Welsh had on social interactions' (this volume, 121). Hutson, who has lived in south Wales for over thirty years and whose research benefits from the added credibility and acceptance extended to those who return to previous research sites and informants, still feels that being non-Welsh speaking affects his relationship with some farmers. For Murphy, herself a resident of The Field where she carries out her research, the issue of Welsh identity does not even arise. And Segrott, English-born and raised, became fluent in the Welsh language while attending university in Wales and 'embarked upon a deeply personal engagement with the Welsh culture and language' (this volume, 183).

As all this clearly suggests, the question of being a 'native' anthropologist is not necessarily the same as being an 'insider'. 'Native' anthropology generally refers to research among people with whom the anthropologist shares ethnic or national identity. The concept is a result of anthropology's developing conscience regarding the long standard practice of sending western anthropologists to research 'natives' in Third World societies. The antidote to the resonances of this practice with colonial exploitation – in this case extracting knowledge solely for the benefit of Western anthropologists without regard to its effect on colonized peoples – was to encourage individuals from these societies to pursue research there, an enterprise not without its own complications and ambiguities (cf. Abu-Lughod 1991). In contrast, the question of 'insider' status has as its referent the rather more limited collectivity of those the anthropologist is explicitly studying and among whom research (particularly participant observation) is carried out. Belonging to groups such as these may be linked to ethnic or national identity, but is not necessarily so, certainly not in any straightforward way. Thus for Murphy her status as 'insider' is undisputed, and unconnected to any question of Welsh identity. Yet, as she found, the question of belonging is never unproblematic. Much as did Panourgia (1995) in an ethnographic study of her own family, Murphy has to separate her self as a resident of The Field, campaigning to retain her home, from her anthropological self, observing and analysing this campaign and its effects. In direct contrast to Murphy's chapter, Williams offers the ironic spectacle of a 'native' anthropologist doing research 'at home' who is nevertheless a comparative 'outsider' to the network of those adopting vegetarian lifestyles whom she is researching. Even so, as the research relationships develop, she finds points of contact in her own biography and, most insightfully, through one of the folk songs of her rural Welsh upbringing. Between these two extremes, the other chapters demonstrate a variety of degrees and ways in which anthropologists may claim to be either 'natives' or 'insiders' or both. Jones as a Welsh woman with a working-class background can certainly claim to belong to the valley mining village where she lived for a year. And her own experiences as a woman living alone and coping with what she would surely regard, in another context, as sexual harassment were clearly integral to her analysis of the role of gender in community identity. But she acknowledges as well her 'vastly different life experience from most people in Blaengwyn, having lived in London and East Anglia as well as Wales, and having spent seven years in higher education' (this volume, 28). Similarly, James, both a 'native' and an 'insider' researching the Welsh village where she had grown up, still reports her identity as an academic researcher affected her 'belonging'. O'Neill, like Murphy a resident in the community he studied and like Jones from a similar Welsh working-class background and locality, nevertheless concludes that in the terms in which residents themselves defined belonging, he was an outsider, in fact the only outsider he managed to locate: 'The only family in the study area that I found had no historical claim to "East-sider" identity was my own' (this volume, 92). Hutson's community, determined by occupation, makes him as anthropologist and university lecturer an outsider by definition. Yet he finds communality in his own relationship with the countryside, as well as in the much greater readiness to accept as 'belonging' someone who returns after an absence, and who is therefore a part of one's own history, a phenomenon that many anthropologists have reported on and benefited from on their return to a former field-site. Segrott, a non-native by birth and upbringing, experiences the power of a shared language in some circumstances to define belonging and bestow insider status, at least for one section of his research subjects. Philpin is the one who most clearly perceives herself as outsider, by virtue of ethnicity, language, and profession. In her case the professional distance is not primarily due to her identity as anthropologist, experienced by all contributors, but to her earlier training as a nurse, which 'engendered a degree of scepticism in me towards wool measuring as a therapeutic intervention' (this volume, 122). Yet her own experience of having her wool measured helps to bridge this professional distance and informs her discussion of the meaning of this practice.

For anthropologists the question of their relationship to those they study is central to the practice of ethnographic research. Yet it is not a question that can be resolved by positivist-inspired attempts to minimize reactivity, that is, to control the researcher's effects on either research subjects or situations. Ethnographic research, by its very nature, requires both involvement with the research subjects and separation from them. The quality of its results is then evaluated, in part, in terms of these research relationships. But this is not to imply that this evaluation is simply a matter of how 'close' these relationships are – or, put another way, whether or not the anthropologist 'truly belongs'. As Frankenberg's study demonstrates, the examination of the anthropologist as a particular kind of 'stranger' can be equally informative of a community's internal dynamics. Nor can full 'insider' status ever be assumed, even in cases where the anthropologist most self-evidently 'belongs'. Robert Murphy, an anthropologist whose disease of the spinal column left him a quadriplegic, took his experiences as an opportunity for 'a kind of extended anthropological field trip' (1987, xi) into the world of the disabled, in which he was to 'act simultaneously as . . . both ethnographer and informant' (1987, 3). Yet even he found that he was still using his persona as anthropologist to distance himself from his subjects, to deny his 'belonging' to that collectivity (1987, 126). Thus, belonging is always problematic and it is not sufficient for anthropologists implicitly to claim validity for their research on anecdotal evidence that they have been accepted by their research subjects. All anthropologists, even those who work 'at home', make journeys of some kind during their fieldwork, from one sort of connection or belonging to another; in the process they are themselves altered and these alterations should form an acknowledged part of their data.

Thus research relationships must be examined and the ways in which they affect analysis made visible. The contributors to this volume demonstrate how their different ways of belonging to a variety of collectivities may be used to inform analysis; they do so in a substantive area of enquiry – that of the nature of communities – in which bases of belonging form an important theoretical focus as well.

References

Abu-Lughod, L. (1991). 'Writing against culture', in R. G. Fox (ed.), *Recapturing Anthropology: Working in the Present* (Santa Fe, New Mexico: School of American Research Press).

Arensberg, C. (1968 [1937]). *The Irish Countryman* (Garden City, NY: Natural History Press).

Aull, C. H. (1978). 'Ethnic nationalism in Wales: an analysis of the factors governing the politicization of ethnic identity' (Ph.D. thesis, Duke University).

Bell, C. and Newby, H. (eds.) (1974). *The Sociology of Community* (London: Frank Cass).

Benhabib, S. (1992). *Situating the Self: Gender, Community and Postmodernism in Contemporary Ethics* (Cambridge: Polity).

Bowie, F. (1993). 'Wales from within: conflicting interpretations of Welsh identity', in S. Macdonald (ed.), *Inside European Identities* (Oxford: Berg).

Carter, H. and Davies, W. K. D. (1976). 'Emeritus Professor E. G. Bowen: a brief introduction to some selected academic papers', in H. Carter and W. K. D. Davies (eds.), *Geography, Culture and Habitat: Selected Essays of E. G. Bowen* (Llandysul: Gomer).

Charles, N. and Davies, C. A. (1997). 'Contested communities: the refuge movement and cultural identities in Wales', *Sociological Review*, 45, 3, 416–36.

Cohen, A. P. (ed.) (1982). *Belonging: Identity and Social Organisation in British Rural Cultures* (Manchester: Manchester University Press).

—— (1985). *The Symbolic Construction of Community* (London: Routledge).

—— (1987). *Whalsay: Symbol, Segment and Boundary in a Shetland Island Community* (Manchester: Manchester University Press).

Crow, G. and Allan, G. (1994). *Community Life: An Introduction to Local Social Relations* (New York: Harvester Wheatsheaf).

Davies, C. A. (1999). *Reflexive Ethnography: A Guide to Researching Selves and Others* (London: Routledge).

Day, G. (1979). 'The sociology of Wales: issues and prospects', *Sociological Review*, 27, 447–74.

—— (1989). '"A million on the move?" population change and rural Wales', *Contemporary Wales*, 3, 137–60.

—— (1998). 'A community of communities? Similarity and difference in Welsh rural community studies', *The Economic and Social Review*, 29 (3), 233–57.

Day, G. and Fitton, M. (1975). 'Religion and social status in rural Wales: "buchedd" and its lessons for concepts of stratification', *Sociological Review*, 23, 4, 867–91.

Day, G. and Murdoch, J. (1993). 'Locality and community: coming to terms with place', *Sociological Review*, 41, 1, 82–111.

Dennis, N., Henriques, F. and Slaughter, C. (1969). *Coal is Our Life: An Analysis of a Yorkshire Mining Community* (London: Tavistock).

Emmett, I. (1964). *A North Wales Village* (London: Routledge and Kegan Paul).

Frankenberg, R. (1990 [1957]). *Village on the Border* (Prospect Heights, Illinois: Waveland).

Frazer, E. and Lacey, N. (1993). *The Politics of Community: A Feminist Critique of the Liberal-Communitarian Debate* (New York: Harvester Wheatsheaf).

Gans, H. J. (1962). *Urban Villagers: Group and Class in the Life of Italian-Americans* (New York: Free Press).

Hastrup, K. and Hervik, P. (eds.) (1994). *Social Experience and Anthropological Knowledge* (London: Routledge).

Hutson, J. (1987). 'Fathers and sons: family farms, family businesses and the farming industry', *Sociology*, 21, 2, 215–29.

Jackson, A. (ed.) (1987). *Anthropology at Home* (London: Tavistock).

Jenkins, D. (1960). 'Aber-porth: a study of a coastal village in south Cardiganshire', in E. Davies and A. D. Rees (eds.), *Welsh Rural Communities* (Cardiff: University of Wales Press).

Jones, S. P. (1997). '"Still a mining community": gender and change in the Upper Dulais Valley' (Ph.D. thesis, University of Wales Swansea).

Khleif, B. B. (1975). *Ethnic Boundaries, Identity and Schooling: A Socio-cultural Study of Welsh–English Relations* (Durham, New Hampshire: University of New Hampshire Press).

Lal, J. (1996). 'Situating locations: the politics of self, identity and "other" in living and writing the text' in D. L. Wolf (ed.), *Feminist Dilemmas in Fieldwork* (Boulder, Colorado: Westview).

Murphy, R. F. (1987). *The Body Silent* (New York: Norton).

Okely, J. (1996). *Own or Other Culture* (London: Routledge).

Owen, T. M. (1986). 'Community studies in Wales: an overview', in

I. Hume and W. T. R. Pryce (eds.), *The Welsh and Their Country* (Llandysul: Gomer).

Panourgia, N. (1995). *Fragments of Death, Fables of Identity: An Athenian Anthropography* (Madison, Wisconsin: University of Wisconsin Press).

Parman, S. (1990). *Scottish Crofters: An Historical Ethnography of a Celtic Village* (Fort Worth, Texas: Holt, Rinehart and Winston).

Rees, A. D. (1950). *Life in a Welsh Countryside* (Cardiff: University of Wales Press).

Rosser, C. and Harris, C. C. (1965). *The Family and Social Change: A Study of Family and Kinship in a South Wales Town* (London: Routledge and Kegan Paul).

Stacey, M. (1960). *Tradition and Change: A Study of Banbury* (Oxford: Oxford University Press).

—— (1969). 'The myth of community studies', *British Journal of Sociology*, 20, 2, 34–47.

Thompson, A. and Day, G. (1999). 'Situating Welshness: "local" experience and national identity', in R. Fevre and A. Thompson (eds.), *Nation, Identity and Social Theory* (Cardiff: University of Wales Press).

Tönnies, F. (1955 [1887]). *Community and Association* (London: Routledge and Kegan Paul).

Trosset, C. (1993). *Welshness Performed: Welsh Concepts of Person and Society* (Tucson, Arizona: University of Arizona Press).

Wellman, B. (1999). 'The network community: an introduction', in B. Wellman (ed.), *Networks in the Global Village: Life in Contemporary Communities* (Boulder, Colorado: Westview).

Wellman, B. and Gulia, M. (1999). 'Net-surfers don't ride alone: virtual communication as communities', in B. Wellman (ed.), *Networks in the Global Village: Life in Contemporary Communities* (Boulder, Colorado: Westview).

Whyte, W. F. (1955). *Street Corner Society: The Social Structure of an Italian Slum* (Chicago: University of Chicago Press).

Williams, G. (1978a). 'Introduction', in G. Williams (ed.), *Social and Cultural Change in Contemporary Wales* (London: Routledge and Kegan Paul).

—— (ed.) (1978b). *Social and Cultural Change in Contemporary Wales* (London: Routledge and Kegan Paul).

—— (1983). 'On class and status groups in Welsh rural society', in G. Williams (ed.), *Crisis of Economy and Ideology: Essays on Welsh Society, 1840–1980* (Bangor: British Sociological Association Sociology of Wales Study Group).

Williams, W. M. (1956). *The Sociology of an English Village: Gosforth* (London: Routledge and Kegan Paul).

—— (1990). 'Introduction: Sociology and Anthropology at Swansea, 1964–1989', in C. C. Harris (ed.), *Family, Economy and Community* (Cardiff: University of Wales Press).

Young, I. M. (1990). 'The ideal of community and the politics of difference', in L. J. Nicholson (ed.), *Feminism/Postmodernism* (London: Routledge).

Young, M. and Willmott, P. (1957). *Family and Kinship in East London* (London: Routledge and Kegan Paul).

Section 1

LOCALITIES and IDENTITIES

2 Supporting the team, sustaining the community: gender and rugby in a former mining village*

Stephanie Jones

Ten years after the momentous 1984–5 coalminers' strike, I conducted ethnographic fieldwork in a village, Blaengwyn, situated in a valley in south Wales. The strike had been a fight against the Thatcher government's pit-closure programme, but to no avail, and five years prior to my fieldwork the last pit in the valley had closed. As the major local employer in the village, the closure of the colliery had a devastating impact on the village. In the 1991 census, male unemployment in the village was 21.25 per cent against a county mean of 13.37 per cent (West Glamorgan County Council 1993). Female unemployment was recorded as 6.19 per cent, a figure which reflects not only that only one spouse could claim benefits and that many women would have been classed as 'housewives', but also that there were increasing job opportunities for women in local electronics and clothing factories during the years immediately prior to and during my fieldwork period.

My research interest lay in investigating how the major structural change of de-industrialization, with fewer jobs for men and more jobs for women, would affect gender identities and relationships at the micro level. In order to gain an understanding of the everyday lives of the villagers, the quotidian practices or *habitus* (Bourdieu 1977) which the villagers produced, reproduced and were constituted by, I lived in the village for twelve months, conducting qualitative fieldwork. This comprised participant observation, a questionnaire survey and semi-structured interviews. I had wanted to do 'anthropology at home' and being Welsh myself I believed that the

---

* All personal and place names have been changed to protect confidentiality.

research would afford me the opportunity to investigate important questions regarding gender as a 'native' anthropologist.

During the last twenty years, critiques of anthropology have brought attention to the problems of research carried out predominantly in the Third World. Talal Asad points out a serious neglect within anthropological discourse: 'there is a reluctance on the part of most professional anthropologists to consider seriously the power structure within which their discipline has taken shape' (Asad 1979, 9). The volume in which his essay 'Anthropology and the colonial encounter' appears, *The Politics of Anthropology*, is an attempt to undertake such consideration, asking 'Why is it that we are concerned about human peculiarities in faraway places rather than confronting ourselves with those in our own street?' (Asad 1979, 20).

More recently, Judith Okely suggests that the 'exotic should be displaced' within anthropology and that the 'avowed aim of anthropology to study all of humanity is spoiled if it excludes the Western "I" while relying mainly on the Western eye/gaze upon "others"' (Okely 1996, 1, 5).

I agree with Diane Lewis, who as early as 1973 said 'I feel, along with a number of other Third World anthropologists, that the time has come for the study of culture from the inside, by the insider' (Lewis 1973, 588). But the fact that 'native' or 'insider' anthropology has never really been accepted by the discipline is demonstrated by the fact that I was discouraged by an eminent anthropology professor from studying in Wales. A recent publication of articles debating the merits or otherwise of 'insider anthropology' and problematizing the concepts of 'native' and 'insider' anthropologists alerts us to the difficulties in asserting that one is an 'insider' in the fieldwork context (Cerroni-Long 1995).

In his article, Walter Goldschmidt reflects on his research in California rural communities and asks if he was really studying his 'own culture' as he was from a different area of the United States and had a German-American background (Goldschmidt 1995, 18). I am Welsh, and from a working-class background, but am from a different geographical area of Wales and have a vastly different life experience from most people in Blaengwyn, having lived in London and East Anglia as well as Wales, and having spent seven years in higher education. But, as Delmos J. Jones points out in his contribution to the same publication, 'The native anthropologist must be seen in relationship to a native population, but the native population must not be viewed as a homogeneous and cohesive entity' (Jones 1995, 59). He also warns that native anthropologists can end up serving native elite interests (Jones 1995, 61, 67), so that echoes of colonialist Western anthropologists' research in Third World cultures can resound in native anthropology too.

In my own research, as a 'reflexive ethnographer' (Davies 1999), I recognize that I was in a privileged position in that I was able to spend a year living in Blaengwyn conducting my fieldwork. During that year I lodged in the local bakery for half the time and rented a bungalow for the remainder. The fact that I am a Welsh woman certainly made it easier for me to be accepted into the village. In addition, the fact that both my grandfathers worked in coalmining facilitated an entry into relationships in the village, as it was seen as proof that I was somehow similar to the villagers themselves, despite the fact that I was doing academic research and was therefore in most respects very different from them. Although not a native of Blaengwyn, and not even a native of a mining community, my research did, I believe, fall into the category of 'native' or 'insider' anthropology. Throughout the research process, however, it was apparent that my 'insider' status was dependent on specific circumstances, and that on many occasions I was definitely an 'outsider'. This outsider status was, however, very useful as it ensured that I was advised by an 'insider', a villager, to attend an event which would help clarify for me social processes in the village.

I here describe that one episode from my year's fieldwork which elucidates social relations in the village and shows that, despite the major structural transformation brought about by de-industrialization, there was a fundamental lag in change at the micro level as the villagers sought to maintain traditional gender and community identities. As might be expected for a village associated closely with the dominant male industry, gender and community identities were found to be inextricably linked. The issue of ethnic identity also proved important in this Welsh context. The event discussed here suggests that an alternative emphasis on a recreational activity as opposed to employment, within a broader framework of traditional gender relations, meant that the inhabitants were able to perpetuate the village's identity as still being a Welsh 'mining community' despite the absence of mining jobs.

An ethnographic metonym

I now describe a rugby trip from Blaengwyn to Cardiff, and I use the trip as an analytical device to explore my data. It seems to me to sum up what life in the village was like when I did my fieldwork, and even though it is an exceptional event, it captured for me the fundamental nature of everyday life in Blaengwyn. This device, in which one particular event is interpreted as a metonym of social relations, is familiar in anthropology, for example from the work of Geertz (1993), who analyses a Balinese cock fight, and Gluckman (1958), who discusses a bridge-opening ceremony in Zululand. Both authors draw out elements from a key event which reflect the wider social situation and elucidate social relations in their locus of study. In this way an ethnographic metonym can highlight important aspects of social processes, or 'practices' in Bourdieu's terms, and aid under-standing of the wider culture. By recounting the events of the day as experienced by me, I believe that an interesting analysis of the community, including my own position in it, can be achieved.

The rugby trip

The Blaengwyn rugby team reached the final of the Prysg Whitbread Welsh Districts Cup during my year of fieldwork. Although not inter-ested in sport myself, I could not help but notice the high regard for the game in Blaengwyn, and had often seen team members practising on the artificial field provided by British Coal Opencast. As it happened, the first match I saw Blaengwyn rugby football team play turned out to be their finest hour, and the first rugby match that I ever went to in my life happened to be in the National Stadium at Cardiff Arms Park. The final of the Cup was played at the end of April, about halfway through my fieldwork. The week before the match, while out celebrating a woman friend's fortieth birthday in the one surviving pub in the village, the club coach, Jeff, said to me about the final: 'You must go, if you're interested in the village, it'll be a great day out.'

As a dutiful anthropologist, I knew I could not miss the match, but I did not look forward to the trip for a number of reasons. Firstly, I had no interest in the game and I thought that the match, though ethnographically interesting, would be boring in itself. Secondly, a male admirer from the village attempted to use the game to entice me to Cardiff for his 'birthday treat'; but I was anxious to ward off his advances. Thirdly, I knew that from the anthropological point of view I should travel to the match with most of the rest of the village, that is, on one of the coaches. But I am very affected by travel sickness, and was dreading the journey.

However, I am now very glad that despite my hesitations I went to the match in Cardiff. Anthropologists usually take a society, village or group of people out of context for consideration in their ethnographies. I am also doing this, of course, but in this case, the village took itself out of context to Cardiff for the day and provided me with an apposite metonym for exploring community and gender identity in the village.

The trip

Seven coaches left the village from the rugby club and two from the pub on the morning of the Cup Final. They were full of supporters going to the game in Cardiff. In addition, some villagers went in their own cars. In all, about 1,000 people went to the match from the village where the total population was only approximately 1,300.

I had put my name down for a seat on one of the rugby club buses. This cost two pounds, and the match ticket cost four pounds. I had to go into the club to find my coach allocation details, and ascertained that I was on bus number five. The club was full of people, and about thirty were standing outside drinking beer when I arrived at the club at about 10 a.m. Children were running around excitedly, drinking cola and eating crisps. Many of their faces were painted with stage make-up: one half vertically up to the middle of the nose red, the other half black, the team colours. There were notices in the back of the coach windows: 'Jeff Rodgers' red and black army' and 'The Blaengwyn girls are on the piss again'.

When I joined the women who had befriended me during my fieldwork, by pushing through the crush of drinking bodies in the downstairs bar and climbing the stairs to the first-floor bar, where they were painting their friends' and children's faces, the Blaengwyn girls were indeed 'on the piss again'. Alcohol was being consumed by adults in this bar as well, which was full of women, mostly sporting red jerseys and black, red and white mining helmets, and children; the men remaining downstairs. After having a chat with my friends and enjoying a beer with them, it was time for the coaches to leave so we all took our places and left the village in a convoy on to the M4.

From my vantage point at the front of the coach I could see an enormous whisky bottle (it must have held at least five litres) being passed around in the coach in front.

I sat in the front seat because of my travel sickness, next to a middle-aged man from a neighbouring village. We talked about where I came from, what I was doing in Blaengwyn, and about his job as a carpet supplier. We also chatted about the rugby team. He emphasized the achievement of the team in getting to the final, as it was made up entirely of local men, and that it was a boost to morale in what was a very deprived area. The opposing team was also from a deprived area, he advised me, a large council estate in Cardiff. He also laughed about the unofficial use of the large opencast site near Blaengwyn for dumping and burying cars involved in insurance claim fiddles.

The coaches soon became separated in the busy motorway traffic, but we all ended up at about half past twelve in the centre of Cardiff at a hotel where the rugby club had paid for all those travelling by coach to have a buffet reception prior to the match. It had cost two pounds fifty per head, and there was much grumbling at the 'cheek of it' because the buffet consisted of one chicken, ham or cheese sandwich each, and these were made from sliced white bread and presented on cardboard plates covered with clingfilm. There was also outrage at the price of drinks, for example 'bloody two pound twenty for a bottle of Budweiser, ridiculous, mun'. However, the prices did not stop the *hwyl* (fun) and people chatted, laughed, posed for photographs and drank their drinks, children ran around and danced to background music. It was a fine day, so some chose to carry their drinks out on to the terrace. By about two o'clock everyone decided to leave the hotel to walk round to the Arms Park.

Cardiff shoppers looked on askance as a line of villagers snaked round the corner to the ground's entrance. As we went, the group of supporters I was with, comprising women and children, sang songs and chants such as 'Fairview (a rival village nearby) went to Rome to see the Pope, Fairview went to Rome to see the Pope, Fairview went to Rome to see the Pope, and this is what he said: "Fuck off!"' and 'Who are, who are, who are we, we are Blaengwyn RFC!'

As we neared the grounds, we were directed by officials into the stand in which both sets of supporters would sit. It was immediately apparent that although the other team was local in the sense that it was from Cardiff, it had about a third as many supporters as

Blaengwyn. Club committee members were sitting in specially reserved seats near the front. As we were arriving, a little boy who was the son of one of the team members and one of my women friends from the bakery, was kicking a ball around the pitch, dressed in Blaengwyn's colours. His mother was sitting next to me. Her daughter Andrea was upset because her friends were ignoring her, and she started crying as the teams came on to the field amidst horn blowing and clapping. Andrea's mother, Mary, said 'Look, Andrea, this is a very important moment for your father, he's playing on the national stadium, so just shut up.' One of the Blaengwyn players kissed the turf as he arrived on the field.

During the match there was much shouting, singing and booing from both sets of supporters. Despite trailing at half-time, Blaengwyn eventually won. The supporters were screaming, and some of them were crying with joy. Both sets of supporters clapped when the teams went to collect the cup, medals and tankards. As we left the stadium, to go back to the hotel, the 'Who are, who are, who are we, we are Blaengwyn RFC' chant started up again. When we got back to the bar, drinking continued until we got back on our coaches in the early evening.

My front seat had been taken by a teenager, and the man in the next seat, whom I did not know, said 'Come and sit by me, love.' Two young men sitting nearby said 'You'll regret that,' and he replied, 'I won't molest her' as he squeezed my knee. He then lit up a cigarette and said 'You don't mind if I do, do you?' but it made me feel instantly nauseous so I went to sit behind the two young men, explaining that I feel sick on coaches and that cigarette smoke makes it worse. 'Good move,' the young men said.

I was joined by a man who introduced himself as 'Whizzo', otherwise known as Owain, from the village of Glanllwybr, situated down the valley from Blaengwyn and classed as part of the same community council ward. I noticed that he had one finger missing from his right hand, and guessed correctly that he was an ex-miner. During the trip back to Blaengwyn, he asked me about my research, and we talked about his political views and his experiences living in the valley. He had been unable to get a job since the last valley pit closed in 1990: 'They saw us as pit fodder, so they didn't educate us too well. Now they complain that we can't do anything else, we can't retrain. Well they can't expect us to read and write well because they never educated us for that.' He told me he was a 'Welsh nationalist, almost a communist', though really he had had enough of politics: 'We need a revolution, not elections, and I hate that Margaret Thatcher,' he said, spitting on the floor of the coach to emphasize his disgust. As we passed a colliery museum, opposite the entrance to some derelict pit baths, he told me 'That's the deepest anthracite mine in the world – go down there and after three days you speak with an Australian accent – they don't have pit ponies down there, they have kangaroos.'

During our conversation, an elderly man, friend of my neighbour for the outward journey, asked me in Welsh if I was all right. I smiled. He then asked me in English, and I replied 'I'm fine, thanks.' He overheard the young men in front of me swearing and asked them if they spoke Welsh. 'No,' they replied, and he said 'Well, you don't speak proper English either.' The young men apologized to me and said they thought that I couldn't hear them. The old man also told off the middle-aged and younger men who got off the bus to relieve themselves behind some bushes, 'Don't you know there are ladies on the bus?' As the bus slowed down to let the old man off outside his house, because he had decided not to return to the club, he said to me 'Fancy coming from west Wales and not speaking Welsh.' I answered 'Dw i'n dysgu' (I'm learning) and Whizzo said, 'Well, you're doing better than me then.' ''Dych chi'n trio' (You're trying), the old man said as he struggled to get off the coach with his two walking sticks. Whizzo remarked, 'As for the language, well, you can't change what's happened over hundreds of years overnight.' Then the bus drew up outside the rugby club, and we all went into the club, myself relieved that I had not been sick on either journey.

I again went upstairs to join my friends from other coaches. Two women with painted faces and miners' helmets were dancing on chairs. We chatted as a group of women and occasionally got up to dance to the disco music provided by a DJ. We were waiting for the victorious team to return. They had been entertained to a meal in Cardiff, but eventually they turned up with the club committee, all dressed in their team blazers, and a loud cheer went up in the upstairs bar.

The disco was interrupted by speeches in which the club president and coach thanked everybody for their support. The coach, Jeff, particularly thanked the players, the sponsors and especially the supporters who had travelled all over Wales to watch the team play. He ended his speech with 'Thank you, girls,' and provoked laughter by sipping champagne from the trophy, and passing it round among the team members, emphasizing that the Spar shop in Fairview had provided the bubbly.

The celebrations continued all night, but some of my friends and I left at about eleven o'clock. On my way out I met the man who had invited me to Cardiff, and I said 'Happy birthday'. He asked me where I was going and looked disappointed when I told him I was going home. I found out later that some men had not left the club until Sunday night, such was their enjoyment of the celebrations.

So much for recounting the day's events as seen through the eyes of a researcher ignorant of sport in general and rugby in particular. How can this help us understand the complexities of life in Blaengwyn and in particular community, ethnic and gender identities? I believe that by looking at an event like the rugby outing, and the things that occurred during it, and by contextualizing it within my whole research experience, useful insights into life in Blaengwyn can be glimpsed. I want to look here at the symbolic aspects of the rugby trip as well as the material events of the day, and combine these with some of the data obtained during the rest of the fieldwork process in order to analyse the various and overlapping identities in the community.

Rugby in Blaengwyn

The rugby team in Blaengwyn was not formed until 1948. This is relatively late compared with other villages in the valley (Evans 1963, 149, 152). Support, I am informed, for the team in Blaengwyn was strong when the team first started, but it had never been stronger than it was when I was conducting my fieldwork. One of the players told me that the team was struggling fifteen to twenty years ago: 'struggling for support and players, the bigger clubs were taking the better players but now they're sticking to Blaengwyn'. I think it is interesting that support increased locally during the period when the mining industry contracted. The same player agreed that there might be a link between the two: 'Yes, when the pits were going strong the club was not very strong, but now the pits have gone, it's thriving.'

References to rugby came up during my interviews, taped conversations and during day-to-day chats. Following international matches, the national team's performance was discussed, and the Rugby

World Cup was a common feature of conversation in the village among men and women. One man advised me that I could definitely not interview him until the World Cup was over. Readers are probably not surprised by this, because my fieldwork was based in Wales, after all, and it is a common stereotype that *all* Welsh people like rugby.

This is clearly not true, as I myself am Welsh, and am not at all interested in the game. But, as in all stereotypes, there is a basis of truth in the representation. As the team coach had emphasized, if I was interested in the village, I had to go to the Cup Final. A member of the community was giving me a very clear pointer to how to find out about life in the community. Rugby is undeniably the national sport of Wales, and to some it is almost a religion. It is also a very masculine game. This point was stressed to me when Gillian, my landlady, once asked me if my husband liked rugby. When I replied 'Not really,' she said, 'Well, what sort of man is he then?'

I believe that in Blaengwyn, masculine identity formerly associated with mining in the community had been transmuted into a masculinity expressed through playing and supporting rugby. The identification of the rugby team with the village is vital here, as is the fact that rugby is the national sport of Wales. All three identities were interwoven in this way, and women's identities as supporters were also expressions of gender, community and national identities.

Smith and Williams (1980) chart the rise in popularity of the game in Wales during the period of rapid industrialization in the late nineteenth century (1980, 15, 29) and dismiss the various claims that it is a traditional Welsh game (1980, 17–19), but through their book go on to demonstrate that it is undoubtedly a Welsh game now. When I was growing up in the 1970s, the Welsh team was very successful, winning the Triple Crown and Grand Slam more often than any other national team during that decade, and uninterested in the game as I was, even I used to boast at school of how my brother had been in college with one of the stars of the Welsh team, Gareth Edwards. When I moved to London after leaving school, my work colleagues presumed that I would be watching all the international games on television, and one manager even asked me to obtain a ticket for a Wales–England match in Cardiff through my family contacts with a local club in Pembrokeshire. So, though I am not a rugby fan myself, I am well acquainted with the passion that rugby arouses, and is expected to arouse in Welsh people.

Rugby is linked to Welsh identity among Welsh people and else-where, through stereotyping and through real enthusiasm for the game. My moving to London at eighteen was instructive in making me aware of how English people see Welsh people. When people learned I was from Wales, they assumed, as already stated, that I must like rugby, and that my father must be a miner, and that I must be from the Valleys. There is an element of pure ignorance in these perceptions, of course, and in my case, none of these was true. However, my own experience of seeing how others see the Welsh has alerted me to how national identity is formed by the interrelationship of those bearing it and those witnessing it through representations in the media and cross-border contact.

During the campaign for an Assembly in Wales, three Welsh rugby team members were among the celebrities used to encourage a 'Yes' vote in the referendum on devolving political power to Wales, consid-ered influential enough, and important enough 'Welsh' personalities to persuade voters on this important decision. David Andrews sets out the historical relationship between masculine and national iden-tity as articulated in playing and supporting rugby in Wales (Andrews 1996, 50–61). He suggests that, during the period of industrialization in south Wales in the late nineteenth and early twen-tieth centuries, 'a maturing, male-dominated, Welsh industrial middle class sought to create a united, harmonious and livable pres-ent through the creation of a unifying Welsh national identity which was relevant to the modern industrial experience', and claims that the game of rugby was the main conduit for this (Andrews 1996, 53). He notes that the new national anthem 'Hen Wlad fy Nhadau' ('Land Of My Fathers') was first sung in a large public gathering at the international rugby match between New Zealand and Wales in 1905, indicative of the development of the game into 'a high-profile symbol of a vibrant, and self-confident, male-oriented Welsh national ideology' (Andrews 1996, 53, 59). Andrews discusses the identification in the popular media of successful Welsh rugby players with Celtic warrior ancestors, a construction of a certain type of 'Welshness' popular at the time (Andrews 1996, 54–61). This image is still present in Wales today. As Chandler and Nauright say, rugby is viewed as 'one of the most masculine and manly of sports', and this association between a Welsh national identity and a masculine sport is important for an understanding of both nationalism and gender (Chandler and Nauright 1996, 2). At the micro level, it is also interesting to examine how this relationship between a gendered identity, expressed and constructed through a masculine sport, and ethnic and community identity, is articulated.

Blaengwyn is in Wales, and therefore, as in many other towns and villages, rugby was an important point of focus in the community. This cross-over between national and local identity was very important, I believe, and was emphasized by the occasion of the Cup Final match because it was played at the national stadium in Cardiff. The significance of this was demonstrated by the player kissing the turf before the match, and Mary's comment to her daughter about how special an occasion it was for her husband. It was also significant that the local team had reached the final of a national cup competition by playing teams from all over Wales at their level. This was regarded as the icing on the cake of their nine consecutive championships in the local league, a timely demonstration of the team's optimistic future as they were moving up to the next level just a few leagues below Fairview.

I had wondered about the derogatory chant about the nearby village, Fairview, and thought the reference to the Pope might have some relationship to the *plant Mair* (Mary's children) insult directed at people one does not like, and which one of my Welsh teachers explained had its origins in the ill-feeling between Nonconformists and Catholics in Wales. But the song about Fairview was not real animosity between the two villages, but rather 'happy niggling' at their side for having poached many good players from the village in the past, as the Blaengwyn Rugby Club president explained to me:

You see Fairview have had a first-class team always, as far as I can remember. In the WRU, which is Welsh Rugby Union, we've always been a junior league side, which, there's a big gap between the two of us, because I mean they're in the upper bracket, especially now in, they're in Division 3 or 4 of the Heineken League. Well, we've won the cup now, the Prysg Cup, at the National Stadium, well, we were just having a little rant over them like. And of course they have actually took a lot of our players, when I say took, I mean a lot of our players went to better themselves, which they did by going to a higher bracket club, but now we are in the bracket they are in, because they're three leagues above, it'll take us three years hopefully and we'll be in the same league as them. Well, a few of their players now, which are our players, can go back to us. So we're just rubbing a bit of salt in the wound.

This friendly rivalry which expressed a sense of 'belonging', as identified by Cohen (1982), could manifest itself in people's choice of where to live, the rugby club often being quoted as a reason for wanting to live in a specific village. For example, an ex-miner who is now disabled and is studying part time explained why he and his wife refused to live in Fairview: 'It's the camaraderie attached to the rugby, isn't it? There's like a stigma attached to it, I'm not going to live there and play with them.' I asked him about my idea that the rugby clubs were taking over as a focus for community identity now that the mines had closed, and he strongly agreed:

> The communities you had years ago when you had a mine, you were held together by the pit. Each village had a pit and you were held by that. Now I think what keeps the communities together is the actual rugby teams, the rugby clubs, 'cause everybody can identify with them, be involved with them.

An ex-miner who worked in seasonal employment on a canal in the neighbouring valley recognized the importance of rugby in bringing members of the community together: 'The community spirit is still there, as you've found yourself from the rugby, the whole village, if I was a good thief, that's the very day I would have come up here, 'cause there was nobody here.' The former National Union of Mineworkers' (NUM) chairman at the last valley pit, Pete, talked about a rugby metaphor associated with industrial disputes in the mine:

> If you had two stubborn heads together it was 'OK, let's go, we're not doing it, OK, we're on our way'. And the call would go out then, you know, 'the ball is in the river', that meant that people wanted to walk, like, you know, and out they'd go.

I asked what that meant and he explained:

> The ball was in the river and that was to signify everything's over, the game has stopped. I think it came from, we were playing, this goes back to when we were playing rugby . . . and obviously they had two balls, they had two match balls in the club and they had this full back that could kick it from anywhere. But when he caught the ball and kicked it into touch, it went in the river, about twenty yards away, you know. And he kicked the first ball in there, the first ball floated down the river, everyone was trying, they couldn't get at it you know, so they brought the second one. About ten minutes later he kicked the second one in, so the

two balls were in the river and everyone had to come off the field and try to get the balls, you know. But in the end we didn't, the game was called off, you know, so it went from that, like, you know.

This demonstrates how the sporting imagery infiltrated the pits, and he also described how rugby was a topic of conversation underground. He associated the two spheres, the rugby field, and the pit, with a certain type of masculinity and talked about the situation (importantly in the present tense) underground: 'It's very macho, it's men and it's men and boys and we talk about rugby and women and things like that, it's a very macho outlook in that sort of set-up.'

Despite the game itself being very 'macho', Peter thought that the rugby club was a means of women being more involved in social activities in the village, and he spoke of the 1960s as a time when women were encouraged to go to the clubs to increase support and revenue:

About the sixties, the clubs started opening up, you know, the rugby clubs pushed on things as far as women were concerned because you had, you know, women's committees being involved, you know, supporters' committees, you know, so they wanted their enjoyment then so they wanted their big bands, and of course the situation of being a loose woman in the clubs went and just died a death, like. There were business pressures from all directions, there were pressures coming as far as, obviously if you wanted a thriving rugby club, I mean, you're not going to have blokes in a rugby club with their macho image dancing with themselves, are you, they need someone to dance with, and that was it, of course. The sixties did make a big difference, a big impact, sixties wasn't it, changes going on all over the place.

This quotation is significant because it refers to women's emerging role as important supporters in the rugby clubs, a role still recognized at the time of my fieldwork and valued in the coach's victory speech at the club after the Cup win. It was not only on the edge of the field that women in Blaengwyn supported the rugby team. Women voluntarily cleaned the club's kitchen area, one of the women working on bread deliveries washed the kit, the baker's wife arranged sponsorship of the team by supplying their kit. Even the steward employed by the club had unpaid help from his wife, Mary, who buttered and filled all the rolls which were on sale in the club. These domestic tasks performed by women were echoed in the wider context of life in the village. For example, many of the women I spoke to said that they relied on other women friends or family members to help with child-care. This is something I had witnessed myself, with one of the bakery workers looking after her son's girlfriend's daughter after school, and an electronics factory-worker's son being looked after by his aunt. Mary described how she had a network of family and friends who would be willing to assist her:

> You know, if I needed anyone, I know there's loads I could turn to like, if I needed to leave the children, I know I've got Gail [friend] up the road there. Like her children come down here, mine go up there, but if I needed anything and Hilda and Powell [parents-in-law] weren't available, I know I could go up there then to Gail. If Gail wasn't there like, then I know of others.

Similarly most domestic tasks in the home were done by women, one ex-miner in his fifties telling me: 'I'm going to say something now and I'm going to upset; I'm old-fashioned, as far as I'm concerned a woman's job is in the home . . . I expect her to do the housework in the house.' Younger men also relied on their wives and mothers to perform jobs in the house, one mother having to 'draw a map to the coal shed' for her son when she went into hospital.

The institution of rugby thus reflected gender roles in the wider community and was important for national, community and gender identity. Gender divisions in work were also reflected in the social sphere.

When the Welsh team played international matches in Scotland every two years, local men went up to a Scottish town to spend the weekend with long-established friends who made a return visit to the area when Scotland's team played in Cardiff in the alternate years, a tradition at least twenty-five years old. Mary's husband had gone every two years since their marriage in 1982, and she told me that the Scottish trips were very much a men-only event:

> Well, no women go on the men's trip. If the women go, it's like, a couple of women have gone this year now, but their husbands organized a different place to go, a different place to stay, you know, so they stay totally different, they go on a different coach as well, the men'd go bloody mental if they were on the same coach!

During my interview with Mary I asked her what she thought went on during these trips and she answered 'I don't care as long as they go; I enjoy myself, I don't care,' and explained that she and her female friends went out to a nightclub in the nearest city on the Saturday night that the husbands were away in Scotland, one of her children staying at her mother-in-law's, the other at her niece's, adding 'Oh, I would have farmed them out anywhere, Steph; he's gone, so I'm going.'

Rugby trips to watch international matches were important in the establishment of another male-only preserve supported by women in the community, the local male-voice choir. The chairman of the choir told me that supporters, who would sing while away on rugby trips, had originally suggested at a Welfare Hall meeting that their musical talents be enhanced by the formation of a choir. The choir was established in 1969 and went on to perform regularly, not just on rugby trips to Scotland but at concerts throughout Britain and Europe. It is also interesting that although an all-male choir, the support of women for it was apparent in catering, fund-raising and secretarial tasks.

Identities

I believe that rugby in Blaengwyn is important in itself for analysing ethnic, community and gender identities. By looking more closely at other aspects of the trip to Cardiff and the prior and ensuing celebrations one can also gain an insight into understanding these identities and how they were interrelated.

My own identity is relevant here, as I was categorically told that, as a researcher interested in the village, I ought to go on the trip to see what the village was like. My position in the community as a married woman whose husband was living elsewhere was considered somewhat dubious, as reflected in the invitation to go to Cardiff with a single man who was quite blatant about wanting to have a sexual relationship with me. His advances were different from those of the man who squeezed my knee on the coach or the men working in the bakery who propositioned me frequently but in jest. These incidences were kept very much on a joking level, and I felt able to answer back in a joking manner myself. The invitation to Cardiff, however, set in the context of regular 'chatting-up' by this man, was more difficult to handle, though in the end when I insisted that I was happily married and not interested, I was left alone. The situation was difficult because the man had given me a present shortly after my arrival in the village, a lump of coal from the colliery he had last worked in, and I did not want to appear ungrateful. A recent volume of essays addresses how problematic such situations in anthropological field-work can be, and Eva Moreno's essay in particular, which recounts her experience of rape in Ethiopia, alerts one to how dangerous field-work as a woman can be (Moreno 1995). As a researcher I needed to maintain good relations with members of the community, but as a woman living for half the fieldwork time on my own, once I had left the bakery and rented a bungalow, I felt vulnerable and, to be honest, sometimes fearful for my safety when I was alone at night. Moreno points out that rape is often used as a means of punishing women who do not conform to the sanctioned notion of femininity in a soci-ety, as was the case in her experience (Moreno 1995, 219–22). This was partly why I felt vulnerable, I think, but I was also concerned that any resentment towards me in the village caused by the fact that I was carrying out the research could result in an attack on me. However, I have and had no evidence of any ill-feeling towards me, so it was probably a completely irrational response, caused by nerv-ousness at being on my own after living with my husband for over fifteen years. My guilty feelings about doing the research at all undoubtedly played a part in my fear, my feeling that I was exploiting the community being reflected back on to punishment of myself. These feelings also made me realize that I was far from feeling 'at home' in the village, and that this had implications for the 'insider anthropology' status of my research.

My gender's part in the research process is evident throughout in that most of my informants were women, as it was much easier for me to make friends with them without speculation about my possible sexual motives in getting to know them. My chief informant was a man, a man in his seventies, at a similar age to my father, and I was mistaken for his daughter-in-law during my fieldwork. But even he was teased about our friendship and his friends joked that I was his girlfriend. I do not think anyone really thought that we were having a sexual relationship, but the mere fact of the joking does indicate that suspicions would have been aroused had I been as friendly with younger men.

This closeness to women rather than men meant that apart from my time on the coach, all my time during the 'big day' was spent with women, the Blaengwyn girls who were 'on the piss again'. Women in Blaengwyn tended to socialize together, and the women's identity as supporters of men's activities was emphasized by the placing of this notice on the back of all the coaches. The notice was placed by young women and alludes not only to the women's enjoyment capabilities, but identifies them with the team and the community, and in a way claims the trip as their own since they isolated themselves on the notice from the male supporters on the coach.

The painting of faces and wearing of miners' helmets identified the women with the rugby team and the dominant industry which was associated with the village. This identification as a mining community is part of the *habitus*, whereby the community was still identifying itself as a mining community, but the women were now its signifiers through their supporters' helmets: they had become substitutes for the men, whose focus of identity was now the rugby team as players and supporters, through committee work and celebrations in the clubhouse lasting days at a time. The women, who supported in a different way, by attending matches and doing catering and cleaning jobs, were complementing the men's masculinity through their gender-crossing dress: in a way they were symbols of the industrial past of Blaengwyn and recognition that the mining industry had gone for ever but had not been forgotten and was still identified with the village.

The deprivation suffered in the area was discussed by my neighbour on the coach journey to Cardiff, and the real experience of this was expressed in shock at the price of drinks in the hotel and the paltry buffet provided for the supporters at a cost of two pounds fifty each.

My neighbour on the return trip, Whizzo, personified the tensions between gender, community and ethnic identity in the village, and he demonstrated a clear analytical understanding of his own position among the major structural changes which had impacted upon the village. He was despondent about his future prospects and realized that the educational system had not prepared him for anything but mining. In a meeting with the former NUM chairman some months after the rugby match, the union official happened to mention Whizzo, during a discussion on the union official's personnel role and danger in the pit, and I then found out that Whizzo had got his nickname through his wizardry as a repair man underground. The former union leader told me:

> He's probably one of the best repairers I've ever come across. Well, inevitably in Welsh coalmining you'd have problems, roof problems, and

they would start off with a little trickle in front of the face until it would open into a huge chasm. And these could be anything up to about twenty or thirty feet. Now you put a novice in there, or a person that's a little bit nervous, and he would go in and probably kill himself because the stones would be coming down all over the place, he wouldn't know where to start. Well, this particular bloke, Whizzo, terrific, and just about the only one I could put in there.

Five years after the last valley pit closed, it was no wonder that this brilliant repairer was feeling bitter towards the Prime Minister who had progressed the closure of pits and was seen as the figurehead of opposition to the miners during the 1984–5 strike. He had not lost his sense of humour, as demonstrated by his jokes about the deep pit going down as far as Australia, and it is significant that he used the present tense to talk about the pit too, again *habitus* from the past imposing on perceptions and identity. Whizzo's inability to speak Welsh and his recognition that this was due to hundreds of years of historical events, including particularly the 1536 decree that Welsh was to be 'utterly expired' following the Act of Union, and the introduction of compulsory English-language education in 1870 (Berresford Ellis, 1968), was a reflection of the tensions within Welsh identity. The old man's conversation with me and the young men sitting in front of me highlights the ambiguities inherent in a community situated in Wales, where some people were able to speak the native tongue but many others could not.

Concluding comments

I have used the rugby metonym to consider the implications of the game itself, and also its wider implications in Blaengwyn, and have argued that it is a means through which masculine and therefore community identity had been transmuted from an association with mining to the rugby team. National identity and women's identity were also linked to this and, whereas women had been supporting the mining community identity through their domestic work, their supportive role had now expanded to include not only the domestic sphere, but also in some cases paid employment in local electronics and clothing factories, and supporting men's activities connected to rugby. Rugby took on some of the characteristics that mining formerly had, as a means of providing a unifying element in the village. The trip also symbolized the way in which gender relations were constructed, internalized and reproduced in Blaengwyn. Although the rugby team was a masculine domain, women's contributions were vital to the success of the team, and this was acknowledged by the male team and committee members, including Jeff in his speech at the club. I believe that a shift had taken place in the village. In a similar way to that described by Frankenberg for the similarly de-industrialized north Wales village Pentrediwaith, a sporting game had been adopted as a symbol of village unity in Blaengwyn, although the game here was rugby whereas it was football in the Pentrediwaith study (Frankenberg 1990, 100). While the village was once associated with mining, during the period of my fieldwork it associated itself with the rugby team, another male activity. However, at the match women wore the mining helmets, recognizing the centrality of their contribution to the community. They contributed not only through their support of the team, but also by maintaining the close-knit nature of the village through their networks of family and friends.

Klaus Eder recognizes the contribution Bourdieu's notion of *habitus* can make to understanding such social processes (Eder 1993, 63–80). Eder suggests that Bourdieu has been able to move on from a materialist conception of social class, to a 'constructivist' model which takes into account how that class's characteristics are reproduced by social actors (Eder 1993, 65–9). The relationship of an individual or class to what Bourdieu terms 'cultural capital' has become more important than her/his/its relationship to 'economic capital', as defined by Marx, although of course the two are inevitably related (Eder 1993, 68).

Eder claims that as well as superseding Marx's analysis of relations under capital, Bourdieu's notion of class *habitus* has also surpassed Weber's notions of class (Eder 1993). Whereas Marx formulated the idea of collective class consciousness, and Weber identified differences in class as being expressed by subjective opinions and practices, Bourdieu's notion of class *habitus* is orientated towards 'the collective schemata of experience' (Eder 1993, 69). Eder says that *habitus* consists of 'the rehearsed self-descriptions and practised modes of perception and experience' of a class (Eder 1993, 72). Extending the notion of *habitus* from social class, my focus of research was the everyday practices whereby gender relations and identity were constituted and reproduced by a group of people living in a village formerly associated with one male-dominated working-class occupation, mining, and I have here focused on one event which I use as a metonym of social processes in the village.

The villagers were able to maintain the village's identity as a *mining* village not by colliery work performed by men, but by the work performed by women in providing a cohesive social network. By providing support with childcare and domestic tasks, and practical assistance for men's leisure activities, women ensured that the close-knit nature of mining communities could continue and the village could still proudly identify itself as a 'mining community'.

References

Andrews, D. (1996). 'Sport and the masculine hegemony of the modern nation: Welsh rugby, culture and society, 1890–1914', in J. Nauright and T. J. L. Chandler (eds.), *Making Men: Rugby and Masculine Identity* (London: Frank Cass).

Asad, T. (1979). 'Anthropology and the colonial encounter', in G. Huizer and B. Mannheim (eds.), *The Politics of Anthropology* (The Hague: Mouton Publishers).

Berresford Ellis, P. (1968). *Wales a Nation Again* (London: Tandem Books).

Bourdieu, P. (1977). *Outline of a Theory of Practice* (Cambridge: Cambridge University Press).

Cerroni-Long, E. L. (1995). 'Insider or native anthropology?', in E. L. Cerroni-Long (ed.), *Insider Anthropology* (American Anthropology Association: National Association for the Practice of Anthropology, 16).

Chandler, T. J. L. and Nauright, J. (1996). 'Rugby, manhood and identity', in J. Nauright and T. J. L. Chandler (eds.), *Making Men: Rugby and Masculine Identity* (London: Frank Cass).

Cohen, A. P. (ed.) (1982). *Belonging* (Manchester: Manchester University Press).

Davies, C. A. (1999). *Reflexive Ethnography* (London: Routledge).

Eder, K. (1993). *The New Politics of Class* (London, Newbury Park, CA: Sage).

Evans, G. (1963). 'Onllwyn: a sociological study of a south Wales mining community 1960–63' (unpublished M.Sc. dissertation, University of Wales).

Frankenberg, R. (1990). *Village on the Border* (Prospect Heights, Illinois: Waveland).

Geertz, C. (1993). *The Interpretation of Cultures* (London: Fontana).

Gluckman, M. (1958). *Analysis of a Social Situation in Modern Zululand* (Manchester: Manchester University Press).

Goldschmidt, W. (1995). 'The unfamiliar in the familiar', in E. L. Cerroni-Long (ed.), *Insider Anthropology* (American Anthropological Association: National Association for the Practice of Anthropology, 16).

Jones, D. J. (1995). 'Anthropology and the oppressed: a reflection on "native anthropology"', in E. L. Cerroni-Long (ed.), *Insider Anthropology* (American Anthropological Association: National Association for the Practice of Anthropology, 16).

Lewis, D. (1973). 'Anthropology and colonialism', *Current Anthropology*, 14, 5, 581–91.

Moreno, E. (1995). 'Rape in the field', in D. Kulick and M. Willson (eds.), *Taboo* (London, New York: Routledge).

Nauright, J. (1996). 'Sustaining masculine hegemony: rugby and the nostalgia of masculinity', in J. Nauright and T. J. L. Chandler (eds.), *Making Men: Rugby and Masculine Identity* (London: Frank Cass).

Okely, J. (1996). *Own or Other Culture* (London: Routledge).

Smith, D. and Williams, G. (1980). *Fields of Praise* (Cardiff: University of Wales Press).

West Glamorgan County Council (1993). *West Glamorgan Selected Variables Derived From the 1991 Census of Population* (Swansea: WGCC).

3 Research on your own doorstep: Welsh rural communities and the perceived effects of in-migration

Emma James

Migratory patterns to and from Wales have always been varied, complex and rapidly changing (Day 1989). Recent attention has focused on a perceived continual onslaught of 'foreigners' that has significantly contributed not only to demographic, economic and social changes within Wales, but also to cultural and linguistic changes. Indeed, 'many areas of rural Wales have witnessed dramatic processes of restructuring in their local economies in the post-war period' (Cloke et al. 1997b, 3). Resultant changes include a decline in agriculture and other primary industries, the increased dominance of service-sector employment in rural Wales and, perhaps the most dramatic, the reversal of depopulation trends which had previously characterized Welsh rural life prior to the 1970s. The impact of such changes has led to the existence of rural deprivation, poverty, employment problems and competition for housing, which in turn have contributed to the continued out-migration of the younger generations from many of these areas, in search of enhanced education and employment opportunities.

While it is acknowledged that changes within the rural areas of Wales cannot be attributed solely to what Lash and Urry (1987) claim to be the 'spectacular renaissance' of rural Britain, this chapter will concentrate on migration into rural Wales since I feel that it is the most significant contributory factor in causing these changes to Welsh rural communities. This migration has added significance, since in-migration has also coincidentally targeted what Balsom (1985, 6) suggests is the Welsh heartland, Y Fro Gymraeg, the core areas of the Welsh culture and language. Indeed, Day (1989) states that rural Wales faces a possible 'crisis' following the potentially rapid and radical transformation of traditional rural societies as a direct result of the impact of large-scale population movements of culturally dissimilar people. Interaction between incomers and the indigenous rural population has intrigued many academics and has been the subject of growing interest since the instigation of this process. In the case of in-migration to Wales, academic and lay interest in the influx of in-migrants has increased steadily over time because in-migrants have targeted the Welsh-speaking heartland (Champion and Townsend 1990; Day 1989; Office of Population and Census Statistics (OPCS) 1990).

My own research interests considered the changing nature of Welsh rural communities and the potential problems that faced the people who reside there, both locals and incomers. Migration into my own village during my teenage years was a factor of everyday life. However, the increasing number of 'strangers' within the village became more evident to me on returning from university. Whether this 'perceived' increase was a reality or my absence made it seem more apparent, I do not know. Although I acknowledge some degree of change is inevitable, the changes I saw were rapid, and this perception was reinforced by discussions with other native villagers about the changing nature of 'the village'. Academic research also concentrated on the radical changes in rural Wales. Day (1989) stressed the possibility of Wales facing a 'deeply troubled future' in light of the transformation of societies within such areas, as a direct result of large-scale population movements, while Giggs and Pattie (1992) considered the cumulative impact on Welsh rural society to be profound. Previous academic evidence therefore supported my research concerns, allowed me to justify my perceptions and also motivated me to investigate the changing nature of rural communities in Wales as a result of in-migration.

Statistical evidence from the *UK Census of Population* (1981, 1991) and the ONS Longitudinal Study (1991) substantiates the claim that Wales is the most 'cosmopolitan' country within the British Isles, having the lowest percentage of indigenous-born individuals (Giggs and Pattie 1992). Indeed, Welsh-born residency decreased from 79.4 per cent in 1981 to 77.2 per cent in 1991. (Country of birth was deemed the most appropriate census variable to establish 'nationality' of population. It is subject to limitations, such as Welsh individuals who are born in England and vice versa.) By 1991 English-born residency in Wales had risen to make up approximately one-fifth of the population and also to contribute

substantially to the overall population figures of the more rural coun-
ties, including Clwyd (37.5 per cent); Dyfed (22.1 per cent);
Gwynedd (29.6 per cent) and Powys (36.9 per cent). These figures
provided hard factual evidence to support the theory that Welsh rural
communities were subject to in-migration and its impact. It is
acknowledged that not all in-migration to Wales is concentrated in
the rural areas. However, the perceived impact of such demographic
changes were anticipated by the researcher (myself) and the local
population to be the most negative in rural areas, hence such areas
were of most interest to this particular study. The following quote
from a local resident illustrates this point: 'You only need one person
who wants to do it their way; the way things were done "at home" to
change things.' Indeed, this respondent emphasizes that the actual
volume of in-migrants is not necessarily a matter of importance, the
simple addition of *any* number of culturally dissimilar individuals to
Welsh rural communities is perceived to alter what are seen as
precious Welsh lifestyles.

As the predominant migrant population in Wales (78.2 per cent of
all incomers to Wales between 1981 and 1991 were English-born) it
was decided that all incomer interviewees were to be English-born
individuals who had moved into the settlements in the fifteen years
prior to the study commencing.

Through ninety qualitative in-depth unstructured exploratory
interviews in three rural settlements in south-west Wales (Llansteffan,
Llandeilo and Llanybydder), I attempted to unravel the complex
nature of rural community lifestyles in Wales, through the perceptions and understanding of those interviewed. Comparisons were
drawn between the perceptions of locals and the in-moving population in order to identify differing or opposing perceptions of these
changing lifestyles. Therefore my own cultural background provided
me with the ideal opportunity to practise ethnographic research 'at
home'.

In attempting to interpret 'the voices' of those interviewed, one of
the concepts considered was that of 'community'. Communication
between people and the need for a collective existence has fascinated
many academics in numerous disciplines, yet no agreement can be
reached as to the meaning of community. Indeed the term 'community' is notorious for its ambiguities. Interviewees were asked to
describe community, and what it constituted to them. They were also
asked whether they considered their own village to be a community

and, if so, they were asked to describe their own community and their role within it. Individuals were invited to discuss what aspects or characteristics of the community they deemed important and why. One of the most important themes to develop was the association that the majority of interviewees made between 'community spirit' and a sense of belonging and their understanding of community. These were deemed crucial elements of the community, without which it could not exist, and the majority of respondents argued that community spirit and the corresponding familial/social relationships were the essence of 'community meaning'. It is this theme in particular which will be developed in this chapter. It will explore my own relationship as a researcher with the communities within which I conducted my interviews, the material that I received and in turn the interpretations I can offer of the understanding of 'community' and 'belonging' within Welsh rural communities in light of my own position within such communities.

The importance of reflexivity

Let me consider therefore my own position within the context of my research. Such 'positioning' has become a practice of increasing importance for the qualitative researcher. Baxter and Eyles (1997) advocate that the recognition of being a 'positioned subject' provides the researcher with the means to validate their own research. Increasingly since the 1970s, however, reflexivity has been seen as 'a positive aspect of ethnographic research, rather than as an undesirable effect to be minimized' (Davies 1999, 178). Davies (1999, 3) points out, 'all researchers are to some degree connected to, a part of, the object of their research. And, depending on the extent and nature of these connections, questions arise as to whether the results of the research are artefacts of the researcher's presence and inevitable influence on the research process.' It is for these reasons that 'considerations of reflexivity are important for all forms of research' (Davies 1999, 3), especially those involved in social research.

Given what has been said about the significance of positionality or reflexivity, it is incumbent upon me to explain who I am, my background and my own status in relation to the research topic. As a female, aged twenty-six (at the time of study), born and raised in the district of Carmarthenshire, west Wales, I began the long process of gathering field material. I am Welsh-born and regard myself as Welsh by nationality, although I do acknowledge that I am also British. I am from a middle-class background, since both parents were teachers. I was educated until the age of eleven in what can now be classified as a category 'A' (Welsh-speaking) primary school, after which I transferred to a bilingual comprehensive school at Carmarthen. After this I attended the University of Wales, Swansea and graduated with a degree in geography, remaining in Swansea for the duration of my Ph.D. My first language is English. I would regard myself as a Welsh learner rather than a Welsh speaker, because since leaving school my ability to speak Welsh has diminished although it still remains with me. My lifestyle up until this time, and indeed since, has meant that I have never lived outside Wales, and for all of my life I have been immersed in the Welsh lifestyle. For all the above reasons I qualify on a number of levels for the category of ethnographer practising research 'at home'. Indeed, in interpreting my own relationship to the research being conducted, an interesting, if slightly complicated, set of explanations emerged. In all three sites my identity and therefore relationship with the communities was based around my 'native' status, as I was a Welsh individual who was living and working in Wales. However, in Llansteffan I also had what could be described as 'insider' status since I am indeed an individual who has grown up within the boundaries, both physical and emotional, of the community. Despite these obvious similarities between my own personal identity and that of some of my interviewees, in some respects my position in the community as an academic researcher made me very different from those I was to interview. Aspects of my identity therefore contributed to my position within the communities with varying degrees of limitation attached to them. These will be considered later in this chapter.

Understanding community

Let us now consider how respondents understood community within the three Welsh rural villages studied. For many the crux of their understanding was associated with connecting sentiments and feelings regarding family, friends and the village. Indeed, the most common definition among the respondents, particularly the local population, is that *community* is seen as a social system, where a set of relationships takes place within a specific locality. The community was therefore thought of as being a network of social relations that occur between individuals living in that locality.

> This is the village I was brought up in. It's a very special place. Because I grew up here, a lot of my memories are of this place, of my family and friends, so you could say I'm attached to it!

> This is my village. It's where I grew up. It's where my family has lived for years. This is the place I know best, it's part of me and how I grew up. I feel that I have a claim on it in some way.

Within the respondents' statements it is evident that both locals and incomers regard the community to be constructed from relationships. Social contact and relationships were cited as the essence of community, and their presence, in turn, created community spirit.

> I stay in the village because this is where my family and friends are. It's nice for the children to have all their friends around them.

> We live quite close to the village, we know a lot of people there, and we're on the committees there.

Locals in particular referred constantly to the apparent continuity and social stability present within the community (see Halfacree 1995). This continuity is reflected in the enduring nature of relationships present among the local population. Locals were keen to emphasize connections with other fellow community members, and stressed the longevity of their relationships. This aspect of community was recognized by one of the most formative thinkers in the development of the theories surrounding the concept of community, Ferdinand Tönnies (1957). He stated that the community, or *Gemeinschaft*, had several crucial characteristics. The first of these was that the *Gemeinschaft* is characterized by intimate relationships, believed to be enduring in nature. The local population appear to relish the fact that the village is a place where everyone is known to everybody else, where 'togetherness' or 'common knowledge' (Halfacree 1995, 9) is seen as an attribute. The local population often referred to the long-term relationships that they believe they have with other villagers. The majority prided themselves on retaining these relationships and claimed that this was one of the very qualities that the community relied upon, to allow it to continue.

My family has strong ties with the village and the people that live here. My Gran has a friend and they were very close. Her daughter and my Mum became friends, and are also very close. I'm friendly with the granddaughter, although we are not in each other's pockets. She's like a cousin. We see each other at Christmas and on birthdays. I look after her kids for her now and then; I suppose our children will be friends too. Our families are linked through the ages. I like that. It's nice; it's safe and familiar, to think that we've had a common link. They're not family but they feel like it, they're an extension of my family.

This interviewee describes her close relationship with another family in the settlement, which she describes with great pride and sincerity. She appears to take great comfort in the enduring nature of her relationship with this family, and emphasizes the length of time and the depth of feeling she has for this group of individuals. The reference made to 'family' and the associated emotional ties are an important and recurring theme in the discourses of the majority of the local population. The term family was used in this particular instance to indicate the level of intimacy in this specific relationship that was perceived to exist beyond that of acquaintances and even that of friendship.

Social organization within the settlements was therefore explained in terms of family and kin or enduring relationships that alluded to these sentiments. Cohen (1982b) describes similar circumstances in his study of Whalsay in the Shetland Islands. Indeed Cohen (1982b, 28) explains that in Whalsay, kinship remains the most common form of 'explanation and legitimation for close association'. He maintains that 'the reconciliation of the two themes change and continuity is the essential feature of the management of social identity in Whalsay'. Clearly, 'the structural basis of the society *has* changed. The relative importance attached to its various elements alters over time and with use.' This change, however, is 'masked by the rhetoric of continuity which Whalsay people employ in their own accounts of their social organisation' (Cohen 1982b, 22). He explains that the structures of social associations in Whalsay are described by the residents in terms which emphasize their historical character and significance, 'the history thereby suggested is itself an expression of the integrity and distinctiveness of the community' (Cohen 1982b, 23). But, as he points out, change has occurred and the 'expression of continuity in structural form requires a social organisation which gives the appearance of great stability whilst also permitting a good deal of flexibility and fluidity of social association' (Cohen 1982b, 23). Family and kin, or in this case enduring relationships, therefore provide the means by which to do this. Reference to the unchanged elements of their society allows locals to emphasize the enduring nature of the community as a whole despite the changes it has to face.

Incomers to the three Welsh villages I studied also recognized the existence of these enduring relationships among the local population: 'People here know so many people. There seems to be a history to these friendships; families seem interlinked. I suppose that is what we came here for.' In contrast, incomers do not refer to their own relationships in the same manner. It is assumed that, due to the short duration of their residence in these villages, few had experienced such relationships actually within the communities themselves. It is not known whether similar relationships can be found among the incomers in relation to their own families and networks of friends elsewhere since they were not discussed.

The importance of community spirit

Community spirit was cited as one of the most important characteristics of a rural community. Many of the local population describe it as the crucial factor that allows the continuation of the village, some stating that without its existence they could not reside within the settlement:

> This village has a definite sense of community spirit, and I personally could not live anywhere that it didn't exist.

> A sense of community spirit; down here we are a small group of people with a communal interest.

Bell and Newby (1978), referring to the work of Schmalenbach (1961), propose the notion of 'communion', which can be compared to the sense of community spirit felt among certain social groupings. Membership of a community involves 'a matter of custom and of shared modes of thought and expression, all of which have no other sanction than tradition' (Schmalenbach 1961, 331–2), while communion, according to Bell and Newby (1978), is radically different. Communion refers to emotional experiences and is the form of human associations which refers to affective bonds. They proposed that belonging to a community is only acknowledged by the locals when that community is under threat, while at any other time it is something that is largely unconscious and often taken for granted. Bell and Newby (1978) suggest that a community does not necessarily involve emotions that characterize a 'communion' and use these emotional ties to distinguish one from the other. Residing in a settlement may promote such experiences, allowing a context for such experiences to occur and then to continue to exist, but not all communities are actually in 'communion' or 'en rapport' (Schmalenbach 1961, 332).

Since community spirit is essentially a feeling that exists among like-minded individuals it is arguable that an attachment to a physical location is not necessary. However, Bell and Newby (1978) do suggest that a concentration within a specific geographical area may encourage such relationships. Continuous social contact with the same individuals can foster emotional ties. In this situation the community has stimulated these experiences, creating an environment in which emotional ties and relationships with other community members develop. It is this that is thought to allow community spirit to mature.

However, although this clearly exists within the study settlements, these distinctions were not recognized by the respondents. The concept of 'communion' appeared to encompass what the majority of individuals described as 'community' (especially where community spirit is believed to exist). Indeed Bell and Newby (1978, 291) state that 'the contemporary yearning for "community" is, however, an expression of the desire for communion'. Thus when respondents from both groups describe the community it is believed that their perception of the settlement is in fact more in line with Schmalenbach's (1961) notion of 'communion'. This type of definition was the most popular explanation for community as described by those individuals who inhabited the study settlements in west Wales.

> Everyone here knows each other. They all belong, and then they come together on carnival day, the boys from the football and the ladies from the WI. You need something to bring them all together; to get some sort of cohesion.

> There is a sense of good feeling here. People help each other. I'm not from here; my husband is, although I'm still Welsh. I came from a different

type of community background, that of the valleys. So now when people want help, like going on the hay, they know not to ask me because I wouldn't know what to do. But my husband does, and I go along and I make some food for them, that is my way of doing my bit. Everyone has a role if you're prepared to take it on.

We like to return this help, and they can see that we appreciate their help and that we are pulling our weight. We're then seen as part of the community or at least trying to be part of it.

Thus it has been noted that many of the locals both recognize and fully embrace the sense of community spirit in their community and regard this as highly desirable. Community spirit will exist only where there are individuals with like-minded ideas willing to participate in the enduring relationships as previously described. It can therefore be argued that community spirit is an imagined collective identity amongst those that wish to belong. This sense of belonging may, or may not, be attached to a particular location. Such a sense of community spirit is acknowledged to exist in the study settlements of west Wales.

Incomers also recognized both community spirit and a sense of belonging as being an essential part of community and their understanding of it. However, contrasting opinions were seen to exist regarding the perception of the importance of these factors to individuals. These seem to stem from the expectations that the incomer has of the destination community and also from whether these factors are important in their migratory agenda. Incomers who perceived community spirit as a positive attribute, something to aspire to, were those who would actively seek out this quality in the destination community. The desire to become part of the community, to belong and to experience community spirit would in turn determine the behaviour of such individuals on arrival. These tended to be the older incomers, many having moved to Wales to retire. These incomers were anxious to belong, and retirement gave them the opportunity to become involved in village life, thus ensuring they achieved the enrichment that they perceived such a move would bring them. The means by which these incomers believed that they could acquire these attributes was to be seen to be actively contributing to the community. For example:

Village life is a lot more than we expected. Much lovelier in fact, in many ways.

> Actually living here has been exactly how I imagined it would be. I thought there would be a community spirit and there definitely is. We've made a lot of new friends, incomers like us, and villagers too. We do lots of things in the village.

These incomers came in search of community spirit. Many hoped to reside in a community in 'communion', and the desire to experience community spirit was recognized as being high on the agenda of incomers. Indeed, such was the lure of the idyll that incomers chose to draw attention to its existence whether they felt that they had experienced it or not. Some incomers state that they are still outsiders, despite having earmarked community spirit as all-important to their perception of community characteristics.

> People keep themselves to themselves. They don't really mix and that wasn't why we moved here. We were looking to make lots of friends and find a real sense of community spirit.

> Although I've lived here for over ten years, I still feel that I am an outsider. I think however that this is partly my fault. I think that I could probably have joined in more if I'd wanted to.

Incomers appeared to prize community spirit when accepted into it. Some incomers resign themselves to never achieving full acceptance, while others satisfy themselves with other aspects of community life, relishing any level of acceptance. In explanation of this lack of acceptance incomers refer to their participation or lack of it in the community, some suggesting that it is this that has hindered their acceptance.

Thus community spirit and the relationships that allow it to exist and continue to exist were deemed very important to the overall understanding respondents held of the community. Both groups deemed it vital to their perception of community life within their own communities. Indeed the actual importance of this factor takes on another level of significance when its role is considered in relation to local/incomer interaction.

Status, acceptance and community spirit

In the situation where two groups of individuals live in a settlement but differ in social, cultural and economic terms, then the issue of social position is a matter for concern. Social position, rank or status in the community was especially important to the local population. Locals felt that their social standing in relation to the incomers was important for two reasons. The first was that they felt it was 'their' community and that since they occupied it first, they should have a position of superiority to the newcomers, regardless of other measures of status such as economic position and social class. Second, and contributing to the first, locals perceived incomers to occupy better economic positions and consequently to belong to higher social classes. This led to the local population perceiving themselves to be threatened by the incomers economically.

On consulting figures derived from the ONS Longitudinal Study (1991) it is possible to consider the socio-economic characteristics of the two most prominent incoming groups to Wales between 1981 and 1991: English-born incomers (78.2 per cent) and Welsh-born incomers (13.7 per cent). James (2000) states that when considering economic activity, the largest flow of both English- and Welsh-born incomers during this period are those individuals that are actively employed (English 48.4 per cent, Welsh 48.9 per cent). Indeed, the most significant proportion of these incomer groups are those individuals who did not experience any change in their economic position; 21.4 per cent of English incomers and 25.4 per cent of Welsh incomers remained in full-time employment between 1981 and 1991. When social class as a proportion of each respective incomer group is considered (see Table 1) it may be seen that two social classes dominate flows for both English and Welsh incomers – firstly, social class II (English 35.3 per cent and Welsh 37.8 per cent) and, secondly, social class IIIN (English 21.8 per cent and Welsh 22.5 per cent) with the Welsh-born individuals exceeding the English-born individuals slightly in each category. Therefore, over 50 per cent of both the Welsh- and English-born incomers are white-collar workers. If the incoming population differs significantly to that of the population as a whole this could have serious implications for the resident Welsh population, especially within the receiving areas. However, it may be suggested that *any* degree of dissimilarity could be offered as an explanation for tensions experienced between incomers and the local population. Indeed it is arguable that this is especially the case in the study areas where incomers were actually perceived to be 'better off' by the local population, regardless of any statistical verification. This view is perhaps not surprising given that significantly

Table 1: Social Class as a proportion of
each respective Incomer Group in 1991

Social Class	% English Incomers	% Welsh Incomers
I	7.0	13.1
II	35.3	37.8
IIIN	21.8	22.5
IIIM	15.2	10.5
IV	14.5	12.6
V	3.9	2.1
Forces	1.6	1.0
Totals*	99.3	99.6

* Totals do not include inactive individuals, thus do not reach 100.
Source: Commissioned from the ONS Longitudinal Study 1991 and OPCS
1991, Crown copyright, ONS.

more English-born incomers are present within the total incomer
population and it may be suggested that this in itself could result in
the local population being overly aware of these particular incomers.

In socio-economic terms, then, it may be suggested that the locals
certainly perceived they were 'challenged', if not actually threatened,
as the following quotes illustrate:

> Incomers are keen to let you know their professions and how much they
> earn. It's as if they think that it will make us accept them. The thing is, it's
> the one thing that puts us off them. In fact it makes me angry to hear
> them boasting, no one here respects that kind of arrogance.

> Incomers think they know everything, have big houses, cars, the best
> education but it's not about that, it's about people and what they are like.

However, this perceived threat was translated into other forms of
intimidation for the locals. As they felt that they could not challenge
the incomers economically, perhaps they felt that other aspects of
their lives were also threatened, such as their community lifestyle and
their culture. In accordance with conventional forms of social organization the locals therefore may have had to take second place to
incomers and, as a direct result of this, status within the community
became an issue. The locals did not want the incomers to challenge
their position in the community, as this would be another component
under threat. Consequently, they appeared to develop a strict attitude
to acceptance in their community.

Community life and the sense of belonging that accompanies this were aspects of rural life that incomers were keen to acquire; to be accepted and to be allowed to experience belonging were important to them. The local population holds the key to acceptance, as they allow individuals to join the community or not. (Indeed, in my opinion acceptance to the community became an issue only when this particular wave of incomers arrived en masse, actively seeking acceptance.) Community status can therefore be equated with acceptance into the community. It appears that this type of status is peculiar to particular communities since it seems to exist in a separate manner from the more conventional forms of status. Although social class and economic position are also acknowledged within the community, community status is the manner by which the community 'hierarchy' is established. Community status is allocated according to respect among the local population and ultimately it is a commitment to the community that commands this respect. However, the allocation of respect is complicated, since each group is treated differently.

Locals in particular appeared to have a definite sense of status – a theme that was also developed by Tönnies (1957). Tönnies believed that individuals have a 'clear understanding of where each individual stands in society' (Bell and Newby 1971, 24). Locals referred to individuals who perform key roles within the community, especially those that were willing to organize committees or events, or indeed those who were willing to help other individuals in an informal capacity. It is revealed that individuals are admired for extending a kind hand to fellow community members:

> People exchange 'favours' of the skills that they have. Someone will help on the hay, and then that farmer will help you. Or someone will be ill and when they are better they will send a gift to the people who called to say 'Thanks for the help', like a cake or something. Some people return gifts at a special time like a wedding or a christening or a twenty-first birthday.

> My neighbour calls every day to check on me and to deliver the paper.

Locals valued conduct, gestures, and actions. To act out a favour, to extend a gesture of practical help or simply to give a gift is symbolic of the desire to be part of the community and was seen as a highly prized gesture in terms of community acceptance. To assist others especially in times of adversity is seen as a key characteristic of the community ethic. Indeed this is a quality that incomers often remarked upon, not having experienced this type of behaviour before, as the following excerpt indicates.

> There is a concern for those that 'belong'. I have a friend from Oxford who moved in, and her husband died. I went to visit her and she was flabbergasted. The neighbours that she said she 'hardly knew' had been and had left gifts of food, cakes and flowers, and she didn't know what to do with them all. I had to explain to her that this was their way of demonstrating that they were sympathizing with her; that they shared her pain. It is the way that the village shows that we know that you are in trouble.

Individuals are also held in esteem within the village if they have a strong sense of respect for others, a pride for the village and a regard for others in the community. Other attributes are also highly revered within the community and they determine the standing of individuals in the community. Such qualities include diligence and perseverance and skills utilized to the good of the community.

> In the village, people value each other, and what everyone gives to the community. Some work really hard, whilst others do small things – but it's all appreciated.

> There is a lot of respect here for hard-working people. Lots of the villagers have been successful in education and the like.

> That's the difference between us and the incomers. Lots of the village children grow up and do well for themselves. . . They may be important councillors, be employed in professional occupations but in the village they are still 'Johnny down the road'. They know their place within the village and they know that they need to remain within the confines of their slot so as to retain their respect in the community.

These quotations also introduce another element to the understanding of status evident within these communities. Many of the local respondents referred to an apparent lack of regard for social class within the study settlements. Such a means of determining status is claimed to be redundant. Similarly, Day and Fitton (1975, 873) refer to the concept of 'the *buchedd* system', a distinctly Welsh variety of social stratification whose foundations are not economic but cultural. They describe the basic dichotomy of this stratification as existing between those whose *buchedd* (way of life) 'lays stress on respectability, self-discipline, deferred gratification and a love of knowledge, and those who fail to live up to these high ideals' (Day and Fitton 1975, 873). The quotations above certainly illustrate these sentiments. It was suggested by the locals that material worth was not a means by which they judged individuals. Locals claimed not to allocate status in accordance with wealth or social class, but via commitment to the community and fellow members of the community. Locals were also keen to compare themselves to the incomers, contrasting their own behaviour favourably with that of the incomers, the locals being portrayed as the 'religious and respectable' and the incomers as the 'irreligious and feckless' members of 'the *buchedd* system' as outlined by Day and Fitton (1975, 873).

> We're not bothered about 'who you are' around here. Money's not important. Everyone just mucks in and does their bit.

> Those that work hard for the community do it quietly. Those that shout about it aren't doing it for the village they're only doing it for their own glory; that's not what it's all about here.

This apparent lack of regard for social class amongst the local population surprised many incomers. Many stating that it was a feature of community life that they had not anticipated, prior to moving.

> Where I used to live, people used to go on about how much they earned and what cars people drove. But here, no one is bothered. I much prefer it that way.

> People in the village mix, and it doesn't seem to matter what class they are. People of different incomes all mix in together.

> There are those incomers that think they are the 'kingpins,' you know. They are the ones that have the first slice of the roast at the pig-roasts; they are on the committees and such. Many of them make huge donations to the community. They think that money buys people, but it doesn't, people admire you as a person.

What must be asked is why the local population wish to present themselves in such a manner, since the majority of individuals do have the desire for material wealth and economic success. A number of reasons can be presented for this. First, the locals may wish to present a positive image of themselves in comparison to the incomers. Subsequently, they claim that the incomers have these negative attributes that exist in contrast with their own. This would be done in the hope that any changes to the community would thus be blamed on the incomers for their negative qualities. By attributing the blame for such changes to the incomers, the locals could also accentuate the sense of loss to the community and paint a very negative picture of their experiences as a result of in-migration. In making the incomers scapegoats the local population demonstrated characteristics of situational prejudice (Allport 1958). Change to a familiar society causes confusion, and a lack of control over destiny results in decreasing self-esteem. To counteract these feelings, locals directed their anger and anxiety at their loss of control into blame. Indeed Allport (1958) suggests whenever anxiety increases and is accompanied by a loss of predictability in life people tend to define their degenerating situation in terms of scapegoats.

The second reason is that, due to feelings of economic inferiority, the local population wished to criticize the incomers for the one thing they cannot compete against. Differentials in social mobility are known causes of prejudice. The locals perceive the incomers to be in a more favourable financial position than theirs. Materialism and greed are considered to be unattractive attributes and, by presenting the incomers in this light, the locals contrived, consciously or subconsciously, to create a negative image of the newcomers.

Thirdly, prior to in-migration there was no real need to assess status in the community; individuals understood their roles and stuck to them. Locals perceive in-migration as a threat; a threat to the environment which incorporates the concept of community and also their national identity (see James 1998, 163–205). After in-migration, this hierarchy was upset and there was a need to reassess both the hierarchy and the manner in which it was controlled. Incomers, who were often in higher social and economic positions than the locals, were perceived as a threat. This was compounded by the fact that incomers had better jobs, better cars and were able to afford properties which local individuals could not afford to purchase. This, married with their attempts to belong to the community, meant their actions matched the fears of the locals. This only served to accentuate feelings of prejudice against the incomers. Ironically, for the locals it was their feelings of economic inadequacy which stimulated their actions and their claims that status in the community was not determined by conventional means of social categorization.

To counteract these feelings of threat the locals have redefined status (and therefore acceptance into the community) as a commitment to the community. Discrediting the more conventional forms of social organization, the locals succeeded in adding a moralistic tone to the allocation of status or social organization in the community, which existed in opposition to what they present as 'vulgar', but conventional, forms of social categorization used by the incomers. The locals were aware that the incomers came in search of community life and a sense of belonging and it was the one aspect of the incomers' migration experience that they had control over. The locals could determine which incomers were accepted and the extent of this acceptance. Regardless of education, occupation or income, all incomers were subjected to the same difficulties in gaining access to the community. Finally, it might be suggested that the action of redefining status established locals in a position of superiority, especially since they deemed it as the only way in which community acceptance/belonging would be judged.

This 'discrediting' or 'reinvention' of social organization to suit the community can perhaps be compared to the notion of cultural reproduction put forward by Bourdieu (1973). In describing the role of education systems in 'the reproduction of the structure of the distribution of cultural capital' Bourdieu (1973, 72) explained the concept of 'cultural capital' as the transmission of cultural wealth from one generation of a society, or perhaps, as in this case, community, to the next. However, he stated 'the inheritance of cultural wealth which has been accumulated and bequeathed by previous generations only really belongs (although it is theoretically offered to everyone) to those endowed with the means of appropriating it for themselves' (Bourdieu 1973, 73). If success within the community is determined by the appropriation of cultural wealth, but such appropriation is enhanced for those who have the predisposition to possess the instruments of appropriation, then it is only they who will be successful. This is certainly seen in the settlements under study, since success or acceptance for incomers was determined by the locals in accordance with the criteria they deemed appropriate. Bourdieu also emphasizes the fact that 'making social hierarchies and the reproduction of these hierarchies appear to be based upon the hierarchy of "gifts", merits or skills established and ratified by its sanctions' or, in other words, by transforming traditional social hierarchies into hierarchies most appropriate to the communities themselves, this then allows these communities to fulfil 'the function of legitimation' (Bourdieu 1973, 84). This allows the community the authority by which to justify its actions, and the manner in which it has reproduced or redefined social organization and status. Indeed, it could even be suggested that community status and the actions deemed necessary to achieve it were not such an important issue within the minds of the locals until large-scale in-migration, after which it became a powerful weapon with which to fight perceived threats to the community.

Participation and community spirit

As has been stated, community spirit and the accompanying sense of belonging were cited as important, if not crucial, attributes of the community, for both incomers and locals. For incomers these are the very qualities that enticed them into making the move to Wales, and which had eluded them prior to migration. Incomers aspire to experience community spirit and a sense of belonging to the community, however, to do so they must first be accepted into the community. Simply to reside within a settlement does not allow an individual access to the community, nor therefore to community spirit or a sense of belonging. For locals, access and consequent acceptance and the acquisition of a sense of belonging are dependent on a number of factors. The first is the tolerance of the local population who are ultimately the 'gatekeepers' of the community. For the locals, the sense of belonging and community spirit are acquired through forging relationships with other community members and a commitment to the community. Locals stated that both of these attributes were achieved through participation and involvement in community activities. Incomers therefore had to pick their way effectively through a minefield of activities, demonstrating their commitment to the community, in order to reach their ultimate goal of community acceptance, respect and belonging.

The local population interpreted attempts to 'belong' by the incomers in a particular manner. Again, the work of Bourdieu (1973) is particularly relevant to an explanation of this. Indeed, it was Bourdieu's belief that the transmission of 'cultural capital' or cultural wealth occurs most successfully between generations present within the dominant culture prevailing within any society. It is these individuals who are in possession of the most suitable 'instruments of appropriation' (Bourdieu 1973, 73). Since 'instruments of appropriation' are unequally distributed among the classes, then it is those who are closest to and most familiar with the dominant culture that understand and interpret the culture most effectively. Those who are part of the dominant culture have at their disposal larger cultural capital than other groups within society. This coupled with the fact that the 'apprehension and possession of cultural goods as symbolic goods ... are possible only for those who hold the code making it possible to decipher them', leads to the assumption that the transmission of cultural wealth among these individuals is very successful (Bourdieu 1973, 73). Bourdieu suggests that when the institutions responsible for the transmission of culture neglect to 'transmit the instruments indispensable to the success of its undertaking', this allows a monopoly within the institutions only of those 'capable of transmitting by their own means' (Bourdieu 1973, 81). It also allows for the perpetuation of the situation where individuals from other groups that are not close to the dominant culture are excluded from this success. Applied to the study communities, such reproduction allows the locals to control who can belong to the community, therefore rendering them proactive 'gatekeepers' of the community. Indeed, it could be suggested that it is a means by which individuals are prevented from ever truly belonging.

Similarly this can be explained by the work of Cloke and Milbourne (1992) who suggest that each individual has a cultural understanding of the rural or 'cultural construct', a set of images, imagined geographies and expectations of rural communities. 'Cultural competences' are the manner in which individuals translate the images and expectations they have of the rural community into actions and attitudes (Cloke and Milbourne 1992; Cloke et al. 1995; Cloke et al. 1997a). Indeed, it may be claimed that they are in fact the 'codes' by which people live their lives. Cloke and Milbourne (1992) suggest that since it is their belief that differing 'cultural constructs' of the rural community exist at national, regional and local levels, then individuals from differing areas may have (to varying degrees) different images and expectations, and consequently may have differing 'cultural competences'. It may be suggested that non-Welsh incomers will have differing, if not opposing, 'cultural competences' of rural communities to those of the local populations, which could result in them engaging in potentially inappropriate behaviour. Rural communities in Wales have, according to Cloke et al. (1995, 48), become potential areas of 'cultural conflict' due to the fact that incomers arrive with imaginations of what rural life is like, fuelled by 'the cultural idylls of rural England'. They suggest that incomers are thus ill equipped to settle or even be made welcome in Wales, since they lack the appropriate 'cultural competences' to do so. It is interesting to note that while Cloke et al. (1997a) do not suggest that 'cultural competences' are fixed or that they can't be learnt, they do suggest that they contribute to the manner in which individuals experience life within rural communities.

Therefore, if 'cultural competences' (Cloke and Milbourne 1992; Cloke et al., 1995; Cloke et al. 1997a) can be described as appropriate behaviour which translates into a 'proper' way in which to live in these settlements, then those individuals that do not live in this manner do not fit into the village community. It is thought that every individual has a lifestyle strategy, a way of expressing themselves in everyday life and a plan for their future life. However, there are certain lifestyle strategies that are deemed inappropriate to specific villages. It is felt that each individual village has a collective set of priorities determined by the local population. Some of these are actually defined, while others are subconscious or hidden 'codes' that are culturally ascribed (see Cloke et al. 1997a). This leads to problems for incomers committing 'accidental transgressions'. If an incomer is seen to be attempting to adopt the cultural 'codes' of that settlement then this makes locals far more tolerant of the individual. However, if no attempt is made to even acknowledge the cultural 'codes', then this will alienate that individual from the local population.

> New people that join the community are so keen to join in that they try to do it too fast. That just gets people's backs up! If they let things take their own course then they wouldn't take as long.

> They just don't know how things are done round here. They arrive and they think that they know everything. They join 'this' club and 'that' committee and then they try to take over, as if we don't know how things should be done. The thing is that we've done all right up till now and we didn't need them before. They don't seem to realize that there are certain ways that things are done round here and that we don't like being told what to do and how to do it.

Incidents arise in which contrasting cultural 'codes' can be seen to be in conflict with each other. For example, in one of the study sites an incomer had bought the local pub. As a focal point in the community this pub had played an important role in the community and its existence. However, the new landlord had renovated the site and 'improved' the interior decoration quite considerably, to the utter dismay of the local community, many declaring that the character of the pub had been destroyed.

> It helps to have a focal point, we're a family here and that having a focal point keeps it going. Every family needs a common place and we have been robbed of ours. I am ashamed to say that it was outsiders who came along and bought the pub and have changed it all. We and a lot of the locals don't go there any more because it's not the same. It used to be all old and worn, and had real character. The wallpaper was going brown because it had been up for so long! Generations of the villagers had drunk in there, like my grandfather. It's just not on that they just changed it. They never asked us how we'd like it to be, or whether we liked it the way it was! They thought that the locals needed to be educated and that they needed to be shown what a good modern pub was like. Even though we were happy with it as it was. They've imposed their ideas on us of what they think life in the village should be like, through the way they've decorated the pub, and I can tell you now the villagers haven't taken too kindly to it.

Alteration of the pub was perceived by the villagers to have also altered the character and personality of the community in some way. This one incident has affected relations between the local population and incomers in general. The locals perceive this building to 'belong' to them as a community; its alteration is thus a reflection of the lack of respect that the incomers are perceived to have for them and their community. The local population has an established set of cultural 'codes', which the incomers have not recognized. The incomers have displayed an alternative set of 'codes' and have gone ahead and changed a significant building within the fabric of the village with no knowledge of committing an 'accidental transgression'.

Therefore, many incomers move to Wales due to their desire to search for a community and a sense of community spirit, but the 'codes' of the settlement prove too subtle for them. As a result the incomers do not behave in the proper manner and are therefore not accepted into the community. Indeed as a direct result some incomers alienated themselves from the village in the first few weeks after their arrival.

I don't mind so much if people join in. It's just when they try to take over that really annoys me! We've managed without them until now, so what makes them think that they have to be in charge now?

The thing is that many incomers take things too far, too soon. Instead of waiting to be asked, they are so keen to be part of the village life that they leap headlong into the committee thing, and really if they'd just waited until people knew them better then things would be easier.

I've no objection to people moving into the village or in-migration in general. Only that some move into the area and try to take over. They think the villagers never lived until they arrived to show them how to. They join in, and try to do things their way. There is a really fine line, I think, between involvement and interference. Some step over this line.

Therefore the incomers are in a 'no-win' situation, since the local population had drawn a fine line between integration and interference. If incomers were seen to be unwilling to enter into the village activities, then they were condemned for not being sociable. However, if they did join in, then they were perceived as 'taking over' and could be perceived as interfering by the local population. Thus the incomers are left wavering on the fine line drawn by the locals, and many factors determine whether they stay on the line, fall off and are not accepted, or whether they are fully accepted into the community. Few incomers realized that to try too hard and to be perceived as overbearing would actually be detrimental to their quest to belong to the community.

We realize that we are sort of on trial here, you know, to see if we fit in or not. But the thing is, we're not always sure what to do. You know, we'd like to be more involved, but we know that we can't do too much or they'll think that we're trying too hard. Sometimes that's worse than not doing anything. There is definitely this 'thing' about interfering.

Finally, a minority of the incomers in the study communities actually recognized these contrasting cultural 'codes'. While some of these incomers took measures to be accepted within the community by attempting to adopt indigenous cultural 'codes' and lifestyle strategies, others stated that there had to be some give and take by both groups, to work towards a compromise of some description so that different lifestyle strategies could be accommodated within the 'cultural competences' of the settlement.

Being accepted into the community is very difficult. There needs to be some level of acceptance on both sides, the locals and the incomers. The thing is they do things differently to us, the way they live, and things like that, it takes a while to get used to it.

People need to be more tolerant of each other and to try to see others' points of view.

Identity of the researcher

As a young female who was born and raised in the study area (indeed within one of the chosen study sites), it was felt that several features of my own personal identity might have hindered my access to the two groups that were interviewed within the three settlements. Firstly, it was initially envisaged that not being fluent in Welsh might prove to be problematic when interviewing Welsh-speaking individuals in the Welsh heartland about the emotive theme of in-migration. However, for many of these Welsh-speaking individuals the very fact that I have a reasonable grasp of the language and admitted to being a learner was well received and was not seen as a flaw in my 'native' identity, as was first anticipated. Indeed, for the majority of the local population my own Welsh or 'native' identity allowed many to feel at ease. Ironically, this was especially the case for those who did not speak Welsh themselves. For them and the majority of incomers my lack of linguistic skills was actually a plus point. The fact that I was not a first-language Welsh speaker was perceived to ease (although it did not entirely eradicate) any potential tension, with many incomers and locals alike identifying with my attempts to learn the language. It has to be acknowledged that, on recognizing a Welsh individual, incomers may have chosen not to impart certain opinions within the confines of the interview. However, it was felt that the large majority were indeed quite frank and were apparently not hindered by my 'native' status. This is to the best of my knowledge, although I do acknowledge that I do not know of any alternative answers that might have been given to me had I not been a Welsh person investigating a Welsh issue in Wales. It is possible that answers given to me were curtailed; this is something that I will never know but nevertheless must acknowledge as a possible bias to the research project.

Secondly, it was also envisaged that my 'insider' status or personal association with one of the chosen settlements could lead to problems of objectivity, initially when conducting interviews and later when interpreting responses, since I myself have experienced the introduction of incomers to Wales and into my own home village. However, I had not resided in the village for over three years upon commencing fieldwork and thus was 'of the village' but not 'in the community'. My detachment from the community on an everyday basis meant that I was not party to the particular problems or issues that were potentially abroad within the community. This allowed me to focus on exploring the issues themselves with my interviewees, rather than actually being involved in their perpetuation myself. This was further enhanced by my identity as a researcher, which also distanced me somewhat from the communities, especially in terms of my 'insider' status in Llansteffan. As a researcher I was not Emma James from Llansteffan but an unknown entity that those with whom I was most familiar did not identify with. Indeed, my 'insider' status was interpreted on many different levels depending on the interviewee and what they wished to associate me with. To many locals in Llansteffan I am a familiar face, but the majority remember me as a child and therefore the relationship I have with many of them is merely as an acquaintance. This proved, in my opinion, to be a positive situation for two reasons. It allowed me to be sufficiently distant from a number of my local interviewees for them not to be inhibited about imparting personal opinions. However, a degree of familiarity proved highly beneficial when developing a sense of rapport with others, many of whom felt that they knew me and imparted information that they might not necessarily have given to an unknown individual. In the case of the incomers (the majority of whom had moved in during the period in which I was growing up), I was not a familiar figure. This in turn allowed the incomers to relax and not feel as threatened by my 'insider' status. Therefore, with each group differing aspects of my identity allowed them to identify with or distance themselves from me, allowing them to discuss with me elements of the lives they led within the context of the Welsh rural community.

Thus, for the purposes of this research I possessed what could be described as a dualistic research identity. Firstly, for all three communities my 'native' status afforded me access and acceptance within the communities overall. My Welsh-learner status allowed me to be accepted by all factions of the community I wished to interview. Welsh-speaking and non-Welsh-speaking locals alike regarded me as acceptable due to my Welsh identity, while incomers who perhaps were wary of talking to a Welsh person about such potentially emotive issues were somewhat reassured by my limited linguistic skills, which for many were on a par with their own. And, secondly, within my own 'home' community I was also viewed as an 'insider'. My detachment from the community, however, allowed me to be accepted by both locals and incomers. For some I was sufficiently removed from the community for individuals to feel comfortable in imparting what could sometimes be personal or even controversial opinions to me. For others my 'insider' status allowed the rapid development of rapport and discussion to flow freely. In having to recognize the potential problem areas of my own positionality in relation to my research and the individuals I was investigating, I was actually able to identify several positive aspects of this relationship. This in turn allowed successful access to the respondents in all communities and allowed me a reasonable degree of confidence in the responses I received.

Finally, it would be naive of me to suggest that, as a researcher, I did not bring some element of myself to the study and that this in turn did not affect my analysis of information received. Problems of bias must always be acknowledged and addressed by ethnographic researchers. While analysing and writing up this material I was constantly asking myself, 'Is this what my respondents are telling me, or is it what I want to hear?' Did my own experience, and therefore perceptions, of life within a rural community in Wales cloud my interpretation of those experiences recounted by the interviewees? I feel that this issue was particularly at the forefront of my mind because I was conducting research 'at home', had I been investigating a more 'exotic' cultural environment possibly it would not have taken on such an important role in the formation of my methodology. Nevertheless, I feel that both my 'native' and 'insider' status while conducting this research were in fact attributes that contributed positively to the research experience, rather than being the hindrances to objectivity as which they were first envisaged. Had I not been a Welsh individual in Wales, researching the emotive topic of in-migration to Wales, it is arguable that I would not have received the wealth of ethnographic material that I gleaned from my interviewees, especially the locals. It is also arguable that my own 'insider' knowledge of the workings of a Welsh rural community informed me, firstly, of the types of issues which would need to be discussed and, secondly, and perhaps more importantly of the manner in which to interpret the material received in order to fit the jigsaw together. This was certainly the case in relation to the understanding of community spirit, belonging and acceptance. Therefore my overall opinion of researching 'at home' is that it has been a positive experience.

Conclusions

In conclusion, several key issues emerge when considering the perceptions of residents of Welsh rural communities regarding the communities in which they live. The vast majority, incomers and locals alike, understood community to be constructed from relationships. These relationships were perceived to allow the sense of belonging and therefore community spirit to exist and continue to exist within these communities. Certainly the perpetuation of the community was crucial, particularly to the local population. To them, social stability and continuity were essential to the longevity of the community and were perceived to be symbolized by such features as enduring relationships. Reliance on historical characteristics for the verification of the continuation of the community is recognized by Cohen (1982b), who suggests that it is indeed a manner by which locals perhaps negotiate the changing elements of their community, especially those which they perceive as a threat. Referring to those elements which make up community which had *not* changed and continue to exist, such as friendships and kinship bonds, locals therefore sought to emphasize the enduring nature of the community as a whole, in the face of community change. Change and continuity were thus seen as essential elements to the identity and therefore the understanding of the community, certainly within the minds of the locals. In addition, understandings of community were related to the existence of 'community spirit', tied to an emotional sense of belonging, which allowed the community to be in 'communion' (Schmalenbach 1961; Bell and Newby 1978). For incomers the need to belong, to be accepted and therefore experience community spirit, was a key factor, often acting as the instigation for migration to such communities. For locals it was the essence of what inspires the community to exist, without which it does not function. Indeed, the enduring relationships, which they describe as important, allowed the very existence of community spirit.

As a direct result of its importance to both groups it is not surprising that community spirit and the sense of belonging which accompanies it had become a bargaining tool between locals and incomers. Faced with the changes which invariably are brought about by an incoming population with perceivably superior socio-economic characteristics, the locals used the incomers' desire to experience community spirit as a means of controlling acceptance and influencing social organization within the community. Indeed, it may be suggested that locals went as far as to redefine or reproduce the social organization of the community (in line with the sentiments put forward by Bourdieu 1973) in order to assure their status within the communities. It was perceived that status and respect were earned via demonstrations of commitment to the community. However, such demonstrations of commitment were subject to limitations. It was believed that incomers were unaware of the correct manner in which to behave in such communities since they possessed differing 'cultural constructs' of the rural environment (Cloke and Milbourne 1992). As a result they did not possess the appropriate 'cultural competences' (Cloke and Milbourne 1992; Cloke et al. 1995; Cloke et al. 1997a) or 'codes' by which to live their lives in rural Welsh communities. Similarly Bourdieu (1973) suggests that the dominant or, in this case, the local population may neglect to transmit what he terms 'instruments of appropriation' which allow individuals to understand and interpret the 'codes' of the culture in which they are living. Hence incomers often commit 'accidental transgressions' or inappropriate behaviour, which prevent them from proving their commitment to the community. Since locals determined which behaviour was appropriate in their community they effectively acted as 'gatekeepers' to acceptance. As such they controlled the acquisition of community spirit and therefore assured their superior role within the social hierarchy of the community.

Bell and Newby (1978) suggest that membership of community is largely unconscious unless it is threatened in some way. Indeed Cohen (1982a, 3) argues that people only become aware of their culture when they stand at its boundaries. In the case of the Welsh rural community the distinctive culture of each settlement is set against the boundary of the differing culture of the incoming group. Arguably the cultural distinction between the two groups is twofold in this particular case, it is not merely the culture of the community itself which acts as a boundary but also the dissimilarity between the

Welshness of the locals and the 'otherness' of the incomers. Cohen (1982a, 6) suggests that the awareness of commitment and of belonging to a culture is a 'ubiquitous feature of peripheral communities'. Where communities perceive themselves to be peripheral or marginal to society, economically or politically this can result in the locality viewing itself as 'misunderstood, powerless, misrepresented, exploited, ignored or patronised' (Cohen 1982a, 7). He goes on to state 'when peripherality as a self image is complemented by a positive commitment to "the culture" one often finds something like a widespread "politicisation" of social life in which almost any event can assume the proportions of a social crisis, and any crisis can be depicted as threatening the very survival of the culture' (Cohen 1982a, 7). Indeed, in crisis situations the effective maintenance of the culture, rather than allowing it to diminish, becomes what Cohen refers to as the 'raison d'être of the peripheral community'. This is certainly the case in the rural communities of west Wales. Perceiving that the changes in-migration will bring to their communities and their culture are inevitable, locals manage and, to a certain extent, manipulate the only aspect of the process of in-migration in which they feel they have any say: acceptance into their community.

References

Allport, G. (1958). *The Nature of Prejudice* (New York: Addison-Wesley).

Balsom, D. (1985). 'The three Wales model', in J. Osmond (ed.), *The National Question Again: Welsh Political Identity in the 1980s* (Llandysul: Gomer).

Baxter, J. and Eyles, J. (1997). 'Evaluating research in social geography: establishing "rigour" in interview analysis', *Transactions, Institute of British Geographers*, 22, 4, 505–25.

Bell, C. and Newby, H. (1971). *Community Studies: An Introduction to the Sociology of the Local Community* (London: George Allen and Unwin).

Bell, C. and Newby, H. (1978). 'Community, communion, class and community action: the social sources of the new urban politics', in D. T. Herbert and R. J. Johnston (eds.), *Social Areas in Cities: Processes, Patterns and Problems* (Chichester: John Wiley).

Bourdieu, P. (1973). 'Cultural reproduction and social reproduction', in R. Brown (ed.), *Knowledge, Education and Cultural Change* (London: Tavistock).

Champion, A. G. and Townsend, A. R. (1990). *Contemporary Britain: A Geographical Perspective* (London: Edward Arnold).

Cloke, P. J. and Milbourne, P. (1992). 'Deprivation and lifestyles in rural Wales: II, rurality and cultural dimension', *Journal of Rural Studies*, 8, 360–74.

Cloke, P. J., Goodwin, M. and Milbourne, P. (1995). '"There's so many strangers in the village now": marginalization and change in 1990s Welsh rural lifestyles', *Contemporary Wales*, 8, 47–73.

Cloke, P. J., Goodwin, M. and Milbourne, P. (1997a). 'Inside looking out; outside looking in. Different experiences of cultural competence in rural lifestyle', in P. J. Boyle and K. H. Halfacree (eds.), *Migration to Rural Areas: Theories and Issues* (Chichester: John Wiley).

—— (1997b). *Rural Wales: Community and Marginalization* (Cardiff: University of Wales Press).

Cloke, P. J., Phillips, M. and Thrift, N. (1997c). 'Class, colonisation and lifestyle strategies in Gower', in P. J. Boyle and K. H. Halfacree (eds.), *Migration to Rural Areas: Theories and Issues* (Chichester: John Wiley).

Cohen, A. P. (1982a). 'Belonging: the experience of culture', in A. P. Cohen (ed.), *Belonging: Identity and Social Organisation in British Rural Cultures* (Manchester: Manchester University Press).

—— (1982b). 'A sense of time, a sense of place: the meaning of close social association in Whalsay, Shetland', in A. P. Cohen (ed.), *Belonging: Identity and Social Organisation in British Rural Cultures* (Manchester: Manchester University Press).

Davies, C. A. (1999). *Reflexive Ethnography: A Guide to Researching Selves and Others* (London: Routledge).

Day, G. (1989) '"A million on the move?" Population change and rural Wales', *Contemporary Wales*, 3, 137–60.

Day, G. and Fitton, M. (1975). 'Religion and social status in rural Wales: "buchedd" and its lessons for concepts of stratification in community studies', *Sociological Review*, 23, 4, 867–91.

Giggs, J. and Pattie, C. (1992). '"Croeso i Gymru – Welcome to Wales": but welcome to whose Wales?', *Area*, 24, 3, 268–82.

Halfacree, K. H. (1995). 'Talking about rurality: social representations of the rural as expressed by residents of six English parishes', *Journal of Rural Studies*, 11, 1–20.

James, E. (1998). 'Welsh rural communities: perceptions of the effects of in-migration' (Ph.D. thesis, University of Wales Swansea).

James, E. (2000). 'Immigration flows to Wales: in-migration and change in rural Welsh communities', in R. Creeser and S. Gleave (eds.), *Migration within England and Wales using the ONS Longitudinal Study*, Series LS 9 (London: HMSO).

Lash, S. and Urry, J. (1987) *The End of Organised Capitalism* (Cambridge: Polity).

Office of National Statistics (ONS) (1991). *ONS Longitudinal Study* (All ONS Longitudinal Study data remains Crown Copyright and the author alone is responsible for their interpretation. I would like to thank ONS for allowing use of the ONS Longitudinal Study and members of the LS User Support Programme at the Centre for Longitudinal Studies (CLS), Institute of Education for assistance with accessing the data.) The views expressed in this publication are not necessarily those of the ONS or CLS.

Office of Population and Census Statistics (1990). *Population Trends* (London: HMSO).

—— (1981). *UK Census of Population 1981* (Crown Copyright, ONS).

—— (1991). *UK Census of Population 1991* (Crown Copyright, ONS).

Schmalenbach, H. (1961). 'The sociological category of communion', in T. Parsons et al. (eds.), *Theories of Society* (New York: Free Press of Glencoe).

Tönnies, F. (1957). *Community and Society* (New York: Harper and Row).

4 Family and social change in an urban street community

Martin O'Neill

> Community is that entity to which one belongs, greater than kinship but more immediately than that abstraction we call 'society'. (Cohen 1985, 15)

As this quote highlights, community is a concept that people identify with in the most immediate sense, while 'society' and 'culture' are abstract entities of which, even within the grand theorizing of the academic tradition, people have only the most tenuous grasp. Indeed, so abstract and ethereal are these notions that in recent political history a British leader claimed that there was no such thing as society but only a collection of individuals. However, one of the most immediate and tangible manifestations of community is neighbourhood and any political leader who denied the existence of neighbourhood would not be taken seriously, for it is something that most people experience on a daily basis.

C. C. Harris, whose co-authored study of Swansea in the 1950s and 1960s inspired the research outlined in this chapter (Rosser and Harris 1965), has concluded that even in this period of social change and the increasing significance of the globalization process, people still have a sense of 'belonging' to an area, and space is as important as it ever has been in structuring relationships. However, although spatial boundaries of networks have now extended, this in no way negates the importance of spatial clustering in the formation and maintenance of social networks. These developments have led Harris to argue that community studies should be replaced by locality studies. He believes the question 'what else do territory members share apart from occupancy of a spatially located and defined social category?' should be replaced by 'how far has greater spatial mobility led to the spatial disaggregation of social spheres of the inhabitants of a given place?' (Harris 1990, 194).

The following study will demonstrate that in modern-day society the importance of immediate neighbours appears to be still of significance, at least in certain areas. In support of this perspective, in contemporary North American culture it appears that neighbourhood continues to be of importance to certain sections of society, as is illustrated by popular notions of 'boys from the hood' and 'home boys'. These are very powerful notions, particularly to the young dispossessed of urban environments.

From the time of Plato and before, philosophers have concerned themselves with the nature of community and particularly with how changes in the structure of society could affect the nature of community relations. As an example of this tradition during and after the industrial revolution, many of the classical social theorists, such as Comte, Durkheim, Marx and Tönnies, somewhat prematurely predicted the death of community. Today, again, as society experiences the so-called 'information revolution', there are those who argue that such developments will result in the demise of the importance of community to individuals. The purpose of this chapter is to examine the significance of recent social trends and the implications that they may have for the nature of community. In following Harris's suggestion of investigating localities in order better to understand the nature of community, I examine a case study of a contemporary neighbourhood in Swansea.

Theorizing neigbourhood: new conceptions, new directions

Recent theorizing as to the effect of social change on the nature of neighbourhood has again addressed the importance of increased geographical mobility and proposes that there is a growing significance in invented communities. Lash and Urry, in *Economies of Signs and Space* (1994), have considered the nature of this reinvention of community in the post-modern age. They argue that modernity is characterized by the globalization of economic and social life, which is increasingly subject to 'time–space distanciation' (Giddens 1990, 14). Capital, labour, commodities, information and images increasingly become disembedded from concrete space and time, as their mobility steadily expands. This, in turn, contributes to the emergence of new information technologies and post-Fordist restructuring of manufacturing and service industries. They hypothesize that these processes, linked with the growing privatization of social life, lead to old neighbourhoods and communities being replaced by new 'imagined' or 'invented' communities, which could be categorized as subcultures or 'communities of interest', such as the ecological movement. They state:

> To a greater or lesser extent we are not so much thrown into communities, but decide which communities to throw ourselves into ... the invention of communities is a sort of conduct which we more frequently enter into, new communities are being ever more frequently invented so that such innovation becomes almost chronic. (Lash and Urry, 1994, 316)

While not completely discounting the significance of physical proximity, they advocate that information technology and greater social and geographical mobility have, for the most part, made this factor redundant. In the world they describe, characterized by increasing impersonality, face-to-face interaction becomes desirable only as an ecological factor on a par with landscape or environment (Hirsch 1976).

However, although it may be true that there is a degree of invention of new types of community via such entities as chat-rooms and other spatially spread-out communities of interest, this is paralleled by emerging locality-based invented communities such as 'neighbourhood watch schemes' and tenants' and residents' groups, which appear to indicate the continued importance of locality. Therefore, in the evaluation of contemporary theories of neighbourhood and social change, such as Lash and Urry's, there is a need to consider whether such models apply equally to all neighbourhoods and whether such choice is uniformly available to all, or is predominantly a feature of Western middle-class neighbourhoods. Quilly (1995) in his review of Lash and Urry argues that this choice, almost by definition, is an attribute of the middle class. To exercise these choices one must have sufficient economic and cultural resources. The so-called 'middle class' has the capacity to draw upon economic and cultural capital to distinguish itself. This applies not only to housing, but also to entire neighbourhoods, as the process of gentrification bestows cultural and economic value on particularly favoured areas.

Cohen (1985) has highlighted the importance of the symbolic in relation to conceptions of community. He, like Lash and Urry, has observed that globalization processes result in neighbourhoods and communities around the world becoming increasingly influenced by factors outside their physical boundaries. This process, he feels, leads to a flattening of difference in cultural forms, such as language, family structure, political and educational institutions, economic processes and religious and recreational practices. However, he does not believe that these apparent similarities mean that old community boundaries have become redundant and anachronistic. His hypothesis is that the more structural pressures there are on communities to conform and blur their boundaries, the more they reassert their boundaries symbolically. As he states: 'The structural bases of boundary become blurred, so the symbolic bases are strengthened through flourishes and decorations, aesthetic frills and so forth' (Cohen 1985, 44).

This argument appears to be supported by some of the recent developments in European political history, where greater national integration between states has been mirrored by the rise in national sentiment not only in Wales and Scotland, but also more widely across Europe in such areas as Piedmont, Bavaria, Brittany and the Basque country. This notion is also supported by the following study of an East-side Swansea community in which people held on to and reasserted their identity as 'East-siders' and saw themselves as quite distinct from those they term 'Swansea Jacks' from the other side of the river Tawe. This study was conducted at the time of the VE Day fiftieth anniversary celebrations. The distinct identities within the area were further reinforced by overt displays of street decorations that were used not only to mark the East-side as distinct from other areas of Swansea, but also to mark out the particular neighbourhoods within the East-side itself. Various streets and areas competed with each other to present the most ornate display for the street festival.

Cohen's work suggests that the model of the outside world enveloping neighbourhoods or bounded communities is too simplistic. A neighbourhood does not simply become subsumed by the influences of the larger society, but rather, through a system of communal *bricolage,* transforms the alien structural forms that originate from outside, in a process of importation, reconstitution and negotiation with indigenous meaning.

From the literature reviewed, it would appear that neighbourhood is a highly complex social entity that has many different nuances, all of which need to be addressed in order to formulate an understanding of any particular neighbourhood. Reports of the death of community in industrial society, by such writers as Tönnies, seem now to be discredited. Also Lash and Urry's argument concerning the replacement of neighbourhood by new imagined communities that people choose to belong to in a 'post-industrial' environment does not seem to be supported by this study. Although new forms of community may be emerging, as they always have done, in certain areas of society, the evidence of the following case study does not support the theory that they are universally replacing more traditional forms of neighbourhood. A more useful analysis appears to be Harris's observation that changes in the economy and wider social sphere can produce changes in particular neighbourhoods.

Over the years, various theorists have postulated that one or other of these theoretical perspectives was the most fitting to address the nature of the relationship between social change and the nature of neighbourhood. However, a more profitable approach would be to view these various theories as structural models, each identifying certain aspects of certain neighbourhoods. Although one or another may predominate in a locality it is likely that such theories may reflect some of the dynamic processes that can be at play within different areas. Indeed, an individual's own personal network could well be a composite of more than one model, in that individuals who are thoroughly embedded in a traditional-style neighbourhood may well have many networks, both familial and social, that extend beyond any physical boundaries of their local neighbourhood. In general, the formulation of grand theories or laws concerning the relationship between neighbourhood and social change are problematic for, as this study will demonstrate, neighbourhoods can be as varied and complex as the individuals who form them. As Lewis observed as long ago as 1965:

> The variables of number, density, and heterogeneity . . . are not the crucial determinants of social life or of personality. There are many intervening variables. Social life is not a mass phenomenon. It occurs for the most part in small groups, within the family, within households, within neighbourhoods, within the Church, in both formal and informal groups. Any generalizations about the nature of social life in the city must be based upon careful studies of these smaller universes rather than upon a priori statements about the city as a whole (1965, 497).

Neighbourhood: a present-day case study

Having outlined some of the basic theories concerning factors that affect neighbourhood and the nature of neighbouring processes, it is possible to consider how such factors actually operate in a modern-day case study. The case study in question recounts my own research carried out in a Swansea East-side neighbourhood in the summer of 1995. The concept behind the research was to return to St Thomas in east Swansea, one of the areas studied by Rosser and Harris in the late 1950s and early 1960s, and presented in *The Family and Social Change* (1965), one of the classic studies of British neighbourhoods conducted in the post-war period. This research, like Young and Willmott's (1957), found strong evidence of the continued importance of kinship networks in an urban industrial neighbourhood. Rosser and Harris believed that neighbourhood performed two major functions, that of social identification, and also social support in a crisis. They felt that these structures had survived so strongly in this particular area, which they found to be one of the most traditional working-class areas of Swansea (1965, 139), due to the emphasis on employment in the docks at the time of their study.

Indeed, when Rosser and Harris conducted their study, Swansea docks handled more cargo annually than any other south Wales port. By the time of my research this was no longer the case; the docks had ceased to be a major employer in the area. Through the research it was hoped to find if this change in the economic base had produced changes in the nature of neighbourhood, neighbouring and the importance of kinship links.

Various studies of Swansea, such as those by Rosser and Harris, Bell (1968) and Hall (1976), have all shown that Swansea consisted of a number of what Gans has called 'urban villages' with which people identify more immediately than with the city itself. My research supported this perspective. The local residents of St Thomas talked of going to Swansea to do their shopping. There is a historical and geographical context to this, inasmuch as the area has strong geographical boundaries, with the river Tawe separating it from the main city of Swansea. This had only been spanned by an adequate bridge in the 1920s. Not only is there the river Tawe to the west of the settlement but also a dual carriageway arterial road to the south and a large wooded hill to the north. These physical boundaries added to the separation of this neighbourhood from other areas of the city.

There was a strong personal influence in my choice of research topic. I had been living in the area for some six years prior to conducting this research. I was originally from the south Wales Valleys and had left south Wales in my late teens, returning in my early thirties. In the intervening period I had lived in large cities and had noticed there was a difference to their 'way of life' from that of the Valley town of my childhood and early youth. However, when I went to live in this East-side neighbourhood, although it was in a city, I felt it was not of the city. I noticed there were strong similarities to the Valley communities of my youth, which tended to support the analysis of the neighbourhood as an urban village. It was in my mid thirties that I started studying sociology at advanced level and came across Rosser and Harris's study. I was very influenced by this work as I recognized in it truths as to the nature of my neighbourhood that I had observed on an anecdotal level when I knew nothing of socio-logical theory or community studies.

In the first part of the research I interviewed people in the area and asked how they felt things had changed in the past thirty-five years, since the time of Rosser and Harris's study. Local people expressed the sentiment that the neighbourhood was not as close-knit as it had been at that time and that there had been a breakdown in the trad-itional extended family structure of the area. People felt that this had been caused by the children of the traditional families receiving a better education than their parents and then moving out of the area to obtain the employment that this education afforded. Another major factor identified was the influx of 'newcomers'. Therefore, through my research I endeavoured to discover who these 'newcom-ers' were and where they had come from. Again, my own personal identity was central to this for at the time I had only been living in the area for some four years and prior to that had had no connection with the area whatsoever. Therefore, I was one of these 'newcomers' that people were talking about.

The methodology of the study was to return to a particular street where Rosser and Harris had identified the distinctive living and kinship arrangements of the Matthews family. At the time of their study different members of the Matthews family had occupied vari-ous houses in the street, and these family members ate, slept and took part in social activities in whichever house was most suitable. This

led to Rosser and Harris having a problem in defining what constituted a household. In my approach I asked every household in the
area to complete a questionnaire, which attempted to identify
'newcomers' to the area and where they had originated. In many
ways, though, the true purpose behind this questionnaire was for it
to act as a 'blind' in the same way as Ditton (1977, 6) had used one in
his work. That is, its main purpose was to engage the residents in
conversation. Answering the inquiries of a questionnaire for a
research project gave me a reasonable and valid excuse to start the
conversation and ask the questions I wanted, which otherwise could
have been seen as impertinent or invasive. In the end the questionnaire became the 'blind' for a type of semi-structured interview.
There was also a participant observation aspect to this research, for
my being a resident and member of the local dockers' club provided
an excellent opportunity for talking to people about the history of
families in the area.

Hall has stated: 'Neighbourliness implies not simply an exchange
of services, but also a resource of friendship and warmth, which
sociologists have seen particularly characteristic of working class
communities' (1976, 57). At the outset of my research it became
obvious that although some aspects of this are true, any stereotypical
image of working-class communities all pulling together in some
functional response to adversity is far too simplistic and fails to
address the complexities of the relationships within neighbourhoods.
Although neighbourhoods are characterized by reciprocity, the
nature of these relationships may just as easily consist of conflict and
animosity as friendship and warmth. Therefore, to fully understand
the dynamics of this community it would be necessary to understand
the reciprocal nature of animosity as well as that of cooperation.

The different aspects of this neighbourhood were graphically illustrated by the street parties organized to celebrate the fiftieth
anniversary of VE Day in May 1995. During this period one could
observe the most overt displays of neighbourliness, particularly in
relation to the provision of food and other resources for the party,
and in the practical help offered to the old, the infirm and those with
young children. It was a time, however, when inter- and intra-family
feuds became more apparent, on one occasion resulting in violence in
the street. These feuds had long histories, and were very important in
the construction of network identification and the alliances and
antagonisms that permeated the neighbourhood. Although the

bonds of kinship are still important, the animosity involved in these feuds could be strong enough to negate kinship ties.

The violent incident, although proving problematic to resolve in relation to my role not only as a researcher but also as a resident of the street who had to continue living there after the research period, provided insight into areas that might otherwise have been denied to an 'outsider' such as myself. The day of the street party had been characterized by much good humour where a number of the petty feuds and disagreements between neighbours had been forgotten. The vast majority of residents of the street had joined in the festivities and there was no real resentment against those who had not: they were just seen as people who wanted to 'keep themselves to themselves'. However, throughout the day a lot of alcohol had been drunk and emotions, both negative and positive, were running high.

It had been my intention as part of the research undertaking, but also to contribute to the social history of the community, to do some videotaped interviews with some of the older members of the neighbourhood relating to how it had changed since VE Day. I had intended to do this after the afternoon meal, before the evening festivities commenced.

Prior to going to university I had worked in the ambulance service and I still had a residual identity within the community as a first-aider. Neighbours would knock on my door if they were experiencing chest pains or if they or their children had an accident at home. On the day of the VE Day celebrations, as I was setting up the video equipment, a neighbour came running down the street to tell me that someone had been 'knocked down' at the top of the street. I left the video equipment and ran to the top of the street to be confronted with a body lying face down on the pavement by the side of the road, surrounded by blood. I turned the individual over and saw quite severe head and facial injuries. I told a bystander to call an ambulance while I started to clean up some of the blood in order to see where the person was bleeding from and try to stop it. I did not recognize the casualty at all, and indeed was unsure whether it was a male or a female. The casualty at this time was only semi-conscious and could answer none of my questions. As I cleaned the blood away from the badly battered face I was shocked to realize that this person was a neighbour whom I saw on a daily basis, but who, due to the extent of the injuries, I had been completely unable to recognize. At this point the person started to regain consciousness and tried to get up. I asked him to stay on the ground until the ambulance arrived in case he should exacerbate some injury. However, he did not want to and started to get abusive and aggressive towards me.

Although he was still being abusive to me I asked him what had happened and he replied, 'The bastards beat me up.' By this time I was starting to hypothesize as to what had happened. The person who had been beaten up was a known homosexual in the community. He lived with his boyfriend in one of the streets. However, they were well accepted and a known part of the community. In the four years that I had lived there I had never heard any antagonism expressed about the couple due to their sexuality. The general attitude seemed to be it was their own business and as long as they kept themselves to themselves nobody cared. Also, my neighbour did not conform to any stereotypical image as an effeminate homosexual; he was a well-built and powerful man who was known in the community as someone who could 'take care of himself'. Therefore, I began to think that some 'outsiders' who might have been passing through the neighbourhood had indulged in a bit of 'queer bashing'. However, for the time being my main concern was treating this individual's injuries.

I told him that I had called an ambulance and that I thought he should go to hospital due to the extent of his injuries and the fact that he had been unconscious. However, he would have none of it and insisted that all he wanted to do was go home. It was not my position to stop him so I followed him home and asked if he would let me treat his injuries, but he refused and locked the door. I waited outside for the ambulance to arrive so I could explain the situation to the crew. I had not been there long when the man's partner opened the door and told me he had collapsed in the bathroom and urged me to go and assist him. In the bathroom the man had slumped on the floor and although not unconscious was very dizzy. I started to clean him up and this time he seemed a lot mellower. We started to engage in conversation. He asked me how long I'd been doing first aid and what made me want to do it. This seemed to break the ice. As the situation was a lot better now I asked him if he had any idea who his attackers were. He replied, 'Of course I do, it was my fucking brother.' I was quite surprised at this but then he went on: 'That wouldn't have been so bad, I could have taken him. It was when that bitch jumped on my back and got me on the floor. As soon as I was down he just kicked the shit out of me.' I asked who the 'bitch' was. He replied 'my fucking sister'.

At this point the ambulance crew arrived. I explained the basics of the situation to them and as the casualty had calmed down quite a bit by now he went with them to the hospital. I started to tidy up the bathroom a bit, as there were a large amount of bloody dressings. As I was doing this the man's partner came in, very distressed, and started crying. I sat him down on the toilet to comfort him and he started to tell me of the background that had led to the assault. Both he and his partner came from long-established East-side families. Apparently in the past, back in the 1950s, a feud had started between these two families over the member of one family siring an illegitimate child born to a member of the other family, both of whom were married to other people at the time. This feud had continued right up to the mid-1980s, when it was brought to a head by these two individuals starting an openly homosexual relationship with one another and moving into a house together in the same neighbourhood. The man I was now comforting seemed to believe that the father of his partner was behind the attack. He believed that he had 'ordered' his son and daughter to attack his partner because of the shame that he had brought on the family, not only by being homosexual but also for betraying the feud.

While I must admit I was somewhat intrigued by this Shakespearean plot, the partner then went on to tell me a number of salacious stories that concerned various other members of the neighbourhood and spanned the past seventy years. The insight that this occurrence had given me enabled me, not only through the research period, but also for the rest of the time that I lived in the area, to contextualize the animosities and allegiances that were at play within the neighbourhood. This is an area I believe that few locality researchers ever effectively tap, as one needs to live in the locality for a lifetime to get this sort of access. In my case I was fortunate (or unfortunate, as the case may be) to be given access to this dimension of neighbourhood relations due to a very special set of circumstances.

This incident illustrates the multifaceted nature of the reciprocity of neighbourly relationships. The reason that this intimacy had been shared with me on this occasion is that I had provided my neighbour with something, namely care and support at a time of crisis. In return I had been granted access to the intimacy of their private life; I was being given a special sort of friendship reserved for close friends. This, in turn, is illustrative of how often in the ethnographic enterprise the researcher becomes the central tool of the research.

Through interacting in the neighbourhood on a daily basis I had entered into reciprocal relationships that enabled me to gain access to areas of knowledge that no other method would have allowed.

East-side neighbourhoods

In order to understand why different localities come to be as they are, there is a need to consider how social processes interact with the social organization of a place. One way to achieve this is to look at the social process of neighbouring itself. Between 1976 and 1981 Philip Abrams directed several research projects in different neighbourhoods in the United Kingdom and formulated theories concerning the nature of neighbouring practices (Bulmer 1986). Abrams's analysis provides a useful theoretical framework for understanding some of the subtle social dynamics of the neighbouring process. From his studies Abrams proposed that the most apt concept for understanding the nature of neighbourhood relations was as an expression of reciprocity. Care, for example, can be seen meaningfully as an exchange rather than a gift. Abrams observed that reciprocity is a multifaceted phenomenon. It does not necessarily have to concern itself with a simple exchange of equivalent services or even be within a bilateral relationship. As this study has shown, this reciprocity may concern the antagonisms of a feud or the alliances involved in mutual support through provision of childcare.

As the previous case study indicates, and from the responses to the interviews and questionnaires, there appeared to be a settled community with established networks who seemed to be staying in the area. As soon as I started conducting the interviews I found that although the family identified in the Rosser and Harris study were no longer living in that particular street, their descendants were living in the next street. Many people living in the study area, even younger ones, could give me accounts of various members of the family, and where various branches of the family were now. I found this observation very interesting as studies by Young and Willmott (1957) and Hall (1976) had identified how the history of a family could act as credentials and a 'doorway to the community'.

However, as previously mentioned, the people in the area *felt* that the area was not as close-knit as it had been, and believed that a major factor behind this was the increase in 'newcomers'. I was particularly interested in this categorization of people as 'newcomers', so I asked some of my respondents to identify individuals who belonged to this category and then interviewed them. When I conducted the interviews with these individuals I could not find one who did not have strong family connections to the East-side of Swansea. Although these so-called 'newcomers' were not from the St Thomas area itself my research demonstrated that not one was from a community more than four miles distant, and all were East-siders.

The categorization of 'newcomer', on investigation, appeared to be formulated in relation to the knowledge that was held by members of the neighbourhood of an individual's family history. The perceived breakdown in the close-knit aspect of the neighbourhood seemed to be related to the structural factor that different members of the family group were no longer living in the same street, the way they had done thirty-five years previously, as illustrated by the case of the Matthews family. This decreasing propinquity of family members, rather than leading to an attenuation of family ties, which were being maintained via phone and car, had led to an attenuation of networks of knowledge within the community relating to family history. This, in turn, had led to feelings in the wider community of a breakdown of 'closeness'. The only family in the study area that I found had no historical claim to 'East-sider' identity was my own. Therefore, this research is indicative that knowledge networks are an important component in maintaining the social networks that are a constituent part of neighbourhood.

In relation to my own identity within the neighbourhood, at the time of the study I had been living there for the relatively short period of five years. Two years after the research period, after completing my university education, I moved out of the neighbourhood to a more affluent area on the western side of the city. I had nothing to keep me in St Thomas. Although my children were young I had no family in the area to assist with childcare. Also, I had no historical identity as an East-sider.

Historically, this was a community composed of newcomers. It was originally a docks community populated predominantly by dockworkers and seafarers who had moved into the area when port trade was at its highest. It was the first area of Swansea to have a mosque and some of the families in the area are known as 'lascar' families, which means that they are of African or Asian descent. The community had grown in response to the labour demands of the expanding docks during the late nineteenth and early twentieth century. However, during the first half of the twentieth century the neighbourhood had gone through a period of relative stability as a settled neighbourhood based on a specific industry. The removal of this economic base, as this study has highlighted, has inevitably had implications for the nature of neighbourhood. However, the nature of these changes are complex and multifaceted and display a number of elements highlighted by the theorists mentioned earlier in this chapter.

Conclusion: the importance of space and place

In the examination of the impact of social change on the nature of neighbourhood, an understanding of space, economic base and kinship are all important features, and all three deserve investigation. As C. C. Harris has stated: 'What else do the members of a territorial category share apart from physical proximity? It is frequently membership of the same economic category' (1990, 191). While the basis of residential clustering is often economic, in the UK generally and in Wales in particular in recent times, due to the collapse of trad-itional industries and an increase in car ownership, there has been a decline in the importance of occupation, industry or class as the basis for grouping. There is not the same need in contemporary society for people to live near their place of work. This is not to say, however, that economic homogeneity is not still an important component of neighbourhood.

Kinship is linked to space in neighbourhood analysis, for while there is continued importance for local kin networks in territorial group formation, in recent times there has been a great trans-formation brought about by developments in communication, as highlighted by Bell (1968). This has meant that kinship networks can now be maintained over wider areas, and personal networks need not end at the boundaries of a settlement. Therefore, there is a possi-bility for an individual's networks to be distributed over a plurality of localities. While realizing that society is undergoing something of a communications revolution, the continued importance of space as a principle of structuring social relationships should not be underesti-mated. As Harris has observed, communication systems, such as phone and other electronic systems, have more power to maintain social networks and relationships than to establish them. Reciprocal relationships, be they positive or negative, which, as I argue, are central to understanding the nature of neighbourhood, tend to originate in continued personal interaction, which factors such as propinquity and kinship tend to facilitate. Therefore, spatial proximity is a major determinant in the establishment of neighbourly relationships between people and, in turn, can often be the foundation for kin and territorial groupings.

The findings of this research should be related to what has changed and what has stayed the same since the Rosser and Harris study. At the time of their study they noted that most of the property in the area was rented from private landlords, and that the tenancies were inherited through family connections. Today most people in the area are owner-occupiers and therefore are no longer tied by having to rely on the housing stock of a particular landlord. This gives people greater choice as to whether to live in a particular area or not.

It appears that established kinship networks are still important in the area. These can provide systems of mutual support in the same way as Bell (1968) had identified in his study of a middle-class community in the western area of Swansea but, as illustrated, they can also act as a foundation for group alliance. Neighbourhood and kinship networks were particularly important in relation to the role they played in childcare. For families with young children there was a great motivation to stay in the general area or to return at particular times in the lifespan. The empirical data found that most families had extended kinship networks in the East-side of Swansea, which could form the basis of local social networks. Hall (1976), in her study of a nearby East-side community twenty years previously, had found that many of these networks centred on the old and the infirm and those with children. Therefore, although there may be elements of antagonism, a central feature is that such networks more normally concern care responsibilities.

The sense of identity of being an 'East-sider' in general still appeared to be very strong, as demonstrated by the street parties. The area also seemed to be maintaining its identity as an urban village, with various networks centred on the family in the locality, the community centre, church and the local dockers' club. These urban networks continue to survive in the area even after the decline of the traditional industry, and the other social changes of the past twenty to thirty years.

Not only have there been changes in economic base but also in family structure in this neighbourhood in the intervening period. There are various factors that have influenced this such as cohabitation, divorce, remarriage and the growth of female employment. This has led to the creation of a range of new family structures. However, it remains unclear whether these changes have resulted in any straightforward change in individual lifestyle and values.

The findings of this research indicate that the descendants of the 1960s population are staying in the area. This is quite possibly motivated by the material help that having family nearby affords, and also maybe by the sense of identity that individuals feel with the area; the very two factors identified by Rosser and Harris in their study. However, it also appears to be the case that kinship networks now cover greater spatial areas. Members are not found in the same street as much as they were, but are tending to spread out through the Eastside. This has led to the inhabitant's perception that the area today is less close-knit than it used to be. However, as outlined previously, technological developments such as the car and the telephone mean that families can interact and networks can be maintained without there being a need for continued face-to-face interaction. Although these changes may alter the nature of these relationships it does not necessarily lead to their attenuation. Therefore, what this study demonstrates is that the changes in the relationships of this particular neighbourhood appear to be more qualitative than quantitative.

This study demonstrates that the social structures of locality are not homogeneous, static entities, but rather dynamic, constantly changing nuanced phenomena. Crow and Allan state that in a neighbourhood:

> People are embedded in local relationships to different degrees and in different ways . . . equally the manner in which people were incorporated was shaped by their own circumstances and social identities. Within the communities fine gradations separated those whom outsiders looking in at the community might tend to lump together. (1994, 186)

It is still true that local social practice and tradition continue to shape specific family values and lifestyles. Locality continues to be defined by the individuals who live within it, and remains an important constituent of an individual's identities. This research indicates that in this particular neighbourhood kinship groupings are shifting from being centred on a cluster of a few streets. These groupings still appear to be maintained but they are now expanding into the wider locality, from being centred on a particular street to the East-side in general. From this limited research it is impossible to assume that this is a general overall trend in the wider society, but this particular case study is indicative of how social change may affect conceptions of neighbourhood in a particular locality.

My thanks to Ron Trott and family, my key informants, and to the people of the East-side community, particularly the history group, for putting up with my questions. Personal details have been changed to maintain individuals' anonymity.

References

Bell, C. (1968). *Middle Class Families: Social and Geographical Mobility* (London: Routledge and Kegan Paul).

Bell, C. and Newby, H. (1971). *Community Studies: An Introduction to the Sociology of the Local Community* (London: Allen and Unwin).

Bulmer, M. (1986). *Neighbours: The Work of Philip Abrams* (Cambridge: Cambridge University Press).

Cohen, A. (1985). *The Symbolic Construction of Community* (London: Tavistock).

Crow, G. and Allan, G. (1994). *Community Life: An Introduction to Local Social Relations* (London: Harvester Wheatsheaf).

Ditton, J. (1977). *Part-Time Crime: An Ethnography of Fiddling and Pilferage* (London: Macmillan).

Gans, Herbert J. (1962). *The Urban Villagers* (New York: Free Press).

Giddens, A. (1990). *The Consequences of Modernity* (Cambridge: Polity Press).

Hall, I. (1976). *Community Action Versus Pollution: A Study of a Residents' Group in a Welsh Urban Area* (Cardiff: University of Wales Press).

Harris, C. C. (1987). *Redundancy and Recession in South Wales* (Oxford: Basil Blackwell).

—— (1990). 'Conclusion: reflections on family, economy and community', in C. C. Harris (ed.), *Family, Economy and Community* (Cardiff: University of Wales Press).

Lash, S. and Urry, J. (1994). *Economies of Signs and Space* (London: Sage).

Lewis, O. (1965). 'Further observations on the folk urban continuum and urbanisation with special reference to Mexico City', in P. M. Hauser and L. F. Schnore (eds.), *The Study of Urbanization* (New York: Wiley).

Quilly, S. (1995). 'Review of *Economies of Signs and Space*', *Antipode*, 27, 1, 108–11.

Rosser, C. and Harris, C. C. (1965). *The Family and Social Change: A Study of Family and Kinship in a South Wales Town* (London: Routledge and Kegan Paul).

Tönnies, F. (1957). *Community and Society* (New York: Harper and Row).

Young, M. and Willmott, P. (1957). *Family and Kinship in East London* (London: Pelican).

5 Being here and there in The Field: a look at insider ethnography*

Dé Murphy

The original idea for this research grew from my witnessing the extraordinary transformation that overcame the residents of The Field (I being one of them) when faced with the threat of eviction from their (our) homes. People began to live on The Field (for that is what it is) during the 1930s, paying an annual licence fee for the plots their chalets stood on. They were used initially as holiday homes, but became permanent dwellings during the war and the numbers living there increased on an ad hoc basis over the years. The land was sold to a property developer after the death of the landowner in 1988. This developer issued the residents with an order to quit in the following year. In an almost overnight response to this, the diverse group of people living there were describing themselves as a *community* and impressively drew on all their resources – symbolic as well as practical – to withstand a legal and emotional battle that lasted for over ten years. This chapter touches on some of the ways in which this sense of community was experienced and represented, but concentrates more fully on exploring the issue of insider and outsider research by considering my own place in The Field.

The insider/outsider debate

In the past, the anthropological ideal was to study people other than our own. Today, few anthropologists believe that this is still essential. In the so-called age of anthropology, researchers had a wide range of choices of faraway places and distinctive cultures but today anthropologists find they have to look to new horizons. Ironically these new

* All personal and place names have been changed to protect confidentiality, including 'The Field'.

horizons have often been found at home. But do we possess the required objectivity, and will the traditional methods and theories of doing anthropology suffice? In my case, not only was I researching at home, but I, myself, was one of my own subjects. Further reading revealed that insider research was not without its critics. If I was to carry out insider research then I should be aware of these criticisms and, I hoped, by the end of my study be able to refute some of them. Researching at home often means studying our family, friends, neighbours and colleagues in professional life. Instead of attempting to go native, anthropologists at home *are* the natives. This, of course, poses questions about being an insider/outsider – the identity of the researcher.

Though not new, and on the increase, the study of one's own society has been met with strong criticism from many quarters in anthropology. And this is not surprising, for it is essentially an attack on what has been the foundation of the discipline – the study of other cultures. Advocates of insider research have responded to these criticisms with an impressive array of counter-arguments, maintaining that because outsiders lack member knowledge, their research results are necessarily superficial. Critics of insider anthropology, on the other hand, characterize such knowledge as mere subjective involvement. Insider research is seen as inherently biased; this claim has been particularly levelled at ethnic studies in the USA, where it has been claimed the anthropologists function as advocates rather than social scientists. By contrast, the outsider enjoys what Beattie (in Aguilar 1981, 17) has called 'stranger value', which allows for a more disinterested scientific study. It is the stranger who sees the familiar as unfamiliar and is more likely to raise questions than the insider. It is also claimed that the outsider is more likely to have access to secret information and opinions because s/he is a non-interested party. But advocates of insider research also make a strong counter-claim. They point out that insiders do not have to deal with culture shock, something they see as a research obstacle. Culture shock, far from being fleeting, is in reality a chronic experience that can last for most of the fieldwork process. For insider researchers the most positive advantage is their ability to blend into social settings without radically altering them and for this reason they can engage in participant observation to a greater extent than the outsider can.

Another obvious advantage is their linguistic competence and their greater ability to read non-verbal messages. These abilities allow the researcher to pick up on the subtle nuances of the language and on behavioural cues. Claims are also made by those doing research from the inside of enhanced rapport, because as well as sharing cultural characteristics the researcher is also seen as being in the same socio-political boat as those s/he is researching. No matter how hard the outsider researcher tries to fit in and be accepted, s/he is always seen as alien to the community and, while not necessarily being excluded from the social life, remains excluded from many of its meanings. Ethnic scholars also argue that as insiders they are less likely to stereotype the people they study. Insiders are better able to get past any front presented to them and are able to penetrate the real life of the community. The amount of information and history insiders will have of their own community will also allow them to get to the heart of their research more quickly. But insider status can sometimes involve serious constraints, especially suspicion and resentment from your own community. This stems from the fact that the insider researcher can never be wholly insider, as the role of researcher defines her/him also as outsider.

As I have said, one of the main criticisms levelled at insider research is that it is inherently biased. But is there not always a measure of bias present in every research situation whether the researcher is termed *insider* or *outsider*? These biases stem from the cultural baggage every researcher brings to the field, as well as being informed by the nature of the research project and who is funding it. Strathern (1987) is concerned that there is an assumption that those doing anthropology at home can achieve a greater understanding than can those doing anthropology away from home, on the grounds that they will not have cultural or linguistic barriers to overcome. She points out that the implication that the ethnographer achieves greater reflexivity at home is erroneous, because it does not automatically follow that being a member of the society you are studying will result in your adopting local cultural genres. You might end up with a work that is unrecognizable to your subjects. She stresses the differences between common-sense descriptions and indigenous understandings, and the analytical concepts used in translating understanding into ethnography.

Hastrup is another who questions the usefulness of native attempts at self-description since, she says, this is just what anthropology is meant to transcend. According to Hastrup, who quotes Taylor (1995, 148), 'to assimilate interpretation with the adoption of the native's point of view is crippling to theory'. When her own research in Iceland was criticized by an Icelandic native, she points out that 'a genuinely anthropological understanding is different from *mere knowing*' (emphasis mine) and that 'natives' voices never tell the full story about the world' (1995, 149). And yet she had earlier quoted Cohen who says, 'If nothing else, anthropology gives another version of reality' (1995, 148). Anthropology, then, is just another discourse, and like the 'mere knowing' of the native, it also can 'never tell the full story about the world'. Hastrup claims that the only way to define an anthropology at home is through the resulting writings which alone will show, and she quotes Strathern (1987, 17), 'whether there is cultural continuity between his/her labours and what people in the society being studied produce by way of accounts of themselves'. She argues that it is this continuity which defines a proper auto-anthropology. But how are these accounts the natives have produced of themselves to be made visible to the reader if not in the ethnographic text? How else can an intra-cultural comparison be made? When we do anthropology far from home, the distance, cultural and geographical, is made apparent at the outset – in the introductory chapters, in setting the scene. But the distance in an anthropology at home (and there is always distance, no matter how close to home) can be made visible only by placing the accounts of the natives and the native anthropologist side by side. Only then can a proper scrutiny be possible. And should there emerge a lack of cultural continuity between the two, does this make the claim to an auto-anthropology invalid? Or does it cause us to ask more questions about how we can know and understand a culture, even our own?

Hastrup argues that there are no neutral positions in the local discourse, but surely there are no neutral positions per se. She is correct in stating that one must step out of the local discourse when writing and analysing. Surely that is unavoidable; fieldwork and writing-up is recognized as part of the same process; fieldwork is characterized by immersion while what characterizes writing-up is withdrawal or removal (usually physical removal) from the field-work site. I personally found this to be the boundary where insider becomes outsider.

An anthropologist doing anthropology at home need not be the paradox Hastrup suggests. She says that for the professional anthropologist the rules of the discipline are implicit; for the native the rules and knowledge of one's own society are implicit. In carrying out ethnographic research at home the researcher is at once native/ anthropologist and self/other. Hastrup claims that it is 'logically impossible to speak from an inside and an outside position at the same time' (1995, 159). But I would suggest that the Self not only becomes Other in the process of writing up, but that the Other can analyse the Self, as suggested by Mascarenhas-Keyes (1987).

Each of us knows our own culture, though it is true that the knowledge we have of it is not anthropological knowledge; however, it does not follow that a trained anthropologist cannot know it in that way because they are insider. The result of an insider's analysis, interpretation and eventual published work may reveal results very different from the outsider doing research in the same community, but what can we conclude from that observation? If we take the examples of outsiders studying the same society – Freeman (1983) and Mead (1928), Redfield (1930) and Lewis (1960) – they also reached very different conclusions. If insider research can be criticized for a bias which is the result of too much involvement, then outsider research can be faulted for a bias that comes from too much detachment.

Hastrup claims to have dismantled the notion of the native anthropologist; she emphatically states that 'there is no way in which one can claim privileged access to anthropological knowledge – except by being native to anthropology' (1995, 159). I can agree with this statement, but being native to the research setting and native to anthropology are not incompatible. I would argue that the former position can only serve to enlighten the latter.

The Field's story

My home for over ten years has been at The Field, which is situated at the edge of a nature reserve in south-west Wales. It is in a secluded semi-woodland of some fourteen acres and contains a seemingly random settlement of twenty-seven small, single-storey chalets of timber and lightweight materials built during the inter-war years. The Field was designated a Conservation Area by the local council in 1990. It is occupied by some sixty people in total, twenty-four of whom are children. Three of the adults are pensioners, while the others have a variety of occupations, from a footpaths officer to a manager of a care-home. There is a high proportion of artists living there, consisting of painters, a sculptor, a woodturner, a potter, a photographer and many musicians. In my ten years living there, there have been no instances of antisocial or socially disruptive behaviour.

The people of The Field who did not inherit their homes bought them from previous owners, and up to 1989 were granted individual yearly licences by the landowners, with whom we enjoyed a friendly relationship. In the two years before I moved to The Field the residents made several attempts to purchase it, but due to a number of problems, mainly financial, their attempts were unsuccessful. In 1989 the freehold was bought by a development company, and in the following year the company offered a new six-month licence to the residents, but increased the charge dramatically from £85 per annum to £1,000 for the six months. Furthermore, we were given a deadline of the end of that month, leaving very little time for us to make financial arrangements or to obtain legal advice. Most of the residents were unwilling and many unable to pay the sum requested, and we tried to negotiate a more reasonable and secure arrangement. But the company's offer was quickly withdrawn. Instead, the director of the company wrote to the residents advising us that he was going to develop the land into a housing estate, thus forcing the residents to leave their homes. The company's applications for planning permission were refused, as the land was protected by its Conservation Area status. The company appealed to the Welsh Office and the courts, but was unsuccessful on both occasions. However, the director pursued his aims despite these setbacks and wrote again to the residents, asking us to leave, informing us also that we had no right of access to The Field. Other parcels of land surrounding it were bought by the company and fenced off.

We responded legally, claiming that as well as having common rights by virtue of having lived here for such a long time, we also had tenants' rights and that the licences which had been regularly granted by the previous owners had in effect been tenancies. But in 1991 the first summonses for possession of land from the development company were received by the residents. It was then we realized what a serious and unpredictable situation we were in. An extended phase of hearings, claims and counter-claims, delays and fruitless negotiations followed. In 1992, our solicitor and that of the company managed to agree that all residents fell into one of five different categories in terms of how long they had been living on The Field, and whether they were, for example, owner-occupiers or subtenants.

From each of these categories one lead case was chosen to be dealt with in court. The result of each of these lead cases would then also determine all other cases within the same category. The cases were heard in court in 1994, and before rulings were made the development company issued Notices to Quit to all the residents of The Field. When the judgement eventually came it was favourable to the majority of residents. Further legal battles followed, with a successful appeal by the development company and another appeal by the residents to the House of Lords. Negotiation was attempted, but failed, and in 1995 evictions started. We offered to buy the land, but our offer was rejected and our only hope seemed to be the House of Lords appeal. The provisional date for this was in March 1997 and we decided to march to London to coincide with the hearing. At the hearing, most of the residents were granted security as protected tenants but at the time of writing there is still doubt as to the outcome for The Field and its residents.

As can be seen, the story related above is very much my story as much as it is that of any of the other residents, and it is one that evoked many emotions from sadness to anger, from hope to despair. Stepping outside this story and coming back in as an anthropologist was to be my challenge.

The research's story

The subject of my research was outside threat and the creation of community, and the question I asked was 'how does a loose collectivity transform itself into an organized and self-conscious community?' My hypothesis was that the members reinvent themselves on a number of levels and use their newly constructed identities as a primary tool in their campaign for survival. The process involved is a self-conscious elaboration and emphasizing of difference to suit the prospective audience – the wider community, government/local officials and the media. A variety of symbolic resources are developed and deployed, occasional spontaneous events become transformed into folk tradition and individuality is sacrificed as commonality is stressed.

One of the main themes that emerged from my research was how successfully the community had reconstructed and packaged their community identity and how this presentation had become one of the central tools in their campaign for survival. Another theme was that of conflicting individual and group rights and how they were managed. Finally, as I had been a resident in The Field for over ten years, I was particularly interested in the ethical and methodological considerations that arise from doing anthropology at home (in my case, literally *at home*). I intended to examine these issues through the lens of autobiography and anthropology, drawing particularly on the work of Okely (1996).

The theoretical starting point for my research was the body of work by Anthony P. Cohen (1982, 1985, 1986, 1992) on the symbolic construction of community, belonging and identity.

The journey from being 'friends and neighbours' to becoming 'community'

In accordance with Cohen's thesis that communities symbolically construct identities for themselves when under threat (Cohen 1985), the residents of The Field found themselves asserting that their home was a 'community' to be saved, even though some of them had not viewed The Field in this way before. This is demonstrated in an extract from an interview with Gareth, resident of The Field for over thirty years:

> The media, I think it was they who started that, they identified us as a community, it was easier for them to see us that way – completely separate . . . you were asked what this community meant to you, so you had to define what community meant, which is very, very, hard. And I think their concept of community was a bunch of like-minded people getting together, coming to live here, but it certainly, certainly wasn't like that. And it still isn't like that. There's different age groups, different lifestyles, different values.

While the residents may not have previously identified themselves as a community, people from outside The Field, including local people, the City Council and the media, did. One of the residents, when asked why this might be, explained:

> . . . just the geographical position of The Field, a few hundred yards off the road. Like, once you come down that lane, the four hundred yards becomes four hundred miles, a long way from the streetlights, down an unmade track, the boundaries of The Field are identifiable. We're

surrounded by woods and fields and the only way in is down the track, and that puts a lot of people off. When I went around and collected names for our petition, I realised a lot of people didn't know where The Field was, they knew it was there, but didn't know exactly where.

This notion of being geographically separate, leading to perceptions of an identifiably 'bounded' community, is also identified in Cohen's work on Whalsay, one of the Shetland Islands (Cohen 1987). Sarah, one of the younger people who had lived in The Field since she was seven years old, but who has since moved to the nearby town, concurs with this idea that an essential ingredient in the make-up of community is 'separateness':

I feel I am part of a community still, I think everywhere there is communities, but maybe to a lesser degree. Where I am now, I work in the local shop, drink in the local pub, know all the people from there, but The Field is different, here it's not as true, people are not true friends they just know each other. But then I think The Field is the way it is because it's separate.

As the date of the evictions drew nearer, and court cases were threatened, Rachel, a resident for twenty-five years, describes how the notion of community was utilized. She also describes some of the communal activities, which residents took part in before the eviction threats began and have carried on since, which define The Field as a community for her:

I think that we realized we were under threat and we had to defend ourselves in some form, and we realized that our common identity made us strong . . . But it was true anyway, we were all friends, we were a community. We didn't bother going anywhere else for our entertainment, all our friends were here, we had parties, bonfires, boules competitions, card games. We went to the beach together, so we were a community, but we had never thought of ourselves in that way before.

Rachel's account above is echoed in Gareth's description of how the threat of eviction created a previously unarticulated awareness of The Field as a self-conscious community.

Well, it was just this common enemy wasn't it? We owe him a favour in a way, because he made us aware of what we've got here. It wasn't something we'd really thought about before, until it was threatened. But then the press started coming down and getting involved, and then we had to suddenly justify our existence, put a name to ourselves, call ourselves something.

He goes on to suggest that different strategies were used for different audiences:

> Dealing with the council, we gave them facts, figures, a 10,000 signature petition, we were businesslike. But with the media, they wanted emotion, and we gave them that, we played that a bit, like Maisie, we wheeled her out every time, sweet ninety-year-old lady, we used her. We didn't force her, she loved every bit of it, so we let it go on, because we knew that was a way to get public opinion on our side. But that is what people want to see.

As the campaign to protect our homes progressed, the importance of presenting ourselves as a close-knit community increased. From the public's response it was clear that it was this aspect that brought us support. Consequently, it became crucial to maintain and present a united front, as Gareth describes: 'Collectively we didn't want to appear discordant, be seen as a bunch of people who didn't know what the hell they were doing. We knew that wasn't going to help our cause.'

It is over four years since the House of Lords decreed that of the twenty-seven homes, fifteen were Rent Act Protected, which has given those residents security for their lifetimes, and the lifetimes of their children. The remaining twelve homes still have evictions hanging over them, though the property developer has not acted on that threat to date. Despite the difference in the residential status of the tenants, the community still stands firmly together. Gareth sums up the situation as it is now:

> We knew it was what the property developer wanted to happen, to create a 'them and us' scenario, but it never really worked, off the top of my head, it may be because he never pursued those people, though he still could, and probably will one day. Though there is a real division now, in that those who are protected are paying rents set by the Rent Officer, £20 to £22 a week, and those who aren't protected could be potentially paying £70 a week. There's a big difference there. I think in the past he underestimated us. But now I think he has an impression of us as all solid, and that's put him off. He knows we will stick together no matter what.

Rachel also points out that, while some things have changed, the residents of The Field remain bound by their experiences:

Well certainly there is less going on, less meetings, fund-raising, which I think is a shame. But I think the community is just as strong as it used to be, but now we are allowing ourselves to get on with our own development. I definitely see that the common enemy brought us together as a community, we did learn a lot more about each other, our different needs, different strengths.

When I asked Rachel if the residents in The Field saw me in a different way since I carried out my research there, she told me: 'No, I don't think people saw you as any different then, remember we had radio and TV crews here every second week, students doing projects, students doing photography, film, we were so used to it by then.' My current position in The Field is as one of the unprotected tenants, and at the back of my mind there is always the thought that one day I may again be faced with eviction. If that moment ever arrives, I have no doubt that the community would once again mobilize itself in response to that threat as it first did in 1989. What follows now is a snapshot of my own experience as researcher and resident of The Field.

My Story

I had somehow imagined that doing anthropology at home was taking the easy option; it would be easier to obtain access, I would not have the language to overcome, consent had already been negotiated and I would avoid the intense feelings of alienation and loneliness so often described by anthropologists doing fieldwork far from home and in another culture. In truth, I did avoid many of those problems but experienced in their stead a different set of problems. I adopted Okely's (1996) suggestion to incorporate a personal anthropology and separate to my fieldwork journal I was keeping a personal diary relating to my research, from which brief extracts are included for consideration below. In this I was consciously being as reflexive as possible, not only recording my mental and emotional responses to events as an anthropologist doing anthropology at home and among friends, but also as a resident of The Field. This I felt would be crucial in the analysis of my data. I wanted to emphasize from the outset its unavoidably biased nature, while also suggesting that this should not detract from its relevance as an anthropological study. An example of the confusion of roles I experienced during some of my fieldwork is captured in extracts from my fieldwork notes, which I now discuss.

As mentioned above, as part of The Field's campaign we undertook a 250-mile walk from our homes to the House of Lords in London, where a final decision would be reached as to the legal status of the residents. We were fully aware of the symbolism of what we were doing and that we followed in the great tradition of the Jarrow marchers and, closer to home, the Welsh miners. While we did not aspire to anything so grand, we did feel that we were marching to meet our fate rather than passively waiting. For three weeks a fluctuating number of residents (between six and twenty) walked together, and I had hoped to conduct interviews as we went along. I did not. The experience was physically exhausting and intensely emotional. However, I carried my dictaphone as I walked, in which I recorded my every thought and emotion; about myself as resident, as anthropologist, how I related to others I walked with, and how I perceived the dynamics within the group. An analysis of these taped recordings shows them as a diary of the Self, not as fieldworker, but as one of the subjects of my research, as the following excerpt illustrates:

> I'm finding today really hard, my blisters have still not healed and are killing me. I'm last in the line today, everyone is way ahead. Last night I had a big row with Bill over having the electric heaters on in the Church Hall we stayed in. He said it was a waste of energy, I said I was frozen. There is a bad feeling between us this morning. I don't want to be here any more, I don't feel close to anyone, I'm wondering where is the community spirit now. (Excerpt from a recording of my thoughts, day 8 of walk, somewhere between Bristol and Bath.)

My fieldwork diary, which I filled in every evening when we stopped, I now read as the fieldwork notebook where I the anthropologist am Other to my Self.

> The Walkers walked 18 miles today over hilly terrain. Some were obviously struggling. Jean's feet are looking bad and she is very quiet. Spirits are low generally and there has been some bickering among a few people. The talk around the table is about the purpose of the walk, and if there was/is any point to it. Some are talking of old grievances and wondering where 'the community' will be when all this is over. I am one of those.

This is in marked contrast to last night when there was a lot of positive talk and a strong feeling of camaraderie. This fieldwork diary is a way of stepping out of the situation and regaining some perspective. (Data extract, fieldwork diary, 8 March 1997.)

As an anthropologist for whom home is the field and is The Field, reaching a cut-off point was always going to be a problem – and it continues to be problematic, even after the formal completion of the research. Sometimes a week can go by where I am Myself as Resident, and for the following few days it is Me the Anthropologist and then again other days when I am stepping in and out of both roles so often that I no longer know who *I* am. I argue that this duality is less a drawback than an effective research tool which should be employed, not repressed (Okely 1996).

A return to the insider/outsider debate

If one chooses the 'other' to study (traditionally the more *other* the better), there is an assumption that, because the subjects of your study are strangers to you, objectivity will be easier to achieve; you will be able to keep your distance. I would argue that the opposite is true; in assuming an objectivity you can easily fail to take into account your cultural conditioning, your class, race and gender which necessarily inform how you perceive the world. On the other hand, when doing anthropology at home in your own society, because of an assumed subjectivity, your situation forces you to be acutely self-conscious. Your total involvement forces you into an awareness, an alertness, regarding the role of the self in your research. For the native anthropologist, objectivity is what you aim for, whether you can achieve it is less important than that you strive for it. But should objectivity be a desired goal? Do not those insights gained as an insider researcher outweigh those conclusions reached by the anthropologist as outsider?

The native anthropologist is less likely to generalize about her or his own people, for to do so would be to generalize the Self and, as Cohen has pointed out, we tend not to think of ourselves as generalizable (Cohen 1992). It is also true that the ethnography that is produced by the native anthropologist is more likely to be read by the subjects of their research; this knowledge would inform the researcher's text. Accountability and responsibility would necessarily be high on their agenda.

It is accepted that the native anthropologist has insider knowledge, granted it is non-anthropological knowledge, of the cultural and political milieu in which they are carrying out their fieldwork, something the outsider researcher is cut off from. I believe a professional anthropologist has the skills and resources to transform this knowledge into anthropological data.

Stepping in and out of the society being studied is what characterizes the native anthropologist: to use the term 'insider' to describe a person researching their own society is somewhat misleading. I found that the researcher cannot be wholly insider and would suggest rather that the anthropologist researching at home occupies the insider/outsider position.

The problem of verification, I would argue, can be more easily dealt with when the anthropologist conducts research at home. Far from the closeness of the fieldworker to her/his subjects being a drawback, I would suggest that knowing that your work can be scrutinized easily both by the subjects of your research and by your academic contemporaries would result in a succinctness in the text and a transparency of data sources that those doing anthropology far away from home might not deliver. I do not mean to imply that the work of anthropologists researching abroad would not stand up to scrutiny, only to suggest that knowing other anthropologists were looking over your shoulder would induce a healthy self-consciousness.

What is the role of self when doing insider anthropology? As one of the subjects of their own research, the anthropologist researching their own community becomes a virtual other; this is the case if we agree that other is a cultural construct utilized for the purpose of comparisons. The insider anthropologist is called on to research the Self as Other. When researching in The Field, I had to ask myself how can I begin to make sense of how others understand this experience we are going through if I have not yet begun to know how I myself understand it. It has to be through a self-conscious autobiography. But we need to be careful how we position ourselves in the ethnography, for in an attempt to be that not invisible author we may find that we obscure/exclude the Other subjects/informants and end up with too much Self and too little Other.

If we, as Okely (1992) suggests, position ourselves as subject in the text then we are obliged to accept the moral and political consequences of our actions. I would argue that doing anthropology abroad, that is, in a geographically faraway place, allows the ethnographer off the hook, inasmuch as the subjects of the research may never see the final product and so not have the input they should have. Anthropology needs to come home before it can become fully accountable and, though it can never be totally free of the charge of exploitation of the Other, it can be hoped that the relationship may be more reciprocal. I am further convinced that whether we term it auto-ethnography, indigenous anthropology, native research, insider research or auto-anthropology, as Jackson notes, 'doing anthropology at home is here to stay' (Jackson, 1987, 1).

References

Aguilar, J. L. (1981). 'Insider research: an ethnography of a debate', in D. A. Messerschmidt (ed.), *Anthropology at Home in North America* (Cambridge: Cambridge University Press).

Cohen, A. P. (1982). *Belonging: Identity and Social Organisation in British Rural Cultures* (Manchester: Manchester University Press).

—— (1985). *The Symbolic Construction of Community* (London: Tavistock).

—— (1986). *Symbolising Boundaries: Identity and Diversity in British Cultures* (Manchester: Manchester University Press).

—— (1987). *Whalsay: Symbol, Segment and Boundary in a Shetland Island Community* (Manchester: Manchester University Press).

—— (1992). 'Self-conscious anthropology', in J. Okely and H. Callaway (eds.), *Anthropology and Autobiography* (London: Routledge).

Freeman, D. (1983). *Margaret Mead and Samoa: The Making and Unmaking of an Anthropological Myth* (Cambridge, Mass.: Harvard University Press).

Hastrup, K. (1995). *A Passage to Autobiography: Between Experience and Theory* (London: Routledge).

Jackson, A. (1987). 'Reflections on ethnography at home and the ASA', in A. Jackson (ed.), *Anthropology at Home* (London: Tavistock).

Lewis, O. (1960). *Tepoztlan: Village in Mexico* (New York: Holt, Rinehart and Winston).

Mascarenhas-Keyes, S. (1987). 'The native anthropologist: constraints and strategies in research', in A. Jackson (ed.), *Anthropology at Home* (London: Tavistock).

Mead, M. (1928). *Coming of Age in Samoa: A Study of Adolescence and Sex in Primitive Societies* (New York: Morrow).

Okely, J. (1992). 'Anthropology and autobiography: participatory experience and embodied knowledge', in J. Okely and H. Callaway (eds.),
Anthropology and Autobiography (London: Routledge).
—— (1996). *Own or Other Culture* (London: Routledge).
Redfield, R. (1930). *Tepoztlan* (Chicago: University of Chicago Press).
Strathern, M. (1987). 'The limits of auto-anthropology', in A. Jackson
(ed.), *Anthropology at Home* (London: Tavistock).

Section 2

SOCIAL NETWORKS and BELONGING

6 Wool measurement: community and healing in rural Wales

Sue Philpin

This ethnographic study is an exploration of a particular type of folk healing described in Welsh folk literature from the late nineteenth and early twentieth centuries and rooted in antiquity; it is the method of healing through wool measuring, the practice of which has survived as a treatment for depression in parts of rural mid-Wales to the present day. (Depression is the term used by respondents in this study to describe their emotional state; it does not necessarily correspond to the medical diagnosis of depression.) The research is concerned with two broad questions: first, how does people's understanding of the nature of health and illness, and thus their choice of healing, derive from the cultural belief systems of their community? That is, in what way does the therapeutic process stem from shared beliefs about the origins, meanings and treatments of illness? Second, focusing specifically on 'wool measuring', is this process sought out and used as a consequence of shared beliefs about the origins, meanings and treatments of a particular illness, in this case, depression? In short, does the culture of this particular community provide an aetiology, diagnosis and method of healing for depression that is different from those offered by mainstream biomedicine?

In order to address these issues, this study has focused on a community where wool measuring has persisted and sought to determine the meaning of the practice of wool measuring to those involved. It starts with an exploration of the therapeutic process of wool measuring and then examines the nature of illness currently treated by wool measuring, attempting to ascertain the ways in which people within the community studied perceive this illness. Accounts of wool measuring from the folk literature are also drawn on throughout this chapter for comparison and to allow consideration of the process in terms of continuity and change.

Wool measurement – a brief description

Wool measurement is a method of healing that, unusually, does not involve the application of any direct treatment to the sufferer. Instead it consists of an activity, a particular form of self-measurement, undertaken by the healer on the sufferer's behalf. Although there are variations, the following method used by a female healer, one of the participants of my research, is the most usual form that wool measuring takes in the present day. (A more detailed discussion of the entire therapeutic process is provided in a subsequent section.) An essential preliminary requirement to wool measurement is precise information regarding the sufferer's full name and date of birth (I use the term 'sufferer' to describe a person deemed (by him/herself or others) to require healing). Having noted these details, the healer takes hold of one end of a predetermined length of wool, the other end of which is firmly attached to a solid object. She then proceeds to 'measure' the length of this thread of wool against the distance from her inner elbow to the tip of her middle finger, a distance that she defines as a 'cubit', three times. Sound health is indicated if the length of wool corresponds, in each person's measuring process, to three cubits; if, however, all is not well with an individual, the healer finds the thread to be either shorter or longer in length than three cubits. Moreover, a measure of the severity of the illness is indicated by the amount of discrepancy between the actual and desired lengths of the wool. The same thread of wool is used for all measurings performed on each of her clients until the yarn becomes too worn to use.

After a seemingly arbitrary interval, the healer repeats the measuring process, sometimes three or four times a day, the length of the wool informing her of the sufferer's progress. The measuring continues, for each individual, until the thread reaches the correct length, indicating that the sufferer is cured. Thus, 'diagnosis' and 'treatment' of the sufferer's problem are both encompassed in the measuring process. However, all of the healers studied actually distinguished diagnosis from healing to the extent that they made a point of informing sufferers, or their surrogates, what the wool was showing about their state of health.

It is important to note that sufferers do not necessarily have to be in the presence of the healer while their wool is being measured, or even to be aware that measurement is taking place. It is enough for a request for healing to be made (either by the sufferer or on their behalf by a relative or friend) by telephone or letter.

None of the healers interviewed charged for their services, although one of them made the acceptability of a 'donation' clear, informing prospective clients that 'I don't charge but people give'; sufferers usually made a donation of between five and thirty pounds to this particular healer following wool measuring.

Methods

The ethnography draws its data from direct participant (on one occasion I had my wool measured) and non-participant observation of the process of wool measuring, including conversations and/or unstructured interviews with those involved. Additionally (with permission and attention to the maintenance of anonymity) documentary material, such as letters written to healers requesting help or expressing gratitude for healing, is also used. Nineteenth-century Welsh folk literature, pertaining to popular belief concerning healing, is also drawn upon to frame the research questions and provide background information and temporal comparisons.

Principal informants

The principal informants were people who practised wool measuring, people who had received wool measuring and people who had witnessed wool measuring and/or lived in a locality where wool measuring is practised. The number of healers interviewed and observed was small; although six people who currently practise wool measuring in rural Wales were identified, of these six only four agreed to take part in the study. Gender does not appear to be an issue today in this small sample group of healers in that they are evenly divided into three men and three women; moreover none of the healers, sufferers or other informants made any comments on the healers' gender. However, the folk literature refers to female healers less frequently than men. Three of the healers are in their eighties and three aged between forty and the late sixties; all speak Welsh as their first language. Twelve sufferers and five witnesses/community members were interviewed. Of the twelve sufferers interviewed, three of the subjects were under the age of thirty; the other nine were over fifty-five. There were seven females to five males, and all subjects except one lived either in the same village as the healer or within a five-mile radius. The sufferers were all Welsh speaking and predominantly from skilled manual occupations.

Reflexivity

Writers concerned with 'reflexivity' in the research process have noted *inter alia* that the ethnographer is part of the field being studied, that the relationship between the ethnographer and subjects shapes the research findings, and that the 'self' of the researcher becomes part of the data. Davies's (1999) broad definition of reflexivity as 'a turning back on oneself, a process of self-reference' hints at the connection between reflexivity and G. H. Mead's work on the 'self' and symbolic interactionism. That is, the notion that the self actually develops (both in infancy and throughout life) through social experiences and reflections on those experiences.

Authors such as Davies (1999) and Coffey (1999) have noted the need for recognition that the 'self' of the researcher not only influences the behaviour and relationships in the group under research, but is also 'itself' in the process of being changed by the relationships of the research process; and that, moreover, this changed self is also part of the data. A significant consequence of this dynamic connection between the self of the researcher and the group under research is that the relationship between the researcher and the researched (rather than just the researched group per se) produces the ethnography. As Hastrup observes, 'the reality experienced in the field is of a peculiar nature. It is not the unmediated world of the "others", but the world *between* ourselves and the others' (1992, 117).

With regard to issues of reflexivity in this study, there are a number of aspects of my biography that need to be addressed in that my present identity, including my status as a stranger or an insider, has been shaped by this biography. Moreover, I am also aware that my sense of identity and insider/outsider status were not static during the research experience, rather, there was movement, influenced by relationships in the field, back and forth across the boundaries separating these identities.

The first aspect of my personal biography that added layers of complexity to my insider/outsider status is my sense of ethnic identity, which, being English/Australian by birth and upbringing, marginalized me in a rural Welsh community; I return to the issues engendered by this marginality later. However, ethnic identity is not always straightforward; further influencing aspects of my biography are historical family connections with rural mid Wales (although not with this community) which inculcated strong emotional links and, indeed, feelings of belonging to this part of the world and its people.

My fascination with this culture was undoubtedly stimulated by the fact that it was, historically, my family's culture.

As noted earlier, my insider/outsider status was not static; I moved back and forth across the boundary between marginality and 'belongingness'. This marginality, while possibly advantageous in enabling me to adopt the role of the 'anthropological stranger', undoubtedly also limited both social interaction with informants and my understanding of the minutiae of situations and activities. A core feature of ethnic identity in the communities studied is the Welsh language and, despite the fact that all my informants also spoke English, Welsh was their first language. As a non-Welsh speaker I was inhibited in my attempts to understand certain situations and I was sensitive to the impact my lack of Welsh had on social interactions. Invariably, the first question I was asked at my initial meeting with informants was whether I spoke Welsh. I sensed disappointment from them at my negative reply, and also felt that they were having difficulty at times in translating some concepts from Welsh to English. If other family members were present while I was interviewing, conversational asides between them were made in Welsh. On a number of occasions when informants wanted to obtain pertinent information for my questions from other members of their families or neighbours they would telephone them and there would follow a rapid discussion from which I would recognize the odd word. Occasionally they would arrange further interviews with appropriate people while I was there, and again these arrangements would be conducted in Welsh. I was also often asked where 'my people' came from. On reflection, this question involved more than simple curiosity about my history, or even a desire to 'make sense' of me; rather, I suggest that as core cultural practices were being shared with me, this was an attempt to include me as 'one of them'.

The second influential aspect of my biography is that, because of my personal history as a qualified nurse, I am sensitive to the fact that my knowledge and beliefs about the conditions described by sufferers are influenced by my previous enculturation into the world of biomedicine. Thus, from my perspective, the word 'depression' is associated with a particular – though often diffuse – collection of symptoms, treated by medical and/or psychotherapeutic interventions. This necessitated a conscious bracketing of this particular understanding of the terminology in order to consider sufferers' perspectives of the illness. This enculturation into biomedicine also engendered a degree of scepticism in me towards wool measuring as a therapeutic intervention; again, a conscious bracketing of this way of thinking was required throughout the study. Despite this bracketing of my own knowledge and understanding of appropriate therapeutic interventions, my biomedical background distanced me from the shared beliefs of the community and thus reinforced my sense of self identity as a stranger. Thus, while my anthropological background encouraged me to look at the practice from a local perspective, my nursing background tended to produce a more sceptical point of view.

The shifting insider/outsider nature of my identity was also apparent on the occasion when one of the healers, ostensibly in an attempt to clarify the wool-measuring process, suggested that the procedure should be performed on me. I perceived that not only had my status changed radically from researcher to client, but that I was also being helped by this healer to 'belong' to the community; she was attempting to include me. Again, the reasons for this may be as suggested earlier, that as I was now privy to these important cultural practices, it was necessary for me to be an insider. On reflection, this incident did indeed enhance my understanding of the nature of healing through wool measuring in that I was aware, at an emotional rather than intellectual level, that I was experiencing very positive feelings at being drawn in and connected to this community in this way; I felt 'better'.

Stages of the therapeutic process

Having presented outlines of the wool-measuring procedure and the methods it is now pertinent to consider the stages of this process in more depth.

1 The taking of the sufferer's details

The need for the sufferer's full name and date of birth was considered an essential preliminary in all of the cases studied. Some healers wanted more precise information about dates of birth than others and some also required the sufferer's exact place of residence. For example, as one healer explained, 'I must know their full name and exactly when they were born, right down to the month, and their address, even the county.' In view of the fact that the wool-measuring process was diagnostic as well as curative, it is possible that the naming of the condition also required the sufferer's name. The name and age requirement, and particularly the place of residence, is suggestive of the ways in which close-knit rural communities are structured; that is, these communities are based on knowledge about the various families, people need to know where individuals 'fit' in the community. Moreover, these details about sufferers appeared to give substance, in the mind of the healer, to the person requiring healing; this was all the more necessary in view of the fact that some sufferers were not present to be measured. Such information gave them an image to focus on. One healer commented that once he had the sufferer's details he would 'think about them very hard, forget about everything else'. Similarly, another informant described a deceased healer who, when given the details of absent sufferers by a surrogate, would close his eyes saying 'let me have a look at them'.

2 Diagnosis – 'seeing what the wool shows'

The question of diagnosis or identification of the problem for both sufferer and healer raises two issues. Firstly, as noted earlier, diagnosis and healing are encompassed in the same measuring procedure and, as with many other 'traditional' healing systems, it is not possible to separate out these two phenomena. Csordas and Kleinman, citing examples of traditional Chinese and Navajo medicine, comment that the distinction between diagnosis and treatment, 'reflects our own cultural presuppositions about the nature of healing . . . borrowed from clinical practice, [it] breaks down almost as soon as it is applied in comparative therapeutic systems' (1990, 12). It could also be argued, as does Helman, that diagnosis, in a psychological sense, is a form of treatment 'converting the unknown to the known, and reducing the uncertainty and anxiety of patient and family' (1994, 239). Moreover, diagnosis, especially in terms of differentiating between illness conditions, was relevant to the healers' practice; that is, they regarded it as important that sufferers with conditions other than depression sought appropriate help. As one healer commented: 'If they felt ill and the wool wasn't showing anything at all, well, you'd have to tell them to go to the doctor's. But on the other hand if I keep measuring their wool it will help them along.'

The second issue regarding diagnosis is that very often this happened prior to consultation, inasmuch as the sufferers or their families may have already self-diagnosed 'depression', and hence the need to seek wool measurement. In these cases, measuring served to confirm existence of a problem, possibly validating the illness and selection of healer; additionally, as previously noted, measuring indicated the severity of the illness by the amount of the discrepancy in the length of the wool.

In some instances healers made a diagnosis prior to the consultation based on information concerning sufferers gleaned from the community or from their own observations of sufferers' appearance. Again, wool measuring confirmed the healer's diagnosis, indicating the severity of the illness and providing justification for continued measuring.

A further salient point regarding diagnosis was that it might be accomplished without the healer having sight of the client; provided the healer had the required information of full name and date of birth, measuring could proceed and a diagnosis be made. This situation is obviously in marked contrast to most other forms of 'alternative' healing where establishing rapport with clients and taking a long personal and illness history is deemed to be of paramount importance, indeed the efficacy of the healing usually depends on it. Moreover the practice of spending *time* with clients is often regarded as a particular strength of alternative therapies as opposed to biomedicine. Even accepting the oft-quoted 'six minutes for the patient', conventional medical practitioners would ordinarily allocate more time to patients than do wool measurers.

3 The measuring of the wool

The language used by one healer – 'I measured his wool and he was measuring terrible' – suggests that the wool contains or indicates the sufferer's state of wellness, but it is difficult to apprehend from either fieldwork data or folk literature what was actually being measured; neither sufferer nor healer could explain this, and their apparent lack of concern was perplexing. For example, when questioned as to what, specifically, was being measured, most sufferers replied that it was 'their wool', requests for further elaboration would elicit vague responses of the nature of 'well, it's how you are, you know, what your health is like'. Healers were similarly imprecise with their responses to questions regarding what was being measured: 'Well, it's their wool, it shows how they are.'

As mentioned earlier, wool measurement is both diagnostic and healing, thus it is possible that the measurement unit – the length of wool – is more than simply an indication of the state of the sufferer's health; as Hand proposes, it may be 'a sort of intermediate agent . . . to which disease is communicated in the process of measurement' (1980, 94). This concept of healing by the transference of illness through an intermediate channel is frequently referred to in folk-healing literature (cf. Davies 1938; Jones 1969; Jones 1980). Measurement sometimes also implies containment of the illness and prevention of further damage. Hand, with regard to various meas-urement practices in North America, notes that

> Common to these forms, as well as to certain other kinds of magical measurement for disease, is the notion that the unit of measure, the length marked, or the area circumscribed somehow prevents the ravage of the disease beyond the confines measured. (1980, 93)

Thus, it may be that by measuring the sufferer's wool the sickness is perceived to be kept in check in some way; as though by the healer 'having the measure of it' the sickness is under control. The notion of containment also fits with healers' description of the wool shortening with subsequent measurements – indicating improvement – and suggesting that the measurement has stopped the illness getting out of hand.

4 After the measurement

Sufferers' progress following measurement was monitored (and further healing given if necessary) by continued measuring. One of the healers also prescribed a choice of what she described as 'tonics'. These were either a concoction of gin and saffron, a mixture of egg and sherry or beer stirred with a red-hot steel rod. This particular healer, who had learned her recipes from the same source as her measuring skill, commented that she recommended tonics in addi-tion to wool measuring because she always found them to be efficacious and was of the opinion that they were more effective than medically prescribed antidepressants. The folk literature regarding wool measuring frequently refers to the use of potions (Jones 1930; Winstanley and Rose 1926) and it seems feasible that their symbolic value lies in their belonging to local folklore in the same way as does wool measuring. Alternatively, prescribing tonics may be a ritual borrowed from biomedicine and/or indicative of the penetration of biomedicine, with its reliance on the prescription of medication, into lay beliefs.

5 The efficacy of the wool-measuring process

If 'feeling better' is evidence of efficacy, then wool measuring achieves its goals in that all the sufferers interviewed said that they felt noticeably better following measuring. A yardstick of how much better people felt was very often their ability to return to their normal activities, especially to activities outside the home, that is, back into their local community. Hence, their accounts of improvement were frequently framed in terms of what they were able to do and where they were able to go. For example, a sufferer (after wool measuring) commented, 'I feel like my old self again, I'll go out.' While an informant describing improvement in a friend who she had referred for measuring reported: 'In a few days [following measuring] I rang her, and I said "You feeling better, X?" And she said "Well I must be, I'm up the ladder painting".'

It seems that whereas depressive illness had caused them to withdraw from society, in many cases to take to their beds, the healing had enabled them to return to their previous place in the community. Failure in healing appeared to be extremely rare and was invariably explained in terms of the original condition being more serious than depression, as exemplified by the following response from one healer: 'Well, I haven't found anyone that I can't heal, they've all said that they're much better. But if there's something *else* on them that you can't heal, well the only thing you can do is keep their spirits up, if they're suffering from something else.' This example also illustrates the difficulty of evaluating a successful outcome in that 'feeling better', while not necessarily indicating that they were cured (that is, made free of their condition), especially in biomedical terms, surely indicates success. The person was healed in as much as they no longer felt ill, which was the purpose of seeking wool measuring.

The nature of the illnesses for which people seek wool measuring

The main category of illness currently treated by wool measuring is the condition that members of the communities studied define as 'depression'; people usually used the Welsh expression *clefyd y galon* which, in fact, translates as 'sick at heart'. All informants referred to depressive illness, although this was often broadened to include anxiety, 'nerves', breakdowns, or even to being 'run-down'. This is in marked contrast with the folk literature of rural mid-Wales (cf. Jones 1930; Hancock 1873; Williams 1888) which suggests that wool measuring was used in the past to treat a variety of illnesses of apparently physical origin.

The language used by sufferers and other informants, as well as in the folk literature, to describe depressive illness is interesting and significant. First, the illness was often described vaguely, sometimes as if depression, nerves, anxiety and breakdowns are perceived as much the same thing. Depression seemed to be a catch-all term used to describe the sufferers' experiences of not feeling 'right'.

Second, and perhaps more significantly, in both English and Welsh languages, depression was expressed in physical terms. For example, they would describe feelings of 'being really down'; 'at rock bottom'; 'something pressing on you'; 'something is pressing on your heart'; and 'when the pain is hanging heavy on you'. Although informants certainly frequently incorporated the biomedical category 'depression' into their description of the condition, its meaning was expanded to include reference to the physical experience of the illness. They would also describe how their daily lives were affected by it, inasmuch as they would withdraw from society, often, as previously noted, taking to their beds for long periods.

This apparent perception of emotional feelings as mainly physical symptoms may suggest somatization, which a number of writers, for example Helman (1994) and Kleinman (1980), have found to be characteristic of the clinical presentation of the biomedical category of 'clinical depression'. Helman comments that 'these depressed patients often complain of a variety of diffuse, and often changeable physical symptoms: such as 'tired all the time', headaches, palpitations, weight loss, dizziness, vague aches and pains, and so on' (1994, 267). However, caution is required here. As Mumford argues, it is important to distinguish between the experience of somatic sensations and the expression of somatic symptoms; that is, 'ethnic differences in somatic presentations may have more to do with complaint behaviour than with differences in symptom perception' (1993, 237).

Thus, it is possible that people suffering depression in the community studied may deem it more appropriate to present symptoms (of emotional distress) to folk healers through the metaphor of 'heart sickness' rather than of mental illness. Mumford (1993), noting that the use of somatic metaphors is one of the ways in which people 'give verbal expression to their emotional experience', comments on the widespread use of metaphors referring to the heart. An interesting example is Good's (1997) description of 'heart distress' in Maragheh, north-west Iran, as a condition in which sufferers complain of both physical sensations – 'palpitations, pressure on the chest, and a sensation of the heart being squeezed' – and psychological feelings of anxiety and unhappiness. Good proposes that for the people of Maragheh heart distress 'includes and links together both physical sensations of abnormality in the heartbeat and feelings of anxiety, sadness, or anger' (1997, 36).

As noted earlier, the old Welsh expression used for depression in the folk literature and by many informants was *clefyd y galon* which translates as 'heart sickness', or, as a number of informants said, 'sick at heart'. Again, there is a suggestion that this emotional state is experienced by sufferers in physical terms. This terminology is also intriguing because it suggests a perception of the heart and spirit as one, a notion which predates Cartesian distinctions between mind and body. Linked to this notion of the unity of the heart and spirit is the idea that it is the whole person that is ill, rather than a part of the body. As one of the sufferers said after having undergone successful wool measuring for depression, anaemia and a 'generally poor condition': 'It didn't matter which she was treating me for, anaemia, depression, whatever, because she was treating me the person, not the condition.'

It is apparent that there is a narrowing down of the range of conditions for which wool measuring is now regarded as an appropriate treatment. Thus, while the folk literature suggests that in the past it was utilized for a variety of both physical and psychological complaints (although physical complaints are most frequently mentioned) – notably jaundice, tuberculosis, 'wasting' conditions and 'nervous prostration' – wool measuring is now almost exclusively used for depression, the earlier-mentioned physical maladies having been transferred to biomedicine. It is very significant that the illnesses for which present-day sufferers and their families seek recourse to wool measuring are the type that do not fit easily into the biomedical classification and are not 'cured' by biomedicine.

The evidence suggests that people today turn to wool measuring for depression because (unlike jaundice and tuberculosis) it is perceived as an area where biomedicine does not have a good record of accomplishment. However, in some cases sufferers had sought biomedical treatment as a first choice for depression, only moving on to wool measuring when they considered biomedical treatment (which in all instances consisted of medication) to be ineffective. There are also examples of eclecticism in people's choice of treatment, with movement back and forth between biomedicine and wool measuring depending on which treatment was considered to be most appropriate for specific conditions. The decision to select wool measuring as the most appropriate treatment for depression was often influenced by other people in the community, particularly family members, and sometimes by neighbours.

In terms of aetiology, depression was perceived as a common problem that could befall anyone, arising from familiar problems of living, including personal relationship problems, financial worries and/or following an episode of ill health. For example, a sufferer in his early seventies who had both been healed by wool measuring and had often watched the procedure performed on other people commented that: 'depression or *clefyd y galon* as we call it often follows jaundice.'

Bereavement was also seen as an important causative factor for depression, especially the loss of partners, but also the loss of family or friends. This is borne out by the interviews in that three of the twelve sufferers described depression following bereavement. Additionally the healers commented that many of the sufferers or their surrogates identified bereavement as contributing to their (the sufferers') depression. I suggest that what is significant about these causative factors (as perceived by those involved) is the fact that they are the stuff of everyday life, there is no avoiding them. Consequently, the illness provoked by these factors is also perceived as unavoidable, and therefore this condition is less likely to have blame or stigma attached to it. It was apparent in the interviews with sufferers and healers that depressive illnesses did not carry stigma or shame, rather, it was something that happened to people at various stages of life and needed to be treated. This was also made explicit in the contrast between biomedical approaches to treatment for depression and wool measuring. Whereas biomedical treatment is firmly committed to keeping the diagnosis of any sort of mental illness confidential, a sufferer's need for wool measuring was discussed without qualms within the community; it was not seen as anything to be secretive or ashamed about. A by-product of sufferers' conditions being made public knowledge was that the rest of the community were aware of the need to offer help and support.

As noted earlier, the condition frequently, though not always, resulted in sufferers withdrawing from society, in many instances taking to their beds for considerable periods. Again, this response was not seen as extraordinary, it was quite an expected way to behave in these circumstances and it seems that the perceived ord-inariness mitigated against the likelihood of sufferers of depression being stigmatized in the way sufferers of other types of mental illness frequently are. Indeed, I would even suggest that the illness was not regarded in this community as a *mental* illness at all, that is, it arose from everyday problems of living and was experienced physically and socially.

I suggest that it is this perception of the condition of depression in highly subjective terms, that is, in terms of the experience of feeling depressed, which informed sufferers' choice of treatment. Rather than having a disease which required (or was amenable to) curing, they regarded themselves as having an illness – feeling ill – and in need of healing. The work of Kleinman is instructive here. He notes that: 'One reason why indigenous folk healers do not disappear when modernisation creates modern professional medical systems is that they are often skilled at treating illness' (1986, 39).

A community where wool measuring has persisted

The community that this study has chiefly focused on is a small, rural mid-Wales village. I endeavoured to ascertain what it was about this community that has encouraged the maintenance of traditional culture and beliefs and the transmission of those beliefs between certain community members.

The village was found to be a close-knit community, the members of which are bound by multiple ties of kinship, affinity, neighbourli-ness, chapel membership and, significantly, the Welsh language. Moreover, these ties, especially of language, also connect community members to a wider Welsh culture; they serve to define 'Welshness' for the people of this community. Wool measuring, as a further mani-festation of Welsh culture and identity, presents another link connecting village inhabitants to each other and to their specific local variety of Welshness.

All the healers interviewed, residing in parts of rural mid-Wales, belonged to extensive local kinship and affinity networks and also participated in key local institutions such as the chapel; moreover, all were natives of rural mid-Wales and spoke Welsh as a first language. I suggest that the healers as very localized persons are more than just 'nodes' in local networks, they are important base points or anchors in a number of networks and this may contribute to the high regard in which wool measuring and measurers are held by the community. There is a complex interrelationship between language, nationality and culture (cf. Jones 1993; Bowie 1993); it would appear that the Welsh language was a key factor in framing villagers' perceived national/ethnic identity, both in terms of reinforcing 'belonging' and defining cultural boundaries. Moreover, Welsh was found to play a very important role in the transmission of cultural knowledge and traditions, including knowledge about wool measuring.

These dense social networks facilitate the passage of information between people in the local area. The village studied was also somewhat isolated geographically and less affected than many other rural Welsh villages by outward and inward migration (cf. Jones 1993), which may have contributed to the maintenance of traditional beliefs (albeit with some modifications) and practices in this community. People commented that 'wool measuring was always there for us, we always knew about it', which suggests that the practice was firmly embedded in their culture; indeed, it was part of what bound their community together.

The hierarchy of resort in the community

The decision-making process and choosing of options by people, when illness is first recognized, have been explored by a number of writers. For example, Romanucci-Ross (1977) refers to the 'hierarchy of resorts' model of treatment selection, whereby sufferers and/ or their families select what they perceive as the appropriate treatment from a variety of options. In this study, the decision to select wool measuring as the most appropriate treatment for depression was often influenced by other people in the community, particularly family members, and sometimes by neighbours. When questioned as to the reasons for their selection of wool measuring, the sufferers often commented that this type of healing was the most appropriate choice for depression, since it was felt to be more efficacious and quicker than visiting a doctor. As one informant commented: 'No one goes to the doctor for depression.' Or as another said: 'They choose this treatment for depression because doctors can't treat depression.' Comments were made about doctors 'just giving you tablets for depression' which were not considered to be of much use.

In some cases, family members would take it upon themselves to seek help from the healer – by letter, telephone or a personal visit – without necessarily informing the sufferer beforehand. For instance, one sufferer who described himself as having been at 'rock bottom', was told by his mother, after the event, that she had been to the healer on his behalf. Some informants pointed out that the nature of depressive illness often made patients unable to visit a doctor of their own accord because 'they were feeling too low to go to the doctor'. The fact that a third party was able to get healing on their behalf without necessarily involving them was deemed very useful.

Conclusion

This study has found that in certain rural Welsh-speaking communities in mid-Wales, the particular illness defined by community members – both sufferers and healers – as depression was firmly situated, in terms of both its aetiology and its consequences, in the culture of everyday life. Taking a broader perspective of the shared meaning of depression for these communities, this study also illustrates the way in which they have developed a repertoire of explanatory frameworks for classifying ambiguous events (such as when people withdraw from society and/or take to their beds) and deciding what legitimately counts as illness. Sufferers in these situations are regarded as being ill and in need of help and support but are channelled towards an alternative healing system that no longer applies to most somatic illness. Moreover, the cultural construction of this illness within the community is one manifestation of a shared belief system that links members to a wider, historically situated Welsh culture, while also positioning them in a concrete locality. For the people of these rural Welsh communities, 'depression' is perceived as a condition arising from the trials of everyday life, recognized by particular behaviour and amenable to treatment by the very ancient practice of wool measuring. As noted earlier, my own participation in the wool-measuring process on the occasion when I had my wool measured, was particularly instructive in understanding the relationship between community and healing. On an emotional level, I experienced the measuring process as a way of somehow being drawn in and connected to this community, in that I was included in core cultural practices. This suggests that individuals seeking wool measuring may be helped to 'feel better' by being incorporated (or, for locals, reincorporated) into the community.

I should like to convey special thanks to Robin Gwyndaf of the Museum of Welsh Life, Cardiff, for it was he who initially told me that there are people in Wales still engaged in the ancient practice of wool measuring. He also provided access to the very useful resources of the Museum of Welsh Life.

References

Bowie, F. (1993). 'Wales from within: conflicting interpretations of Welsh identity', in S. Macdonald (ed.), *Inside European Identities* (Oxford: Berg).

Coffey, A. (1999). *The Ethnographic Self* (London: Sage).

Csordas, T. J. and Kleinman, A. (1990). 'The therapeutic process', in T. M. Johnson and C. F. Sargent (eds.), *Medical Anthropology*. (Westport, Connecticut: Greenwood Press).

Davies, C. A. (1999). *Reflexive Ethnography* (London: Routledge).

Davies, W. L. (1938). 'The conjuror in Montgomeryshire', *Montgomeryshire Collections*, 45, 158–70.

Good, B. (1997). 'The heart of what's the matter: the semantics of illness in Iran', *Culture, Medicine and Psychiatry*, 1, 25–58.

Hancock, T. W. (1873). 'Llanrhaidadr-yn-Mochnant, its parochial history and antiquities', *Montgomeryshire Collections*, 6, 319–40.

Hand, W. T. (1980). *Magical Medicine* (Berkeley: University of California Press).

Hastrup, K. (1992). 'Writing ethnography: state of the art', in J. Okely and H. Callaway (eds.), *Anthropology and Autobiography* (London: Routledge).

Helman, C. G. (1994). *Culture, Health and Illness*, 3rd edn. (Oxford: Butterworth-Heinemann).

Jones, A. (1980). 'Folk medicine in living memory in Wales', *Folk-Life*, 18, 58–67.

Jones, G. P. (1969). 'Folk medicine in eighteenth-century Wales', *Folk-Life*, 7, 60–74.

Jones, N. (1993). *Living in Rural Wales* (Cardiff: University of Wales Press).

Jones, T. G. (1930). *Welsh Folk Lore and Folk Custom* (London: Methuen).

Kleinman, A. (1980). *Patients and Healers in the Context of Culture* (Los Angeles: University of California Press).

—— (1986). 'Concepts and a model for the comparison of medical systems as cultural systems', in C. Currer and M. Stacey (eds.), *Concepts of Health, Illness and Disease: A Comparative Perspective* (Leamington Spa: Berg).

Mumford, D. B. (1993). 'Somatization: a transcultural perspective', *International Review of Psychiatry*, 5, 231–42.

Romanucci-Ross, L. (1977). 'The hierarchy of resort in curative practices: the Admiralty Islands, Melanesia', in D. Landy (ed.), *Culture, Disease and Healing: Studies in Medical Anthropology* (New York: Macmillan).

Williams, R. (1888). 'History of the parish of Llanbrynmair', *Montgomeryshire Collections*, 22, 315–28.

Winstanley, L. and Rose, H. J. (1926). 'Scraps of Welsh folklore I', *Folklore*, 38, 154–74.

7 Family farm businesses and the farming community: revisiting farm families in west Wales eighteen years on

John Hutson

This chapter is based on findings from two studies of farm families in Pembrokeshire, south-west Wales. In 1980–1, I talked to some fifty farm families about the link between family and business. With the current crisis in farming, I returned in 1998–9 to do a restudy of these same farms. I discuss the experience of doing research on an occupational 'community' in Wales and show how the current crisis in farming hits some harder than others. I go on to consider the validity of the idea of a farming 'community' and argue that there has been a loss of identity and common purpose with the result that beyond a common, increasing struggle for survival there is probably more to divide farmers than to unite them. However, farming is an activity which is literally inscribed on the landscape and rooted in a place so that local context remains important. Thus, while the existence of a single inclusive farming community may be a questionable idea, many local farming communities are a living reality.

Background

In the autumn of 1980 I embarked on a project to look at family farming in south-west Wales in what had been the old county of Pembrokeshire, recently incorporated into the new county of Dyfed. I had obtained a small research grant, from the then Social Science Research Council (SSRC), to pay my salary for a term and the family moved down to St David's for the autumn term where our daughter and son attended the local primary and nursery schools.

The background to this research interest was earlier fieldwork in the French Alps where peasant farming was giving way to industrial work in an aluminium factory in the main valley and to employment in tourism-related enterprises, most of which were family run (Hutson 1971). From this research, I developed an interest in the link between family and business as well as in how changing economic and social situations influence family forms and strategies. So this was what I wanted to look at in relation to farming in Wales, where Pembrokeshire seemed to have a good mix of farming, industry (oil refineries and a power station around Milford Haven) and tourism. Farming as an occupational sector was also special because it was unique in being a major productive industry in which 97.5 per cent of farms in England were family businesses (Harrison 1975). In Wales, the percentage was certainly as high and likely to have been higher.

There were personal reasons, too. I grew up, and have lived most of my life, in the countryside. I have no background in farming itself but a long-standing interest in how the countryside is created by the farming process and in how farming and the landscape interact with one another. We also had a young, school-age family and did not want to go abroad. Neither did I want to study farms on Gower, where I live. There is a paradox, on which much social research depends, that people will speak with a degree of openness to absolute strangers which they will not grant so readily to neighbours or acquaintances.

Researching farm families

Eighteen years ago, I talked to fifty farm families as well as to some estate agents, auctioneers, bank managers and agricultural merchants. The farm families came from 'snowball' samples which rolled from three main sources – a local farmer contact, a lecturer on the agricultural training course in the local college and a list of county council-owned farms. So it was not a formal random sample, but one which ended up with a reasonably representative variety of region, farm type and size.

People had said that farmers would be difficult people to interview – busy, secretive and hard to contact. In practice, farmers are constantly filling in forms detailing their production or land use and are often involved in university agricultural research programmes. Of course, some did not want to know, but the majority were very willing to be interviewed and quite a few said that because I asked them very different questions from other surveys – not about their ratio of concentrate to silage or their butterfat content, but rather about how they met their partner, what their ambitions were and about their children – they actually rather enjoyed the experience. Also, the issues I was asking about were ones which really did concern them. When I contacted farmers again in 1998 by telephone, one woman said, 'Oh, yes, my husband thinks he remembers you because you asked unusual questions!' Another aspect which anthropologists rely on is that most people love talking about themselves, especially to someone who actually wants to listen. Several times, when a parent had launched into a story about what the farm was like when they first bought it, a son or daughter would say something along the lines of, 'Oh Dad, no, not that old story again!'

Also, since I was quite open about knowing very little about farming techniques and processes, informants took pleasure in explaining, teaching and showing me how their farming was done and what it meant to them. Research was based on open-ended interviews, with the normal scenario being me sat at the kitchen table, usually with a farming couple, but often with a child or two as well, and sometimes up to three generations around the table. In addition, other family members or visitors might drop by and join in with their views. In such situations tape recording was essential. However, this can become difficult if one ends up moving around from room to room or out in the farmyard. When I arrived for one interview the day after a gale, the farmer was on the roof of a shed where I had to join him at first, helping to replace damaged roofing sheets.

But sitting round the kitchen table was the usual venue and it was a very appropriate place because it is the heart of both family and farm. Family meals and daily discussions about work take place here. Family crises and farm decisions are all 'hammered out' here around the kitchen table. It can be quite an atmospheric experience, sitting in an old farmhouse kitchen and realizing that the surrounding countryside has been to a large extent created in this room, by the decisions taken here over the last two hundred years or more, and by the chances of births, deaths and marriages in this house.

Farmers are very busy people who nonetheless often spent two hours or more talking to me. Nearly always over ninety minutes, which is when the tape stops, I check my notes, and say 'Well, I *must* go now and let you get on.' Then I can spend another twenty minutes with my hosts giving me valuable quotes or important financial details while we all stand by the door with no tape running and my notebook packed away. So I then have to drive off a couple of miles, before stopping to scribble down what I can remember of this last conversation. (This is also when several cups of coffee begin to take their toll – another hazard of this kind of research.)

I have lived in south Wales for more than thirty years but I do not speak Welsh. Some farmers clearly would have been happier talking in Welsh, especially about topics such as family, the local community and what mattered to them in the countryside. So, on the one hand, my lack of Welsh language clearly has some effect on my data, especially when this kind of qualitative research does depend so much on picking up on particular terms, phrases or manners of speech that in the final analysis are taken to symbolize certain attitudes, aspirations or feelings about emotive situations. On the other hand, this is compensated for to a degree by my long-term familiarity and involvement with these particular farmers in this specific locality.

Farm families in productionist agriculture

In 1980 I set out to compare family labour farms with hired labour ones, but that did not turn out to be a very significant variable. More important than labour was the family aspect of farm management. This was a very vibrant moment in farming, with growth in farm businesses and agricultural outputs and fast-moving changes in farming practice. These, in turn, were supported and encouraged by developments in new technology, markets, tax regulations, tenancy laws, EEC and government policies and subsidies, as well as by the influence of the large commercial corporations which surround farming – the seed, feed, chemical and machinery companies, supermarkets and banks.

The early 1980s were, then, a time of some prosperity in farming. Maximization of production was still the policy driving farming and everything was geared to increasing output. One consequence of this emphasis on increasing production was a changing relationship between family, farm and business. It seemed that there had been what I then called a move from 'generational fragmentation' to 'generational integration' (Hutson 1987, 1990).

Between the two world wars, on small family farms in south-west Wales, parents would aim to set up sons in farms of their own, usually as tenants, when they married, maybe also giving them some stock or machinery to start up with. After that, they were on their own to make their fortune, building on this basis of occupational succession combined with partial inheritance. Daughters were not expected to farm but to marry farmers. The youngest son would be expected to stay with his ageing parents, working for his father on the farm and eventually inheriting it or the tenancy.

From the 1950s, the emphasis on farm expansion, the rising cost of land, the break-up of large estates and the introduction of new tenancy laws all meant that the logical strategy was for children to remain on the family farm. With the pressure to increase production, farms were growing larger and needed not only children's labour, but even more their management skills, in order to start up new enterprises in the growing family farm businesses. Since these businesses were expanding, children had the opportunity to take on responsibility for running a separate enterprise – such as building up the milking herd or improving lambing rates. The long, restrictive apprenticeships of half a lifetime 'under father's thumb' were ending. Thus the process of succession, bringing children into the management of the farm, became the critical process. Inheritance, the legal transfer of ownership, was put off into the future (Hutson 1987).

Of course, alongside the successes were the failures – those farms that went bankrupt or had no children to succeed. However, these farms coming on to the market gave other farmers the chance to buy more land and expand their businesses. Overall, the result was fewer, larger farms – a process which has continued relentlessly ever since with the 'marginal' size of farms creeping up every year.

What struck me at that time was the continuing importance of the relationship between family and farm. Farming was now fully commercial and a big business, but it was still largely owned and run by families. Moreover, family needs influenced business decisions. A child leaving school or university might precipitate a move to buy land, expand the herd or invest in a new milking parlour even if profit margins, interest rates or currently available grants might not make this the most business-efficient time to do these things.

How control was passed from one generation to another had become a key process, with succession separated from inheritance. The contribution of family members went way beyond simply providing labour. A family farm did not now just mean a family-worked farm but a family-managed farm. Such family farm businesses were ones where the business principals were related by kinship or marriage, and where business ownership was combined with managerial control to be then passed on from one generation to another (Gasson et al. 1988).

This had a direct effect on both family forms and the content of family relationships. There were new forms of extended family business partnerships as well as changes in what it actually meant to be a father, son, wife or daughter-in-law when people worked together in new ways. It was an example of the way in which the form and content of family relationships are linked to relations of production and market forces in particular cultural and social settings (Hutson 1987).

The beginning of the farm crisis

From the mid-1980s, only a few years after my first research ended, there was a major policy change away from a production-oriented agriculture to one which was sustainable and environmentally concerned. This change was motivated by huge EEC production surpluses and by a growing public awareness of the damage done to wildlife, the countryside and the landscape by the regime of intensive farming.

The changing direction of state support, following the reversal of productionist policies, led to the introduction of quotas restricting production. In 1984, milk quotas, the first of the EEC production restrictions to be introduced, were imposed. Other quotas followed and both agricultural and non-agricultural diversification were encouraged – farmers were advised to consider rearing ostriches, running haulage firms or providing services for tourists.

Environmental and conservation programmes were also promoted. The concept of 'stewardship' was introduced to replace that of production. Compensation was offered to farmers who took land out of production as 'set-aside' and incentives were offered for the sympathetic management of newly designated Environmentally Sensitive Areas or areas of Special Scientific Interest. Additionally, in Wales, 80 per cent of agricultural land is classified as being in a Less Favoured Area and is thereby eligible for special subsidy support.

Thus, there began a shift in the public perception of farmers, who were now represented by the media as villains rather than heroes.

They were no longer seen as feeders of the nation but as polluters of nature and food; or as rural 'fat cats' being paid for doing nothing but letting wild geese graze their grass or rare plants grow in undrained bogs. In the 1990s the BSE crisis further undermined the public reputation of farming.

There were concerns on all sides about both the future of farming and the future of the countryside. Farming makes and maintains the countryside. In Wales, 82 per cent of its land area is under some form of agricultural use, and it is estimated that around 25 per cent of the working population of Wales is still directly or indirectly dependent on agriculture and associated businesses (Welsh Office 1995, 1996).

Farmers' reactions to the growing crisis

These were the conditions which prompted me to go back and talk to the Pembrokeshire farmers I had seen in 1980. These farm families also represented a reasonable sample to cope with in three months of research time. We are all too familiar with the acute problems faced by livestock farmers in Wales as markets in lamb and beef have collapsed. Farm produce prices have fallen through the combined effects of a variety of factors: loss of export markets; cheap food imports; the high value of the pound against the euro, in which subsidies are paid; and overproduction at home. Over the last three years average farm incomes (after meeting costs) have fallen by around 82 per cent to a national UK average of around £8,000 a year.

When it came to contacting farmers again, I used the 'Farmers' section in the Yellow Pages directory as a good starting place to check addresses and telephone numbers. About two-thirds of my 1980 sample were still in the telephone book. I wrote to farmers first, then followed up the letter with a telephone call to try to arrange an interview. Farm families were very welcoming, and I was often invited to stay for lunch. I read up my notes from the earlier interview before I telephoned so that I could mention some particular detail from eighteen years back, as a way to re-establish my credentials. For example, 'I remember you said you would never join the Women's Institute. Did you join?' The other side of the coin for me was that a number of farmers then asked me for copies of articles written after the last research.

I talked to members of thirty-five of the original fifty farm families.

There was a wide variation in the sample from those who said they 'had no problems' to those who said they constantly thought, 'Am I going to be here in twelve months' time?' There were those who confidently planned their next strategy to increase production or income as well as those who said 'We live day by day', or 'We just try to hang on and hope it gets better!' However, a common remark was that they were better off than 'many of the upland livestock farmers'. Thirty-two of the fifty farms were still owned by the same families. Indeed, overall, and contrary to my expectations, most households said they had managed to survive the crisis so far, although all had suffered loss of income. Why was this, and what features could account for this contrast with media images?

Dairy farmers made up 69 per cent and milk prices had not fallen as much as stock prices. Nonetheless, a drop of 20p a litre is an annual loss of £13,000 for a seventy-cow herd. Most farms were over two hundred and fifty acres, which has now become the 'marginal' size. They were also established farms without heavy borrowings to service. In addition, those I contacted through the telephone book were, by the very fact that they were still in business after eighteen years, self-selected as currently viable businesses. Those who were not in the telephone book, if I could have found them, might have had a very different story to tell, as had those who were no longer in farming but whom I did manage to contact.

It would appear that most of the farmers I returned to talk to had lost income but were in the type of farming, or at the stage of business and point in their life-course where they could stand such losses – for a time, at least. However, compared to 1980, fewer expected their children to come into farming and more considered retiring. These were both factors which directly affected the way farm businesses were currently run as well as how plans were made for the future.

Many farmers were surprisingly optimistic and entrepreneurial, actively seeking to reduce costs and combat falling prices by embarking on new systems of production such as organic farming, new types of production to add value such as cheese making, new schemes of cooperative marketing, new breeding or management strategies. Economic downturns do not hit everyone in the same way at the same time. Nor are farmers' reactions, or their scope for action in these circumstances, always similar.

Family farms and the farming community

The current crisis in farming has led to much discussion about the plight and future of the 'farming community' – particularly in Wales, where there is a predominance of family-run livestock farms. It seems that there is now a media image of the 'farming community', but how valid is this notion? Farmers are certainly located in the countryside, but is the idea of a farming community perhaps more of an occupational and cultural one than a spatially located one, in today's world of international policy and global markets? To explore the idea that this is a community which is defined by vocation rather than by location, I now turn to look at the characteristics of this so-called 'community'.

Farmers in the early 1980s talked readily about how farming had changed during their lifetimes from a 'way of life' to a 'business'. Farm couples, then in their forties, fifties and sixties, had lived through something of a revolution. They were now running commercial businesses and managing complex financial structures. As one younger farmer said to me back then 'To my grandfather borrowing was immoral; to my father it became a necessity; to me it is normal!' However, even as a business, farming was still closely linked to family goals with family labour, continuity and well-being remaining key themes in discussions about farming. Indeed, by the 1980s, business expansion and innovation depended on children coming into the farm business to make a management team with their parents.

In the late 1990s, while farmers talked more of the downside and tensions of working with family, especially with falling markets and incomes, they still put great store on the security of a family business as 'something you could always come back to', as 'a pool of financial and material assets that you knew you had access to'. Today, many farmers regretted that their children would not be coming into the business, but they knew that it would be a hard life for them if they did. Fewer farms can support two or more families, as many did in the 1980s. The next generation will neither inherit an occupation nor the means to practise it. As one man said to me, 'Thank God I haven't got a son coming in, and thank God I'm fifty and not twenty!'

The re-study showed that, despite a continuing family involvement in farming, many farm businesses now seemed to be placing less emphasis on the family aspect of their identity as farmers. In the Pembrokeshire sample, children had succeeded to control in 53 per cent of the businesses. However, only a quarter spoke of themselves as 'family farms'. Nonetheless, there appeared to me still to be an obvious involvement of family needs in business decisions in many more farms. The farm might pay either for retirement housing or for children's university education. A farmer gave free use of a farm building to one son for his alternative therapy wholesale business and also joined an environmental scheme, so that he could give his other son work laying all the farm hedges and give him a chance to set up his own hedging business. Another couple were in business with their son as well as with their daughter and son-in-law across a business partnership based on three holdings. To me, these were all the kinds of activities where business decisions appeared to be clearly linked to family goals, yet these farmers sought to avoid a 'family farm' label which they associated with small, inefficient and trad-itional enterprises. The idea of a 'family farm' seemed now to be much less an acceptable component of farming identity than it was eighteen years ago.

A whole generation of farmers, working since the end of the Second World War, grew up with constant encouragement to produce food and yet more food. As farm incomes fell, many farmers have been left struggling financially as well as bewildered about the direction they should now take. The very idea of real farming was devalued as farmers were forced to diversify to provide services rather than to produce food. Providing accommodation or tea-rooms for tourists was not considered to be 'proper' farming. To many farmers, the label of 'part-timer' was anathema – they wanted to be real farmers, not just 'playing at it'. No longer required simply to produce food, they suffered crises of both income and identity.

In 1998, a number of farmers I spoke to said that they had lost their sense of purpose and direction. A typical view was, 'Where are we going? We've done everything asked of us. We've turned an indus-try around, we've worked bloody hard, and now what?' This uncertainty in direction has not been helped by the way that subsidy support has tended too often to be in the form of sequential crisis management rather than directed by clear, forward-looking policies.

Policies which encourage and fund schemes redefining farmers as 'stewards' and 'park-keepers' – 'caretakers' of landscape and envir-onment – provide identities which are viewed with reluctance and wariness. 'Stewardship' is seen by most as a given – they do it anyway. Eighteen years ago when I asked what makes a good farmer, the consistent reply was that it was someone who 'looked after the land and maintained soil fertility'. Now this has been extended to the conservation of landscapes and wildlife as well as to increasing public access. But farming has to be about more than these things. They are aspects of its deeper morality but were not seen by farmers as sufficient ends in themselves. Farmers still saw themselves as producers, and it was identifying a viable, modern product which was the current problem for so many small and middle-sized farms.

A number of farms were adapting to find niche markets for their products such as local cheese, organic produce or Welsh Black beef. Those who were successful did seem to find a positive and tradition-ally authentic identity as producers of high-quality food – 'adding value' on the farm and retailing the product locally to minimize value 'leaking out' of the local area (Parrott et al. 1999). However, while this can foster an increasing regionalism, it can also create local competition within small and specialized markets which can serve further to divide rather than to reinforce the idea of a local farming community.

A number of local weekly livestock and produce markets have closed down with a loss of the social opportunities which they afforded farmers to meet to exchange news and information. To some extent farmers I spoke to were realizing the need to unite in resistance to powerful food wholesalers and retailers. A successful vegetable marketing group had been set up and there were also moves to form dairy cooperatives and other producer groups to counter falling market prices, but these were struggling against a long-standing reluctance among farmers to cooperate as well as the differential effects of the farm crisis. Farmers have traditionally helped one another out in emergencies but have seldom joined in longer-term cooperative ventures. Today farmers will use contractors when the purchase of expensive machinery would be uneconomical, rather than share it with, or borrow it from, neighbours as they might have done in the past.

A study in 1990–1 of 427 farms, in seven purposely selected areas across Wales, showed a cultural ideal in Wales that *real* farmers *farm* so that those most likely to go into non-agricultural work on the farm or into off-farm work tended to be wives and children (Hutson and Keddie 1993, 1995; Acheson et al. 1993; Bateman et al. 1993). Thus, farming still has very much a masculine culture, but there has also been a new dependency on farm women for financial viability.

Before, women played a vital, but largely invisible, supportive role – looking after the calves, feeding the men or 'just being around' to help when needed. Now, women were playing a very upfront role, both as farmers in their own right and as wage earners bringing in an extra income not only to keep the family, but often to support the farm itself.

Farming is no longer the driving force in rural economies, but it remains the *raison d'être* of a chain of firms supplying the farming industry and providing local employment for local people – agricultural merchants, machinery suppliers, veterinarians, markets and auctioneers, estate agents and village shops. While Pembrokeshire has already seen its industrial base decline with closure of the oil refineries and power station, its natural beauty makes it attractive to tourists. Pembrokeshire still has above-average employment in agriculture, and in 1994 agricultural production was around £52 million. However, tourism produced £160 million in 1995, which demonstrates its importance to the local economy (Parrott et al. 1999).

Farmers were well aware of their poor current public image and recognized the need to improve it. They were amazed at the public's ignorance of what happens on farms – that so many children had no idea where milk comes from – and they were deeply indignant that the public thinks they all mistreat their animals. Increasingly many have encouraged farm visitors. They might offer bed and breakfast guests a chance to look around the farm, to see how animals are treated or encourage school trips to visit. BSE has been a devastating experience for most of them. They did not feel they deserved as much blame as they have had. Most could identify exactly which batch of feed caused their problem, but said they had had no idea what was in it at the time. And they talked of the cull of cattle as a terrible experience – seeing a generation of cows they had bred and reared as calves just going to slaughter – a further rejection of the work which gave them their livelihood and marked their identity.

There is a growing trend of fragmentation in the farming industry at all levels. Pre-1980, the industry was represented by the National Farmers' Union (NFU) allied with the Ministry of Agriculture, both seeking to increase production and safeguard markets. Wales has also had the Farmers' Union of Wales (FUW), aiming to represent the interests of small farmers, but now there is further fragmentation of political lobbies, of policy and farming practice. Environmental schemes and regional foods are local in their application. There has been the loss of industry-wide institutions such as the Milk Marketing Board and its successor Milk Marque. The NFU has lost overall political power, which is now shared between a whole raft of farming and countryside organizations, as well as consumer, environmental and animal welfare groups and militant farming groups. Non-farming bodies, such as the National Rivers Authority, have legal powers to enforce maintenance of water purity and there is now the Food Standards Agency as a watchdog for food quality. However, against this trend, what other single industry has its own daily radio programme, even if it is now at 5.47 a.m.? Then there is the slightly later (6.35 a.m.) publicity slot on Sundays, *On your Farm*, plus a weekly Welsh-language programme – and, of course, *The Archers*.

Conclusions

So how valid is the idea of a farming community? Certainly there are common characteristics, such as the shared knowledge and experience which come from doing farming and being farmers. In addition, there is a common struggle to survive against adverse market conditions and a negative public image. However, while there have always been regional differences between types of farming and sizes of farm, today such divisions are increased by the unequal effects of recession and a growing economic polarization within the industry. In addition, there is no longer a clear understanding of what farming is about nor a shared idea of where it is going. Diversity of enterprise is encouraged so farmers feel they are more service providers than producers. As producers they compete to add value to their produce before marketing it in specialist market niches. Local market-places, with their opportunities for socialization, are closing, and national marketing bodies such as the Milk Marketing Board are gone. With their businesses under threat, farmers no longer plan strategies around family considerations as fewer children see a place for themselves either on the family farm or in farming. The transmission of a common occupational culture in terms of experience, skills and motivation seems in danger of being broken. A unity is there, but it is perhaps more a unity of resistance, of shared struggle for survival, rather than one based on a positive sense of identity. New entrepreneurial ventures are required with every shift in policy, and farming, it seems, can no longer provide a sense of well-being or achievement in either work or household life in the face of continuing economic insecurity.

However, while this list might seem to confirm the notion that identity and culture can in the modern world no longer be tied to a specific place, or be seen as a unique local product, it is still obvious that locality remains of vital importance in constituting local farming communities. Firstly, farming always has been, and still is, much more than an economic activity. It is a way of life which is still central to the Welsh language and the Welsh landscape (Hughes et al. 1997; Hutson and Byron 1999). In this way it is strongly tied in to place and locality. Secondly, locality is still the basis of a particular type of agricultural production and set of environmental conditions, such that Pembrokeshire farmers would say how they were better off than small, Welsh upland livestock farmers. Today, the growth in clearly labelled local produce also reinforces the idea of locality. Thirdly, farmers, like other rural dwellers, are situated in local networks of family, friends and neighbours which spread way beyond occupational boundaries. Fourthly, farmers are involved in local projects and interests, from committees to hobbies such as birdwatching and, indeed, the spin-offs of these hobbies which can become farm diversifications, such as off-road driving courses. Fifthly, while BSE, and especially foot and mouth disease, may have differentiated the farming community, they have reinforced local communities in terms of suffering or deliverance. Finally, farming is above all an activity which is ultimately territorial, one which is literally inscribed upon the landscape and rooted in the soil of a place.

Farming is not the only occupation, industry or business which suffers in the harsh world of economic restructuring. But it remains a unique productive industry with its structure of small businesses and its role as creator and maintainer of landscape and countryside through its very rootedness in locality. As an endangered species the future of the family farmer is one that affects not only rural communities but us all.

References

Acheson, J., Davies, L. and Edwards, H. (1993). *A Comparative Study of Pluriactivity in the Less-Favoured Farming Areas of Wales: A Final Report to the ESRC* (Aberystwyth: University of Wales).

Bateman, D., Hughes, G., Midmore, P., Lampkin, N. and Ray, C. (1993). *Pluriactivity and the Rural Economy in the Less-Favoured Areas of Wales* (Aberystwyth: Deptarment of Agricultural Economics, University of Wales).

Gasson, R., Crow, G., Errington, A., Hutson, J., Marsden, T. and Winter, D. (1988). 'The farm as a family business: a review', *Journal of Agricultural Economics*, 39, 1, 1–41.

Harrison, A. (1975). *Farmers and Farm Businesses in England* (Reading University: Department of Agricultural Economics, Miscellaneous Study 62).

Hughes, G., Midmore, P. and Sherwood, A.-M. (1997). 'The Welsh language, agricultural changes and sustainability', in R. Byron, J. Walsh and P. Braethnach (eds.), *Sustainable Development on the North Atlantic Margin* (Aldershot: Ashgate).

Hutson, J. K. (1971). 'A politician in Valloire', in F. G. Bailey (ed.), *Gifts and Poison: The Politics of Reputation* (Oxford: Blackwell).

—— (1987). 'Fathers and sons: family farms, family businesses and the farming industry', *Sociology*, 21.

—— (1990). 'Family relationships and farm businesses in south-west Wales', in C. C. Harris (ed.), *Family, Economy and Community* (Cardiff: University of Wales Press).

Hutson, J. K. and Byron, R. (1999). 'Policies to protect family farming in New York State and a devolved Wales: a case of convergence?', in R. Byron and J. K. Hutson (eds.), *Local Enterprise on the North Atlantic Margin* (Aldershot: Ashgate).

Hutson, J. K. and Keddie, D. (1993). *Household Work Strategies in the Brecon/Merthyr and Fishguard Regions: End of Project Report for the ESRC* (Swansea: University of Wales).

—— (1995). 'Pluriactivity as a strategy for the future of family farming in Wales', in R. Byron (ed.), *Economic Futures on the North Atlantic Margin* (Aldershot: Avebury).

Parrott, N., Sherwood, A.-M. and Midmore P. (1999). 'Strengthening links between agriculture and tourism on the rural periphery: a case study of southwest Wales', in R. Byron and J. Hutson (eds.), *Local Enterprise on the North Atlantic Margin* (Aldershot: Ashgate).

Welsh Office (1995). *Welsh Agricultural Statistics* (Wales: HMSO).

—— (1996). *A Working Countryside for Wales* (London: HMSO).

8 Vegetarian biographies in time and space: vegetarians and alternatives in Newport, west Wales

Janice Williams

> Vegetarianism is by no means a straightforward concept, and it has many varieties which shade into one another. The researcher inevitably faces the problem of whether to generate a set of objective definitions of varieties of vegetarianism . . . or . . . to work with subjective self-definitions of respondents . . . In fact, the data available for countries like the UK and USA are sparse and rather fragmentary. (Beardsworth and Keil 1997, 223–4)

Surprisingly little empirical research has been conducted on vegetarianism in the UK, and no one has yet broached the problem of how vegetarianism is subjectively defined in specific social and cultural contexts at a particular time and place. This chapter explores the meanings attached to vegetarianism and meat-eating in a rural Welsh community which has experienced significant social change in recent decades, change that brings this issue to the forefront in community social relations. For the social collectivities to which my research subjects 'belong', categorizing oneself as a vegetarian or meat-eater is a primary act of identification in the construction of the self. The nature of this self emerges as both highly reflexive yet at the same time intrinsically social (cf. Davies 1999, 23–4). Part of an ongoing process of self-definition and assessment in relation to significant others, it is subject to constant and continuous scrutiny, redefinition, negotiation, challenge and compromise. Dealing largely with people who dip in and out of a vegetarian identity, I attempt to make visible individual decisions and choices surrounding food by considering narratives which relate both to historical time, in terms of stages of the life-cycle, and to contemporary time and space, in terms of immediate social relations and understandings of community.

Social context and methodological considerations

For two years between 1994 and 1996, I conducted the Welsh portion of a comparative ethnographic study addressing the question, 'Why do people eat what they do?' Fourteen months of this time were devoted to fieldwork in a rural location in Wales. This was the small seaside town of Newport (Trefdraeth in Welsh) in Pembrokeshire, with a population of some 1,166 inhabitants (1991 census). Newport, like other parts of Wales, has witnessed rapid social changes in recent years, manifested by economic diversification and increased outward migration of young local people and inward migration by retirees and others fleeing the urban rat-race. This is therefore not a homogeneous or 'traditional' community as depicted in the classic early studies of rural Britain, including Wales, of the 1950s and 1960s (e.g. Rees 1950; also cf. Day 1999; Gasson et al. 1988). Thus, for example, the combined inward and outward migrations have resulted in a community that at the time of fieldwork was approximately 50 per cent Welsh-speaking, which represents a steep decline since the early 1960s when over 80 per cent of the population was able to speak Welsh. A further indication of this 'non-traditional' heterogeneity is the fact that this small rural Welsh community sustains a wholefood shop described in an edition of 'Country Living' at the time of fieldwork as one of the best in Britain.

By far the most important social divisions hinged on distinctions between incomer versus local, English versus Welsh- speaking, town-dweller versus rural resident, oppositions which were by no means clear-cut, but intersected one another and were also mediated by other criteria such as age, gender, occupation and class, religion and way of life/lifestyle. Broadly speaking, however, town-dwellers could be socially categorized as: (1) the local, Welsh-speaking Welsh, many of them chapelgoers; (2) 'retired middle class', consisting of incomers, largely from England but also from other parts of Wales, and mostly non-Welsh speaking; and (3) low-income families who straddled the linguistic divide. The inhabitants of the rural hinterland, on the other hand, were broadly categorized as: (1) the farmers, still largely, although by no means exclusively, local Welsh speakers and mostly chapelgoing; and (2) others viewed as 'alternatives' and/or 'hippies'.

I related to this research location not only as a trained anthropologist but also as a 'native'. Thus the fact that I come from a

Welsh-speaking farming background near Carmarthen, some forty miles from Newport, an area which in the last decades has undergone similar rapid social changes in terms of demographic and linguistic shift (cf. Aitchison and Carter 1999; Davies 1993; Jones 1993) had profound implications for the way I related to different categories of informants. As a Welsh speaker I was deeply aware that I was a member of a linguistic 'community' which had in a sense been 'disinherited' (cf. Foley 1997, 398–416; Grillo 1989). Thus, with certain social categories, especially Welsh-speaking farming families, I was considered 'one of us'. (This was much helped by the fact that Pembrokeshire Welsh bears very close dialectical resemblances to Carmarthenshire Welsh.) But there were important differences as well as commonalities, the main one being that I had spent long years away from Wales. In addition, the claim that language is the primary marker of a distinctive Welsh identity is contested by some Welsh people, even those for whom it is the central linchpin; there are also important distinctions arising out of differences in linguistic competence and the complexities of the socio-linguistic situation in Wales. For instance, even though I speak Welsh at home and can hold my own in most Welsh-speaking 'folk' situations, I could not say the same for my 'literary' Welsh, and the standard of my fluency and literacy in English far exceeds that of my Welsh. In some fieldwork situations I therefore found myself conversing with people who inspired in me both shame and admiration by virtue of the fact that their Welsh linguistic competence and, *ipso facto*, their claim to Welshness, far exceeded my own. At the same time, this paradoxically increased my capacity to relate to the great many other Welsh speakers (especially those who had, like myself, returned to Wales after a long absence and wanted to consolidate their knowledge of the language), whose competence was approximately the same as my own. On the reverse side of the coin, among incomers my status as 'native' was highly variable. The fact that I have spent most of my adult life in urban environments in England, forming deep attachments there, meant that I shared as many commonalities with most of them as I did with Welsh speakers, and some informants were unaware that I was Welsh-speaking. Among local people generally, I became known as the 'food lady', and I received enormous support and cooperation partly because I was involved in a national research project about 'their' town and locality and also because most people had a genuine interest in food. Thus another key aspect of my identity that had consequences for the research was my own orientation to food; for example, it was only after I relived my own attempts at being vegetarian years prior to the fieldwork period that I was able to make any headway in conducting fruitful interviews with vegetarians.

Research methods were based mainly on the classic techniques of anthropological fieldwork – participant observation and informal semi-structured interviews. Out of the total number of over 220 interviewed, 133 were what were referred to as general participants living in Newport or in the immediate surrounding area. These were interviewed following a fairly standard semi-structured format, and the in-depth qualitative data collected from one category of twenty-eight such participants forms the main focus of the present chapter. In addition, some follow-up interviews were carried out in 1998 in order to develop some themes more fully. Information was sought on a large number of topics including food preparation and consumption, the division of labour in the household, dietary change, health and healthy eating.

The twenty-eight informants reviewed in this chapter were all in some sense either vegetarian and/or alternative; they include meat-eaters, however, and bearing in mind that the words 'vegetarian' and 'alternative' are problematic ones whose meanings slip and slide, they also include at least four people who were vegetarian but did not regard themselves as alternative. Consisting of eighteen females, ten males, eight married couples and one cohabiting couple, most informants fell into older age categories, the majority being in their forties (thirteen) and fifties (seven). With the exception of one informant, who lived in a nearby village, eleven were town-dwellers and the remaining sixteen lived in more isolated rural surroundings. Predominantly middle-class and highly educated, the great majority fell into Social Class II; over half (sixteen) had attended university, five had attended art college, and most others had some form of professional or vocational qualification. Occupationally they included social-workers, dress designers, authors, microbiologists, consultants, teachers, technicians, midwives, counsellors and engineers. Many had given up such posts to run smallholdings in the Newport area. While the picture that emerges is an overwhelmingly middle-class one, the economic status of some informants was by no means high, eight of the women being single parents, seven of these on low incomes. Nineteen informants were born in England, two in continental Europe; of these twenty-one, eight had learned Welsh as adults to a good standard of spoken fluency. The remaining seven were born in Wales and included two people born locally for whom Welsh was their first language. It is striking that these informants included only two (ex-)chapel members and three couples who were affiliated to the Church. The majority, although not affiliated to any organized religion, expressed strong personal religious or spiritual beliefs and very few asserted they were atheists.

Vegetarianism – theoretical perspectives

The work of three anthropologists is particularly relevant in approaching the topic of vegetarianism: Twigg (1979, 1983), Fiddes (1991) and Willetts (1997). For both Twigg and Fiddes meat-eating and vegetarianism are opposite sides of the same coin, the one providing insights into the other. In Twigg's studies of English vegetarianism from the mid-nineteenth century onwards, there are at least three themes which deserve attention. First is her articulation of an 'ideal-type' culturally constructed food hierarchy which she locates in the dominant meat-eating culture:

> At the top, highest in status, are the red meats – roast beef – lower in status are the bloodless animal meats – chicken, fish – and below them we have the animal products – cheese, eggs. These are sufficiently high in the hierarchy to support a meal being formed around them, though they are confined to lower-status events – the omelette or cheese flan of light lunch or supper. Below these we have the vegetables, regarded as insufficient and merely ancillary in the dominant scheme. (1979, 17)

Second is the manner in which she expands on the distinction between nature versus culture and the way this relates to ambivalence towards meat-eating. Since meat-eating involves a literal incorporation of an animal and a particularly intimate identification with the consumed product, it 'presents us with the ambivalences and complexities of our own attitudes to animals and the animal, nature and the natural' (1983, 18). This ambivalence is shared by meat-eaters and vegetarians alike. For both, the eating of animals represents an ingestion of animal nature, and blood, associated with the living essence of the animal, is the central symbol. Although dominant culture prizes the qualities of red-bloodedness – strength, aggression, sexuality, passion – it does so in a qualified way.

Enough and not too much is the essence of its attitude to this power. Cooking plays a crucial role here . . . Thus western society does not eat raw meat; tearing at an animal's flesh with one's teeth is one of our images of horror, suited to monsters or to semi-humans. If we eat meat, it is only after the disguising transformation of cooking has brought raw animal nature into the realm of culture, so that the strength and the power has been modified and tamed. (1979, 19)

The fears present in dominant culture of ingesting too much animal nature and of breaking down the constructed barrier between humans and beasts become more acute in vegetarianism and, despite their expressed principle of rejecting fish, flesh and fowl equally, the central imagery of vegetarianism also revolves around red meat. For vegetarians, steak dripping with blood is where the revulsion is focused; this is regarded as the most taboo, defiling food. 'It is a commonplace in the process of becoming a vegetarian that you give up first the red meat, then the poultry, then fish, etc.' (1979, 19–20). In choosing to eat down the hierarchy of foods away from red meat, positive associations are inverted, with, for example, virility, strength, aggression and power being redefined as machismo, cruelty and death.

Twigg's third theme deals with recurrent features of vegetarian ideology; she argues that they embody transformations of an under-lying basic structure. Having noted that certain key words, such as wholeness, natural, pure, goodness, bear a heavy symbolic load, Twigg identifies two conflicts within vegetarianism: (1) a strongly puritanical strain, accompanied by a rejection of the body in favour of the spirit, conflicts with a central concern with physical well-being; and (2) an ambivalent attitude to nature, manifested by a fear of it (vegetarians do not eat meat because it makes you one with abhorrent animality) and a desire to be one with it (vegetarians do not eat meat because this is cannibalistic and horrible) (1979, 21).

The resolution of the first conflict, she argues, lies in their notions of wholeness and oneness, best understood by means of the picture of nature they construct. Thus, for vegetarians, nature becomes moral-ized and the ultimate standard of legitimacy. What vegetarians do is to declare that goodness is natural. Nature is not presented as a vast canvas of death and predation, but 'rather is largeness, the eternal harmony of the stars, the round of the seasons' and is seen as 'containing messages of deep emotional impact' (1979, 22). This picture of harmonized nature is in turn projected back on to humankind and used to criticize the social, which is identified with falseness, artificiality and distortion. Humanity is regarded as having a pre-social, social self that is natural to it and good, and vegetarianism, as the natural diet for humanity, is part of this.

In broaching the central concept of wholeness, Twigg argues that the rejection of meat forms a boundary around the pure, within which the ethic of wholeness is unassailed. The whole may be consumed because all is safely pure; the disjunctions, defined as unreal, have been placed outside the system (1979, 23–4). It is not only against the impurity of meat that the purity of wholefoods is contrasted, for equally important in the modern alternative scene is the rejection of junk foods – exemplifying the malignant power of capitalism and multinationals – through which the concepts of impurity and unreality are strongly linked. Twigg emphasizes that it is crucial in the understanding of the vegetarian movement to appreciate that it offers a 'this-worldly' form of salvation which operates through the concept of the pure body. Thus vegetarian food is perceived as light- and life-affirming. Meat, by contrast, represents dead food, vegetarianism repeatedly referring to eating meat as eating corpses: it builds up dead matter in you; the poison fills the system. The ingestion of dead animals is an ingestion of death itself (1979, 24).

In sharp contrast, Fiddes (1991) treats meat-eating as an ideology, and implicitly supplants Twigg's vegetarian 'moralized nature' with a meat-eating 'immoral culture' which projects this stance unethically on to animals and nature. His central thesis is that the symbolism of meat is heavily implicated in the domination and control humans have sought over nature: it tangibly represents human control of the natural world. Thus Western culture has consistently represented the environment as a threat to be conquered, a wilderness to be tamed, a resource to be utilized, an object with few intrinsic needs or rights.

> To believe that humans have no duties towards, or responsibility for, the non-human world, has the implicit consequence of legitimating meat-eating. Taken to its logical conclusion, this argument predicates that if animals have no rights, no feelings, no true independent existence, then there can be no sense in which it is morally suspect to use them for our own purposes as we see fit . . . To dispute that the individual has unlimited rights over animals is to defy an almost sacred tenet of our common ideology. (1991, 63–4)

For Fiddes, then, meat is more than just a meal; it also represents a way of life. Its waning prestige – and outright rejection by many – may be indicative of more than changing tastes in food (1991, 45). It may foretell a replacement of the ideology of environmental control with an alternative ethos in which humanity is conceived of as complementary to nature, rather than opposed to it.

Willetts's (1997) work, based on her analysis of vegetarians in south London, suggests that we need to reappraise what we mean by vegetarianism. She observes that the categories of vegetarian and vegan covered a varied set of dietary practices: 'Self-defined vegetarians did not confine themselves to a meat-free diet, but ate a wide range of meats, most commonly chicken and fish, but also pork and beef. One "vegan" also ate bacon and another ate fish' (1997, 115–16). In accounting for this puzzle, Willetts states:

> eating meat appeared as a momentary 'lapse' in an otherwise unblemished career, and consequently did not impinge on their identity as vegetarian ... Vegetarians who defined their meat-eating as a 'lapse' were more likely to have eaten meat outside the home [e.g. for fear of appearing rude, or because of giving into temptation at the smell of meat cooking] ... However, for the majority of vegetarians meat was something prepared by them at home and was a regular part of their diet, most people taking it for granted that fish, at least, was part of the vegetarian repertoire. (1997, 116)

She therefore argues that vegetarianism is not rigorously defined but rather a permeable category embracing a wide range of food practices. It is also an identity that one can dip in and out of. Furthermore, meat-eating and vegetarianism are not always oppositional world-views.

Willetts's perspective accords well with my Newport data as is elaborated below. However, my data does not permit full agreement with Willetts on two counts. First is her rejection of Twigg's analysis of vegetarianism in terms of the inversion of a food hierarchy in the dominant culture, for which my data provides some modified support. And second is her assertion that 'eating meat does not place vegetarians in a precarious moral position, at least in their own eyes' (1997, 128). I will expand on these points in my discussion of the Newport data, as I consider the variety of ways in which vegetarianism was manifest in this particular Welsh community.

Vegetarian narratives

> . . . vegetarian biographies require attention, in order to reveal the ways in which motivations and accounts vary over time, as well as the patterns of conversion, adjustment and lapsing which commonly occur. (Beardsworth and Keil 1997, 241)

Given that vegetarianism in Western societies is often the result of a deliberate conversion, it should not be a matter of surprise that difficulties are sometimes experienced in renouncing certain foods, or that lapses occur. This research explored informants' narratives about how they became vegetarians, the varying ways in which that identity was actualized and how it changed over time and in response to specific social relations and contexts.

During fieldwork in Newport I initially operated with the common-sense assumption that there was a core conventional agreement as to what constituted vegetarianism. This assumption was substantiated in the responses of some informants when asked how they would define being a vegetarian:

> Somebody who doesn't eat meat or fish. (Newport female)

> Somebody who doesn't eat meat or fish – or anything that has meat products like gelatine. (Newport male)

Note that neither of these informants ate either fish or meat. Leaving aside finer subtleties such as rennet in cheese and wearing leather shoes or handbags, I can unambiguously categorize five of my twenty-eight informants as 'vegetarian' in this strict sense, that is, they ate no meat or fish, either at home or outside the home, although all of them did eat dairy products and eggs, and further this categorization accords with their own self-perceptions. In the same vein, another seven of these informants were readily categorized (and self-defined) as meat-eaters. Significantly, all seven had been – or were – involved in attempting to be as self-sufficient as possible, a point I return to later.

The real difficulties emerge in attempting to pigeon-hole the remaining sixteen informants. To treat this as a mere taxonomic problem would be reductive: we are dealing with representations, perceptions and identities, with typified social categories, objectifications and conventional proprieties which link the subjective individual and the physical embodied self with the social body and the outside world. In 'nutritional terms', it is fair to characterize all of them as being 'predominantly vegetarian' (cf. Willetts 1997). In terms of self-definition, some characterized themselves and/or their diets as vegetarian but qualified this statement by saying 'but I do eat fish' or some other meat; others made statements to the effect that they were 'mostly' or 'largely' vegetarian. In contrast, others who presented themselves as meat-eaters then said they were 'largely vegetarian' or 'rarely ate meat'. Clearly such problems with classification suggest that it would be more informative to look at the assumptions and processes behind the projection of such categories. The narratives provided by informants present a number of themes: pure or strict vegetarianism; lapses and the role of treats; puritanical interpretations and the role of compromise; and links with environmental concerns and animal welfare. It is these themes that must be explored to understand the meanings of vegetarianism to those who claim it as part of their self-identity.

Strict vegetarianism – a matter of principle

Turning first to informants' narratives about how they became vegetarians, among those who were 'strict' in their observance, one feature common to some was their commitment to vegetarianism as a matter of principle, particularly a moral objection to killing animals. In addition, they were not prepared to compromise these principles in spite of their own desires for particular foods. Thus one male (a farmer's son, a native Welsh speaker, who had become a town-dweller and regarded himself as 'conventional' as opposed to 'alternative') acknowledged he really missed the taste of fish: 'you'll find vegetarians miss bacon or fish most', he told me. He recalled eating fish and chips a few years previously at a public event and said he had felt guilty ever since about that one incident. Another strict vegetarian, a female (born in England, who had learnt Welsh and regarded herself as 'alternative'), said she had gone through a stage of finding it difficult to refuse meat in some social settings. She recalled being invited to a meal given by her husband's boss whose wife had cooked duck. At the time, although she had felt sick, she had hidden her vegetarianism and given the meat surreptitiously to the dog; but this phase 'quickly evolved into being able to say "no thank you, I am fine without it"'. She had eaten no meat or fish for some fifteen years and said she was not prepared to take the life of an animal if she did not have to. For both these informants eating meat or fish quite evidently placed them in a precarious moral position which they dealt with by abstention.

Even such strict, principle-driven vegetarianism can, however, be modified during the life course. Thus, one woman (a town-dweller and monoglot English speaker, born in England but who, by virtue of a Welsh grandmother, regarded herself as Welsh and 'a bit alternative') had become vegetarian at the age of thirteen. As a schoolgirl she had become 'strictly vegetarian' because she had a great empathy with animals: 'I didn't feel people had the right to kill anything really, so it was based on that really.' By the time of the research she described herself as 'largely vegetarian' having become less strict in the last five to six years, after having eaten no meat or fish for well over twenty years. When asked to account for this change, she felt it had something to do with being older: 'I feel less passionate about things than when I was younger and although I don't eat meat very often, I don't feel any qualms about it when I do.' She stated that she 'hardly ever' bought meat: 'probably once a month or something like that. I think I have got more selfish – I eat what I want rather than what I think is right,' also volunteering that 'I am compromising my principles'.

Other reasons for becoming vegetarian – and acceptable compromise
Shifting attention to the sixteen informants I have grouped together as 'predominantly vegetarian', there are three, all women, who viewed themselves as vegetarians but qualified this by stating that they do eat fish. The first (born in continental Europe, living in a nearby village and regarding herself as 'alternative') expounded a different ideal standard for her vegetarianism which allowed for the consumption of fish but not meat. Providing evidence in support of Twigg's (1983) analysis of vegetarianism as an inversion of the dominant food hierarchy in which red meat is ascendant because of the symbolic power of blood, she said:

> We go back to white fish sometimes because if you think of it there's not this red blood flowing – so the idea of eating and killing a fish is a little bit more acceptable – it's like killing a slug or anything like that you know – unlike a warm-blooded soul-inspired being like a sheep you know or a pig or a cow.

The other two women who viewed themselves as vegetarian but did eat fish were both married and were interviewed along with their husbands. These couples were in their fifties, non-Welsh speaking, but in each case one member of the couple was Welsh; one couple were town-dwellers, the other rural. These women did not adopt a principled stance, either strict or modified, for their vegetarianism, although one explicitly stated that she approved only of happy slaughtered animals that did not suffer. She had become vegetarian fifteen years previously, explaining that as a child she had a rather low metabolism and a digestive problem and that this – along with being inspired by a friend's vegetarian food and how nice it tasted – was why she decided to try being vegetarian. She gave it a two-month trial period and simply did not feel like eating meat after that, but she said,

> Still I enjoy fish and I adore shellfish. It's not sort of a religious belief, like almost some are almost religious about it that they cannot accept that animals are killed for eating – I don't have that feeling because I actually kill fish myself in summer [abroad].

This woman therefore acknowledged that there was a place for meat protein in her vegetarian diet and she was not opposed in principle to slaughtering animals.

Prior to the interview with the second couple, I had been informed by the husband that his wife was a vegetarian and that he himself had also become one. Faced with my obvious bafflement that she had presented herself as a vegetarian but nevertheless ate fish, she responded, 'Oh yes, I'm not vegetarian on principle.' 'What made you become vegetarian?' I asked.

Wife	I've never eaten meat – from a child – presumably didn't like it or whatever as a child – I wouldn't eat it. I used to have great battles over it and Sunday lunch was an absolute nightmare because my father used to make me sit in front of my plate you know – and ooh you don't do anything until you've eaten your meat – so I used to sit there all afternoon. [laughs]
Interviewer	Good heavens – and you basically just don't like it?
Wife	I just don't like it.
Interviewer	Nothing to do with cruelty to animals or anything like that?
Wife	Oh no, no, no. I just don't like it – I never have. I mean I can eat bacon – and have – if I'm pushed. That's only if

	I'm pushed. [laughs] I mean chicken it just makes me feel ill. Even the smell of chicken. And pork and lamb . . . Beef is the only one I can eat if I'm forced you know – I mean I wouldn't eat it from choice because I think I don't like the texture either . . .
Interviewer	[To husband] And you've become vegetarian?
Husband	I joined the club you see – it was easier. I'll have meat if I go out – occasionally – but even so – it's quite interesting – I couldn't eat very raw meat if I went out – you know red meat – probably the taste now is a bit strong for me – but I mean I'll have beef or lamb if it's well-cooked yes, but not very often. I like gammon – and then it gets a treat for me.
Interviewer	It's a treat?
Husband	Yes.
Interviewer	So you don't crave it occasionally?
Husband	No – no – I mean we eat fish – and I find we do quite well.

In this example, occasional meat-eating, far from being a source of guilt, as was seen to be the case with strict vegetarians who interpreted such events as 'lapses', was an appreciated – if infrequent treat – to be enjoyed. In this interview, as well as in the interview with the first couple, it became clear that the two men, although both meat-eaters, thought of themselves as being largely vegetarian. And indeed they were much of the time, since the division of household labour was such that their wives did most of the cooking, and while one was willing to prepare some meat at home, the second refused to cook meat at all.

Thus another point emphasized in these interviews was the highly context-dependent nature of a vegetarian identity. The same individual can in one situation (e.g. outside the home) regard him or herself as a meat-eater and in another (e.g. at home) as a vegetarian. People dip in and out of a vegetarian identity not only during the course of their life histories, but also contemporaneously, perhaps contingent on person, occasion, time and place.

Social relationships, for example, between couples as above, between friends, between parents and children, are very influential in establishing vegetarian identities, as well as in compromising them. One woman, for example, explained that there was a difference between what she felt she ought to eat and what she actually ate, mainly because her son had made a strong declaration that he was a carnivore, and she had slipped from buying vegetarian Sosmix to buying meat sausages.

> I tend to have a slightly puritanical approach to life, and sometimes you can make your life such a misery by not being willing to compromise, and it's being able to compromise sometimes and acknowledge that it's not – I mean there is the whole moral thing about food – and that's gone with the permaculture – but you can make your life so hard, and that's what happened with sausages – it slipped from just being a very occasional thing to sort of being rather regular, so it's like if you let your principles slip you've got to be sure that it is only a slip and not a beginning of a habit and be very conscious of what you're doing.

She defended what she clearly perceived as 'lapses', prompted by her particular family context, on the basis of her acceptance of 'ideals we stick with most of the time'.

Alternative culture – vegetarianism and animal welfare

In this section I focus on ten informants – mostly in their forties and fifties – who were perceived, by both locals and other incomers, as 'alternatives'. They were either committed to the use of wholefoods and/or were actively engaged in living communally, followed permaculture principles 'in a loose sense' and advocated sustainable living. Permaculture seeks to invert the Enlightenment principle of control over nature by trying – to borrow words from different interviews – 'to fit in with the habitat along with the other creatures in an unexploitative manner', 'where humans have a sense of their own place that is not too dominant within a landscape'. Their vegetarianism was thus rooted in a different set of principles and this 'alternative' position was highly nuanced.

As far as food in their own lives was concerned, a consciously holistic approach was adopted which encompassed the global and the local and the physical embodied self. Such informants prided themselves on having given considerable reflection to the political, economic, moral and environmental aspects of food in all stages of its production. 'Most people', said one interviewee, 'don't think where meat from McDonald's comes from.' As far as healthy eating was concerned, she could not think of health without thinking of the health of the whole planet. For her, the key concept was simplicity, to live as simply as possible and to be as self-sufficient as possible; the notion of a consumer society based on the satisfaction of infinite wants and needs was explicitly rejected. Human impact on the environment was minimized by using compost toilets, turf roofs, reed beds, producing energy by means of solar panels, water sluices and wind power, and eating only local, seasonal and organic foods. This entailed assuming control of all the basic essentials of life, so that they grew most of their own essential foods and kept their own animals 'in the best possible conditions' – the same organic grain for feeding the chickens was used for making their own bread. They also had their own fuel and 'live spring water', the latter connoting the purity of the essence of the earth and symbolically opposed to impure, dead, chemically-treated water.

This 'alternative' view of morality and of the relation between nature and culture represented another orientation to meat-eating and vegetarianism, which emerged particularly clearly in discussions about BSE. So-called 'mad cow disease' was viewed by three informants not in the restricted sense as the result of sub-standard animal feed, but in a much wider symbolic sense, as a symptom of a rupture between nature and culture:

> The way they keep cows now I just think is cruel because they're made to be either over-milk producing or over-meat producing – there's so little natural health left in them – that's what bothers me – you have to keep them alive with all these drugs to stop them catching all sorts of horrible diseases – I think mad cow disease is just a symptom of all that – it's like we'll go on finding diseases to get because we need to have diseases because we're not living in a healthy way.

Another interviewee voiced her surprise that the situation had not been considerably worse: 'Our goats have a huge amount of land to graze – so they won't have an adverse impact on the environment.' Noting that the whole landscape of Britain has been changed by meat-eating and dairy farming, she disliked the fact that cows were over-wintered on concrete, and that intensive farming deprived them of herbs and the wooded environment which she saw as their natural inheritance: 'I am amazed animals can exist in the conditions we give them – amazed the meat industry can exist.' She saw antibiotics and vaccines as the cause of many modern human diseases, and used homeopathic remedies in treating both her family and her animals. Strictly vegetarian in that she ate no meat or fish at home or outside the home, she volunteered that she could imagine a situation in which if she was starving she would eat fish but, stressing that she honoured and respected animals, she said that she would eat the fish with respect. She referred to someone who ate meat three times a day as 'gross'.

For many of these informants meat and meat-eating were made problematic primarily by the way humans treat animals and the countryside. Some also gave reasons of personal health for choosing vegetarianism, but others, previously strict vegetarians, provided similar reasons (such as problems with digesting cheese, tiredness and weakness due to a lack of meat protein) for occasional, if reluctant meat-eating. It was not so much the consumption of meat per se that placed some of these informants in what they saw as a 'precarious moral position' but rather how and where it was produced. Thus one reluctant meat-eater found it acceptable to eat organic lamb once a month. Another justified occasional meat-eating outside the home by saying he had become vegetarian for political not for dietary reasons, the issue of protein related to land use being mentioned by four informants. (The book *Diet for a Small Planet* (Lappé 1971) was specifically mentioned in this connection.)

For some informants involved full-time in sustainable living, the argument about sustainable living actually provided the basis for their meat-eating while also dictating the manner in which meat was acquired and consumed. To illustrate this point, I consider one woman's responses in some detail. On being asked whether she was vegetarian, she replied:

> I guess I am but you know in the sense that that's how I think of myself but I do in fact eat meat if it happens – I occasionally buy it. There's a lot of us who reaching our age who having been strict we are slightly less so and we want to get away from being puritanical.

Influenced by Tibetan Buddhism she said she did not object to eating meat from animals that were bred to be eaten: 'In a sense they have chosen that life whereas wild creatures – they are so endangered now.' But she could not bear to eat fish:

> I feel pained because they are wild. I think it is terrible – people think the sea is a bottomless resource – they think they have the right to dump rubbish. Everyone says cod is endangered but you know they must have cod. I think it is awful. But I mean we all do it – I mean we all find some way of saying we'll do it just this once all the time.

This informant had first become vegetarian in 1984–5 when she came under the influence of vegetarian friends:

> I needed to see if it felt right – to not entangle myself with the karma of all these creatures . . . and brutality [of being killed] and to just eat you know to be lighter. In myself I needed to do that at that time . . . That was my first contact with that sort of alternative world. And I was very much not a vegetarian before that – at that time I could not imagine how you could make a lentil soup without a meat-stock cube.

By the time of interview she had not only reconciled herself to eating meat again, but also to taking her turn in killing their own chickens. Her return to meat-eating occurred some time after meeting her male partner in 1989, who had been through stages of fasting and being vegetarian, but by that time 'was quite clear that killing chickens was OK for him'. She felt she could square this politically and spiritually as being part of sustainable living – 'he would say it is our own chicken' and he did not enjoy the killing:

> It was almost like honouring the chicken itself. Since it had been killed. In fact I didn't particularly enjoy it at first – I would just have a token bit and then just occasionally. Probably I think that would be a natural amount – just once a month – like it is a special occasion – it is not part of my diet that is really a staple.

In assessing what was a 'natural amount' her yardstick was 'a hunting and gathering society': 'They do say the hunting and gathering societies are the ones who preserve the communities the most – preserve nature best in that they rely on very varied resources rather than trying to control nature.' In her account 'nature' is imbued with strong symbolic meanings, many of her views on animals being influenced by Buddhism and New Age philosophies.

For this person, therefore, the consumption of a chicken had a devotional aspect, as did her approach to nature more generally. She commented: 'In this area there is a lot of peace dancing and quite a lot of pagan stuff and it is part of the way we share. I feel that my spiritual community is the local spiritual community of whatever denomination.' Expanding on what she meant by paganism, she said:

> I suppose it means respect for nature and earth and calling to it and dialoguing with it, whether it is mother earth or the mountain or we have songs – here we sing to the mountain. It seems to be feeling – to be aware of the natural cycles in nature and how one is a part of that.

Taken as a whole, there are strong resonances in some interviews of Twigg's portrayal of a vegetarian 'moralized nature' as the ultimate standard of legitimacy with its stress on purity, raw vegetables and its association of meat with rotting corpses. One informant noted that she did not feel very easy with big meat-eaters because 'I think it goes with a lot of aggression and you eat fear when you eat meat'; she thought that meat rotting inside the body caused cancers because it took longer to digest than vegetarian food. Twigg notes:

> There is a strong pantheistic element in vegetarianism; nature is a source of redemptive power and contact with it is prized. Thus we find the emphasis on gardening and growing . . . The flight to farms in the Welsh hills . . . display[s] this deep feeling for organic contact with the land . . . we find connected with vegetarianism a revival in interest in attempts to read [nature] . . . Nature is a framework of meaning, not just an alien object for our regard or exploitation. (1979, 22)

Simultaneously, however, many such informants were deeply informed about environmental issues and the ideological implications of meat being more than just a meal, and representing a way of life. Just as mindful of tropical rainforests as is Fiddes, the previous informant remarked that 'the cow is central to Western culture'. Interviews were full of references expressing disquiet about battery farming, the way pigs and cattle are reared and kept, the abuse of additives, hormones, fertilizers and pesticides and the exploitation of workers in Third World countries supplying the Western world with luxury products. Although not all ten informants associated with alternative lifestyles imbued the consumption of meat with spiritual overtones, compared to habitual meat-eaters, who might take for granted their consumption of animal flesh and eat it on a daily basis, both the frequency and significance of meat-eating was radically transformed. Traditional notions of a 'meat and two veg diet' and the British 'proper meal' (cf. Murcott 1982, 1983) were displaced by a completely different form of eating. Their beliefs regarding sustainability could be employed to argue that meat protein was acceptable if it was organic, local and reared under humane conditions. But in terms of what these informants believed to be a moral relationship between nature and culture, the majority of the British population were seen to be massively overnourished and to consume amounts of meat protein far in excess of what they considered a 'natural' amount.

In concluding this section, it must be emphasized that there is more than one 'alternative' vision of food in Newport. In addition to the ten informants discussed above, there were eleven who had been or were practising self-sufficiency, several having been influenced by John Seymour, who lived in Newport between 1966 and 1980 and wrote a number of books on the subject (e.g. 1977, 1991). These eleven interviewees included smallholders, most of whom were not vegetarians. In fact in Seymour's writing there is a pro-meat argument to the effect that if people were not meat-eaters, many animals would disappear from the world, an argument that was repeated to me by some of the twenty-eight informants. However, and again in line with Seymour, among some smallholders there was an emphasis on whole and organic foods, as well as the espousal of a non-sentimental attitude towards killing one's own animals. One couple illustrated this approach:

> *Husband* I think it's important to say we tried I think successfully not to be sentimental about this – because a lot of farmers won't eat the animals they rear but we did – we killed and ate most of them.
>
> *Wife* I think it's rather hypocritical and sentimental – the two things run together on this in that I think you've got to have worked out in your mind a philosophy what animals are there for – and if – unless you make a choice to be vegetarian – that's well and good and I respect vegetarians – or if you think that animal protein has a place in our diet then you've not got to put up all these barriers . . . if you have a due sense of responsibility and you recognize that you're not doing it for greed – I think that's the other thing – I think we shouldn't eat too much of these things – there should be a proper balance – and then should take quite a responsible attitude to the food you're eating – that it's going to some next stage of use and development.

This couple were formerly practising Christians and still claimed to be deeply influenced by Christian principles. Thus the wife stated that she could get 'excited about my compost heap as a religious symbol', and she had explained to her daughter when she was a little girl that there is a very real sense in which the pigs they kept – who had names and of whom they were very fond – would be playing the cello or piano tomorrow. Among people influenced by Seymour there were some meat-eaters who ate very little meat, less so than some self-defined vegetarians, and there were also instances of another type of ethical vegetarian – people who have nothing in principle against eating meat but often do not do so when they are unable to obtain organic produce. The emphasis on organic and pure foods as well as on wholefoods was also an extremely important theme in very many of these interviews.

In relating the collectivities to which my research subjects 'belong' to the broader community, it is important to note that at least some smallholders, including the couple just quoted, had become deeply involved with their Welsh-speaking farming neighbours, exchanging information, help at harvest-time and borrowing equipment; at least one couple who had set out to be self-sufficient became caught up in the market system and themselves became farmers. Other 'alternative' lifestylers were, however, clearly very separate from Welsh local culture. Thus, one alternative informant, who had even learned Welsh in order to enter university, still acknowledged that she did not really relate to local Welsh culture.

(Although an interview conducted with a Soil Association inspector confirmed that other areas of west Wales are regarded as being among the foremost centres of organic food production in Britain, there were no large-scale commercially oriented organic producers in the immediate vicinity of Newport at the time of the fieldwork. To place the analysis conducted in this chapter in broader perspective, it is worth noting that a major tension exists between, on the one hand, sustainable living which is appropriate to a community or a household and, on the other hand, the idea of making a major breakthrough so that the whole of food marketing is eventually done by organic producers.)

Conclusions and reflections: geographical and social time and space

This chapter approaches issues of community indirectly by considering a particular collectivity – loosely defined as vegetarians and/or 'alternatives' – within the small rural Welsh community of Newport. This collectivity and its relationship to Newport provides a paradox: on the one hand, most of its members, as comparatively recent incomers to Newport, to Wales and to rural lifestyles, were viewed by themselves and local people as 'outsiders'; on the other hand, this collectivity at the end of the twentieth century had come to typify one aspect of Welsh rural community life. For example, as noted earlier, the population in and around Newport was able to sustain what was recognized as one of the best wholefood shops in Britain. At one point in my fieldwork I asked an employee in this shop whether she knew of any vegetarians I could interview; her response was, 'Oh, there must be loads in *this* place', an assumption I had come to share after a few weeks living in Newport.

The reality, as my research began to make clear, was quite different and considerably more complex. Although I found 'strict vegetarians' to be comparatively thin on the ground, those who assumed a vegetarian identity which allowed for a variety of interpretations regarding consumption of meat were much more common. To restrict the category to some predetermined definition of vegetarianism that did not accord with findings on the ground was clearly inappropriate. Thus one of the findings of this research was the heterogeneity of the category of vegetarian. Vegetarian identities might be based on ethical principles, which were found to range from a simple rejection of killing animals through ideas about hierarchies of food and non-food animals to a belief that it was wrong *not* to kill and eat the animals one raised; or they might stem from a completely amoral expression of personal preference. Given these divergent bases for vegetarianism, compromises regarding meat-eating might be interpreted as serious moral failings occasioning long-term personal discomfort or simply as a minor lapse or even a treat. Furthermore, vegetarian identities were found to vary over the life course and as a response to different social relations and contexts.

Heterogeneity within a collectivity that is viewed from outside as homogeneous is, of course, characteristic of communities more generally. The heterogeneity of this particular collectivity of vegetarians means that its relationship to the rural Welsh community of Newport is not simply as oppositional other, but has various strands and manifestations. In the first place, the boundary between this collectivity and the wider community is permeable. As noted earlier, one of the strict vegetarians, the Welsh-speaking son of a local farmer, was clearly a product of the 'traditional' local community. A rather different type of connection between vegetarians and local residents became apparent as I reflected on my own entirely Welsh-speaking upbringing in a farming community in Carmarthenshire. I recalled one of the songs of that childhood, 'Claddu'r Mochyn Du' (Burying the Black Pig), which was composed in the area in which research for this chapter was conducted. (I am grateful to a local resident, Mrs Meriel Van Haeften-Owen, for bringing this last point to my attention. The song was composed by her grandfather, the late John Owen, described as a 'farm labourer who later became a Nonconformist minister' (Hywel 1987, 22–3).)

> Holl drigolion bro a bryniau
> Dewch i wrando hyn o eiriau,
> Fe gewch hanes rhyw hen fochyn
> A fu farw, yn dra sydyn.
>   O mor drwm yr ydym ni,
>   O mor drwm yr ydym ni,
>   Y mae yma alar calon
>   Ar ôl claddu'r mochyn du.

> (All you people come and listen
> Teardrops in your eyes will glisten
> Soon with pain your hearts be rending
> At our Mochyn's sudden ending.
>   O! how sad of heart are we
>   O! how sad of heart are we
>   There was grief and tribulation
>   When we lost the Mochyn Du.)
>   trans. Sir H. Idris Bell

This wonderful old song both regrets and celebrates the death of a pig which dies before slaughter, thereby escaping the cooking pot. Simultaneously evoking laughter and tears, the song exploits both comedy and tragedy, as it plaintively bemoans the loss to human appetite yet takes exultant joy in the pet pig's defiance, in the manner of his victorious exit and triumph over humankind. There are several versions of the lyrics, some verses describing elaborate plans for the burial and mourning (with polished coffin, silver knobs and velvet trimming), others bemoaning the other aspect of the loss:

> Edrych fyny ar y bachau,
> Gweld hwy'n wag heb yr ystlysau,
> Dim un tamaid i roi i undyn –
> Colled fawr oedd colli'r mochyn.

(Look up at the hooks,
See them empty without the sides (of bacon),
Not one bit to give anyone –
Losing the pig was a great loss.)

The chorus, repeated after each verse, is sung with mock solemnity. Exemplifying the argument put forward by some anthropologists that cultures devise forms of release and ways of dealing with their inherent contradictions, the song not only reflects the economic importance of the pig in former times but also resonates with a widespread ambivalence surrounding meat consumption, and provides a point of contact between the Welsh farming community and the vegetarians latterly in their midst. Such an interpretation was borne out in a great number of interviews conducted with Newport locals, for whom the squeals of not-so-fortunate pigs from long ago still haunt and make themselves heard. 'The pig was one of us,' exclaimed one local Welsh-speaking informant; 'he used to follow us to the shop!'

So close is the identification between pig and human that pigs are commonly characterized as having human attributes, and in an extract cited by Fiddes, the sound of a dying pig is likened to a child (1991, 130). As Sahlins states: 'To adopt the conventional incantations of structuralism, "everything happens as if the food system is inflected throughout by a principle of metonymy, such that taken as a whole it composes a sustained metaphor on cannibalism"' (cited by Fiddes 1991, 134).

As already mentioned, and as Twigg points out, because vegetarians desire to be one with nature they do not eat meat since this would be cannibalistic and horrible. Cannibalism can thus be viewed as representing an extreme form of identification with an animal. Meat-eaters, however, share this identification and it is manifest, for instance, in the frequently encountered inability of meat-eaters to contemplate killing their 'own' animals. The theme is of obvious relevance to the song discussed.

Besides this degree of permeability of the boundary between vegetarians and the local Welsh community in terms of personnel and common cultural understandings stemming from ambiguous feelings surrounding meat-eating, the research uncovered ways in which the local community and some of the different categories of incomers appeared to be attempting to accommodate one another. Thus some smallholders involved in self-sufficiency tended to report a relationship with their Welsh farming neighbours based in mutual material aid and facilitated by their activities being fairly readily placed within the local economy.

Other informants also perceived as 'alternatives' were generally not so readily accommodated in local social expectations nor embedded in local networks. However, some of them, especially those who described themselves as being loosely involved in permaculture, were disproportionately likely to attempt to make a connection with local culture in a symbolic way – they tended to learn the local language. Earlier I noted that eight out of twenty-one incomers in this study had learned Welsh to a good standard of spoken fluency. At least five if not six of these would be considered radical in their 'alternative' views, and four pursued a 'completely alternative lifestyle'. These observations suggest that ironically the category that is least well integrated in this community in terms of social relationships still could be perceived as representing less of a threat to the Welsh language, often regarded as the most important characteristic of rural Welsh communities and the main carrier of local culture, than do those who are better integrated socially but then inject the English language into domains where it would not previously have been used. The very high proportion of Welsh learners among these 'alternatives' is remarkable, and the question of why this should be so, and how this relates to their sense of belonging, as well as to their impact on the local community is worthy of further investigation.

This discussion of vegetarian biographies in a rural community in west Wales has rejected any simplistic duality of insider/outsider status even in circumstances that would seem superficially to allow it. Instead, my research has stressed the internal heterogeneity of the category of vegetarians and, as a consequence, the variety of ways in which this category relates to and is accommodated by the local community.

Research for this paper is based upon part of 'The Nation's Diet: the Social Science of Food Choice' research programme, funded by the Economic and Social Research Council (see Murcott 1996). Two anthropology projects were based at Goldsmith's College, University of London, and were conceived and directed by Professor Pat Caplan. One project involved two researchers for three years in an ethically mixed, densely populated inner-city London borough. The other project involved myself for two years in a rural location in Wales. I am deeply indebted to Professor Pat Caplan for her constructive comments.

References

Aitchison, J. and Carter, H. (1999). 'The Welsh language today', in D. Dunkerley and A. Thompson (eds.), *Wales Today* (Cardiff: University of Wales Press).

Beardsworth, A. and Keil, T. (1997). *Sociology on the Menu* (London: Routledge).

Davies, C. A. (1999). *Reflexive Ethnography: A Guide to Researching Selves and Others* (London: Routledge).

Davies, J. (1993). *The Welsh Language* (Cardiff: University of Wales Press).

Day, G. (1999). 'The rural dimension', in D. Dunkerley and A. Thompson (eds.), *Wales Today* (Cardiff: University of Wales Press).

Fiddes, N. (1991). *Meat: A Natural Symbol* (London: Routledge).

Foley, W. A. (1997). *Anthropological Linguistics* (Oxford: Blackwell).

Gasson, R., Crow, G., Errington, A., Hutson, J., Marsden, T. and Winter, D. M. (1988). 'The farm as a family business: a review', *Journal of Agricultural Economics*, 39, 1, 1–41.

Grillo, R. D. (1989). *Dominant Languages: Language and Hierarchy in Britain and France* (Cambridge: Cambridge University Press).

Hywel, J. (1987). *Caneuon Enwog Cymru/Famous Songs of Wales* (Penygroes: Gwynn).

Jones, N. (1993). *Living in Rural Wales* (Llandysul: Gomer).

Lappé, R. M. (1971). *Diet for a Small Planet* (New York: Friends of the Earth/Ballantyne).

Murcott, A. (1982), 'On the social significance of the "cooked dinner" in south Wales', *Social Science Information*, 21, 4/5, 677–96.

—— (1983). '"It's a pleasure to cook for him": food, mealtimes and gender in some south Wales households', in E. Garmarnikow, E. Morgan, J. Purvis and D. Taylorson (eds.), *The Public and the Private* (London: Heinemann).

—— (ed.) (1996). *The Social Science of Food Choice* (London: Longman).

Rees, A. (1950). *Life in a Welsh Countryside* (Cardiff: University of Wales Press).

Seymour, J. (1977). *Keep it Simple* (Llandeilo: Black Pig).

—— (1991). *Changing Lifestyles: Living as though the World Mattered* (London: Victor Gollancz).

Twigg, J. (1979). 'Food for thought: purity and vegetarianism', *Religion*, 9, 13–35.

—— (1983). 'Vegetarianism and the meaning of meat', in A. Murcott (ed.), *The Sociology of Food and Eating: Essays on the Sociological Significance of Food* (Aldershot: Gower).

Willetts, A. (1997) '"Bacon sandwiches got the better of me": meat-eating and vegetarianism in south-east London', in P. Caplan (ed.), *Food, Health and Identity* (London: Routledge).

9   Constructing communities away from home: Welsh identities in London

Jeremy Segrott

This chapter examines the construction of Welsh identities in London. It begins by tracing the history of migration from Wales to London, and the development of Welsh life there. I then consider the research process, and the role that my own identity as a researcher played in shaping the project that I undertook. In particular I focus upon the ways in which language positioned me in relation to those I was studying. The discussion then examines a number of key themes from the research project itself. For many of the Welsh people living in London who took part in the research, belonging to some kind of Welsh society is an extremely important part of maintaining their identities in the city, often linked to issues of language and the maintenance of cultural tradition. Such societies frequently draw upon multiple nodes of belonging in constructing forms of Welshness, such as tying together bonds of nationality and religion. The Welsh in London represent something more complex than a single homogeneous community. Welsh life in the city is cut across by many social axes, such as class, gender, sexuality and, particularly, generation. Recent years have witnessed a shift towards what might be described as more cosmopolitan Welsh identities in the English metropolis (Hannerz 1990). A once highly centralized and structured Welsh community is giving way to more mobile and decentred networks, that are in many ways less rooted in particular localities. As Welsh migrants to London engage more fully with London life, different ways of belonging to a Welsh community in the city are emerging. I argue, however, that the new networks currently developing in London continue to bind Welsh people together – across and within places.

Welsh migration to London

Economic migration and trade have linked Wales with London for many centuries, and can arguably be traced back to the Middle Ages (Francis-Jones 1984). By the end of the fifteenth century a recognizable Welsh community had developed in London, and when King Henry VII came to power he repaid the loyalty of his Welsh supporters with high offices in the Inns of Court (Jones 1981, 2001; Morgan and Thomas 1984). During this period there was a general influx of well-educated Welshmen who worked as officials in the Court, and as doctors, printers and publishers. But Welsh migration to London encompassed workers from across the socio-economic range, including both men and women (Jones 1981; M. Owen 1989). One of the earliest economic connections between Wales and London which began in the thirteenth century was the practice of droving cows and sheep to fairs in Barnet, Brentwood and Smithfield (Morgan and Thomas 1984). Droving connected rural Wales with urban London, and helped sustain networks of people, animals, money and information (Knowles 1997; Jones 2001). The eighteenth century was characterized by the general migration of labourers to London, and a sizeable Welsh population developed in the area to the south of the river Thames. Many found work in the boatyards as carpenters, and Welsh sailors were often present in the docks, on ships that had arrived from Wales (M. Owen 1989). Demand for labourers in the city's commercial gardens increased as its population rose sharply, and women began to migrate to London independently each spring, to take up such work over the summer months. They became known as *merched y gerddi*, or 'the garden girls' (Williams-Davies 1978). From the 1760s onwards increasing flows of permanent migration developed, primarily driven by economic depression in rural Wales which continued throughout the nineteenth century (Knowles 1997). In the 1840s, when many parts of mid-Wales were suffering from severe economic hardship, a number of structural changes took place in the dairy trade in London which provided a means of escape and a livelihood for thousands of Welsh families (Atkins 1977; Philo 1995). This was an occupation whose necessary skills matched those of the rural inhabitants of mid-Wales very closely. Jewin Crescent Welsh chapel in London recorded its first dairy-owner member in 1839, and by the beginning of the twentieth century the Welsh had become dominant within the milk trade in the city. Other economic activities, such as the drapery business, also became key Welsh occupations in London (Jones 2001).

Towards the end of the nineteenth century new economic opportunities opened up in London for Welsh women, reaffirming the place of the city as a key migration destination for those in search of work (Bartholomew 1991). Domestic servants were recruited in large numbers to work in both private homes and hotels and, by 1931 10,000 Welsh women were employed to carry out such work in the city (Beddoe 1988). Their presence highlights the gendered nature of migration, and how both the employment and experiences of women can be distinct from those of male migrants (Bartholomew 1991; Jones 2001; Walter 1999). During the inter-war years south Wales suffered from extremely high levels of unemployment and economic depression, with valleys such as the Rhondda devastated by the collapse in the coalmining industry (Smith 1993). Many workers decided to try to find work in the large cities of England, with London being a key centre. And through a series of mechanisms the government itself sought both to recondition the workforce of the 'distressed' areas and transfer them to areas such as London, where there was demand for workers with the 'right' skills (Linehan 1998). By 1937, 250,000 people had been assisted in finding work in the large cities of England; between 1921 and 1935 47,000 people left the Rhondda Urban District – approximately 28 per cent of the 1921 population (Owen 1937).

The period since 1945 has been characterized by many changes in the flows of migrants from Wales to London (Jones 2001). In the early post-war years many Welsh people found work in newly opened factories in the western suburbs of London, such as Slough and Ealing. Teachers were a key export from Wales during the 1950s, with a surplus in Wales coinciding with a shortage of qualified staff in London's schools. According to Jones (1996, 5), Wales exported teachers on a vast scale, and the London County Council was a generous employer. Clwyd (1987) suggests that during the 1950s up to 70 per cent of teachers in London were from Wales. London hospitals also recruited large numbers of Welsh women as nurses, a fact from which strong parallels can be drawn with the experience of the Irish in Britain (Walter 1997). As economic conditions in Wales have become generally more prosperous, the need to leave Wales for economic survival has to some extent diminished, and today's migrants often come to London in pursuit of a career. Referring to the period since the 1970s, Jones (2001, 30) argues that 'pressures to leave the country eased considerably as the Welsh economy improved and as more foreign investment was attracted, particularly into south Wales'. Increasingly, Welsh people are working in professional occupations, in the financial and public relations sectors, and in the media. Many migrants are also drawn to London by the metropolitan lifestyle that it offers, and the tolerant and diverse culture characteristic of large cities.

London and Welsh culture

Increasing levels of Welsh migration soon led to the formation of a Welsh community in London that was evident by the fifteenth century, and provided the basis for the establishment of Welsh societies to serve that population. But London has functioned as a centre of Welsh life in other ways, effectively operating as the capital of Wales until the growth of sizeable cities within the nation itself (Jones 1981, 1985, 2001). London provided Wales with a metropolitan infrastructure, with most Welsh books published there up until the eighteenth century. Without a major city within the borders of Wales, the Welsh elite lived and worked in London, and during the eighteenth century a number of Welsh literary cultural societies were formed in the city (Jones 1981). The Honourable Society of Cymmrodorion and the Gwyneddigion (the Gwynedd Society) were particularly important examples. Key national Welsh institutions such as the National Eisteddfod, the National Library of Wales and the University of Wales were established primarily through the leadership and finance of the London Welsh (Ellis 1971; Jones 1985). The nineteenth century witnessed the Welsh chapel network mushroom in London, and Nonconformism took over from the literary societies as the controlling institution of Welsh life in the city (Jones 1985; W. T. Owen 1989). The chapels functioned as one of the central Welsh institutions in London, not only providing religious worship, but also playing a key role in Welsh cultural life in the city.

During the opening decades of the twentieth century a number of Welsh institutions were established in London to serve a growing 'exile' population in the city. In 1920 the London Welsh Association opened its doors in Gray's Inn Road, the building having been a gift from Sir Howell J. Williams, who was interested in the welfare of young Welsh people in London (M. Jones 1946; E. Jones 2001). The London Welsh Centre, as it became, has offered accommodation for cultural activities such as drama groups and choirs, and provided a place where young Welsh people can socialize. The Saturday-night dances were once the highlight of the social week, and it was here that many hundreds of Welsh people in the city met their future partners. Gray's Inn Road has been a central point of information on Welsh life in the city, and kept the London Welsh in contact with life back home in Wales. During the 1950s, the London Welsh Rugby Club settled in Richmond, having spent many years moving around London (Becken and Jones 1985). A number of other important institutions were also founded during the same decade, including the Welsh Book Club and Ysgol Gymraeg Llundain (the London Welsh School). The story of the school and its survival through many difficulties is a crucial one, both for the Welsh population of London, and in terms of the issues of ethnicity and national and linguistic identity it raises. It is the only Welsh-medium school in England and represents one of the earliest attempts by an ethnic group in London to gain funding for a dedicated school.

The falling number of Welsh migrants since the Second World War has been largely responsible for the decline of the Welsh chapels in London, and that of other 'traditional' institutions (David 1991; Jones 1985, 2001). But the changing background and needs of the migrants moving to London has also been an important factor. Since the early 1990s, especially, different Welsh networks have been emerging in London that in some ways appeal more to a new generation of migrants. Perhaps best known among contemporary Welsh societies in London is SWS (Social, Welsh and Sexy). *Sws* means 'kiss' in Welsh, and so the acronym is also a play on words. Meeting six times a year, SWS is essentially a social night-out, held in bars and clubs around central London. Gwl@d is an Internet-based group, concerned with Welsh rugby. Although not specifically a London organization, Gwl@d has recently arranged a series of social nights in central London pubs, and also rugby games in Regent's Park. (*Gwlad* is the Welsh word for 'country', and the Internet @ symbol in its title seems to symbolize a fusion of technology and patriotism.) Cymdeithas yr Iaith Gymraeg (the Welsh Language Society) has had a London branch for many years. Apart from activities to promote the use of the language, it has been responsible for running Noson o Hwyl (a night of fun) – a monthly pub-crawl for Welsh speakers and learners. Across London there are many other public networks, such as Y Gymdeithas Hoywon (the Welsh Gay and Lesbian Society), but also numerous other more informal groups of Welsh people who socialize together.

While my own research focused primarily upon traditional Welsh societies and an emerging group of social networks, there are many other aspects of Welsh life in the city (which I am able to mention only briefly here). Welsh-language classes are offered at a number of locations across London. The Welsh business community in London is served by Wales in London, which organizes supper evenings with prominent speakers from the business world, and also by the St David's Club. In terms of politics, Plaid Cymru – The Party of Wales has a very active London branch, which plays an important role in the work of the party.

A Welsh ethnography in London

The research project upon which this chapter is based was under-taken in London during 1998 and 1999. One of its most important aims was to understand how Welsh people in London understand and experience their self-identities, and what it means for them to be Welsh away from home. Part of this enquiry concerned their reasons for joining (or not joining) Welsh societies in London, and how this was linked to the construction of their self-identities. A second major theme considered the ways in which Welsh societies in London construct differing senses of Welshness, and how being outside Wales might shape such constructions. In achieving these aims, the project made extensive use of both unstructured in-depth interviews and participant observation. At times the two techniques were used simultaneously, such as at meetings where it had been arranged to conduct interviews. Participant observation undertaken at organized events also allowed contact to be made with potential interviewees. Approximately sixty taped interviews were conducted, with about another twenty un-taped. The majority of these were undertaken in people's private homes, though interview locations also included pubs and clubs, chapels, schools and other institutions. Throughout the fieldwork I kept a detailed research diary. The fieldwork was carried out both through the medium of Welsh and English, with roughly half of all interviews, participant observation and field notes in each language. The names of all research participants have been altered, as have some personal details. Excerpts from interviews that were conducted in Welsh are followed by 'trans.'.

Throughout the research process, as I engaged with debates on qualitative and, especially, ethnographic research methods, a key point that emerged was an insistence upon research as an intersubjective 'dialogical process, which is structured [both] by the researcher and the participants' (England 1994, 80; Katz 1994). The texts written by the researcher cannot be value-free or objective, because such accounts are partial and strategic, written from ever-shifting but located positions: 'Both the ethnographer and those being studied present, represent, and invent themselves across boundaries of different subjectivities and identities, forged of class, nationality, gender, ethnicity, age, [and] sexual orientation' (Katz 1992, 496). The identity of the researcher is therefore bound up in the constitution of the research process. An objective, scientific approach would seek to eliminate any impact the researcher might have upon the research process, but increasingly such a position is being challenged: 'With greater theoretical understanding of the self, the analyst's intervention is immaterial, so long as it is clearly acknowledged and built into the analysis' (Smith 1988, 26). Evans's (1988) call for a reflexive ethnographic approach is based partly upon the need to make explicit the position of the researcher in relation to those studied, what England (1994, 80) describes as 'the relationship between the researcher and those being researched'. The researcher constantly presents and represents her/his self and the aims of the research to those being studied (Atkinson and Hammersley 1995). And this presentation is highly contextual, changing between different settings and participants (Goffman 1969).

Although ethnographers have increasingly turned to the study of their own cultures in recent years, Katz (1994, 68) suggests that 'ethnographers still generally rely on at least some displacement from home grounds to elsewhere to distinguish and differentiate the objects of their enquiries'. The researcher is therefore normally a stranger, different from those s/he studies. Jackson (1983) describes how ethnographic research can draw on differing combinations of participation and observation, with interviewing, for instance, being at the observation end of the spectrum. It is Atkinson and Hammersley's contention that the ethnographer occupies a marginal position, of being a 'simultaneous insider-outsider' (1995, 112). This

is because doing ethnographic fieldwork 'involves living simultaneously in two worlds, that of participation, and that of research'. The
researcher therefore occupies a space on the edge of the world which
s/he is studying – the position of a 'marginal' member (Jackson
1983). The relationship that one maintains with research participants therefore needs to be a balance between what Whyte (cited in
Jackson 1983) describes as familiarity and detachment. In the view
of many writers, the risk of over-identification with research subjects
is more likely than becoming too detached from the people being
studied. Jackson (1983, 41) discusses the 'problem of "over-rapport"
. . . to the extent that his [the researcher's] observational acuity is
reduced'. Atkinson and Hammersley make the crucial point that
although maintaining a marginal position in the research setting may
often be uncomfortable and stressful, it is vital to do so: 'There must
always remain some part held back, some social and intellectual
"distance". For it is in the space created by this distance that the
analytic work of the ethnographer gets done' (1995, 115). The use of
participant observation in particular entails achieving a balance in
this relationship, between participation and observation, and closeness and distance from those being studied. The researcher should
ideally occupy a position of marginality in the field of study, avoiding
over-identification or familiarity with research participants, which
could reduce a necessary analytical distance (Jackson 1983; Smith
1988).

The relationships that I negotiated with research participants and
the ways in which I positioned myself in relation to them became
central issues in my own project. One of my main concerns was that
I located myself too closely to those I was studying, and to some
extent this was bound up with my own self-identity. In one sense I
was very different from those whose lives I was researching. I was
English and had been brought up in East Anglia without any Welsh
connections at all. The key facet of my identity that tended to align
me with those I was researching was the fact that at the age of eighteen I had moved to Lampeter in mid-Wales to start a degree in
geography. It was here that I learnt Welsh, and embarked upon a
deeply personal engagement with the Welsh culture and language.
This was my key motivation for undertaking the research in London,
linked to a fascination with the displacement of these cultural
processes into London. As I go on to explain, these motivations,
and the way they were played out in the field, were not always

unproblematic. Having learnt Welsh I was very keen to use the language to improve my proficiency in it, and as a medium of the fieldwork to find out how the language was important to Welsh speakers living in London. Being able to speak Welsh was very useful, because it allowed me to read documents in the language and to understand the proceedings at meetings and chapel services. It was also useful in gaining access to situations. But I began to realize that using the language raised important issues, and it played a part in defining the relationships that I negotiated with many research participants. I often found that the fact that I spoke Welsh endeared me to people; it created a sense of trust, and endowed me with a set of credentials. Crucially, I (at least) felt that the common language created an implicit understanding, and an implicit agreement that I shared certain viewpoints expressed by those I was interviewing (at times). Occasionally this had the effect of making me uneasy about asking questions that might challenge the views of other people, though it is entirely possible that this process also worked in reverse.

But in another way, my identity as someone who had learnt the language was very helpful. I was close enough to be viewed as sympathetic and supportive (which I was). I was viewed as Welsh. But because I was English, and had learnt the language, I was able to be different, located outside the culture I was studying. I was simultaneously inside the language and outside the culture. I occupied a position on the edge of the community under study. In certain ways this position was helpful. It meant that I maintained a degree of unfamiliarity with customs, practices and traditions that Welsh speakers who had been brought up in Wales (or in London) would have known, and would not perhaps have been able to ask about. Interviewing one of the Welsh chapel ministers, for instance, I was able to ask about details of the way in which the chapel was managed:

> JS   I was going to ask – one of the things that I don't know a lot about I have to admit, is the structure of the church. There are the chapels – in theory there would be a minister for each one, but you look after them all perhaps. And the, I understand that there are elders in each chapel. Is the Henaduriaeth the next level? (trans.)

In many situations I felt that my ability to speak Welsh provided some kind of justification for my reasons for doing the research. If I was perceived at times as being Welsh, then I presumed that people would not question why I was interested in Welsh life in London; it was after all an important aspect of the national culture. Equally, if I was viewed as someone who had learnt Welsh, and made an engagement with Welsh culture, my interest in it in London was again meaningful. Some of the research settings in which I felt least comfortable were those that were English-language situations. Not only did I sound more English (and therefore more of an outsider), but I found it more difficult to gain empathy with people, and to elucidate why I was undertaking research on Welsh life in London: 'Quite a lot of people intrigued by the fact that I was from Norwich and studying Welsh life in London, and wanted to know why. Of course at this point not being able to speak Welsh to them, I came across, I suppose, as very English' (research diary, 8 September 1999). Language therefore operated simultaneously on a number of levels during my fieldwork. Firstly, it was a medium of fieldwork, used as a 'vehicle' to collect information. Secondly, it was a central aspect of the ways in which I presented myself as a researcher, and how I located myself in relation to those I was studying. Yet at the same time, it was a key aspect of the study itself; I was interested in how language was an important component of Welsh identities being worked out in London. It is to the construction of Welsh identities in London that I now turn, beginning with a consideration of how individual Welsh people in London make sense of their own self-identities.

Welsh identities away from home

Most of my research participants were Welsh people who had decided, for one reason or another, to join a Welsh society in London. One of the potential dangers in the work was reading their experiences as those of Welsh people in London as a whole. In fact, of the many thousands of Welsh people who move to live in London each year, the majority never become involved in official Welsh organizations (Jones 2001), though a great number retain more informal networks. As an ethnic group, the Welsh are perhaps one of the best integrated into London life, and among the least visible (Heald 1983). Whilst many ethnic groups (including the Irish) have tended to live in particular areas (or at the very least create links with them), the Welsh have never lived in one single area of London, and are scattered across the city (Jones 1985, 2001; Walter 1997). The result of such a demographic pattern is that Welsh societies in London are often city-wide groups, devoid of a particular local identity. This has been reinforced by the movement of a generation of established Welsh people further and further into the suburbs of the city. However, as Griffiths (2001, 172) suggests: 'It has been a characteristic of London chapels that people have generally retained their loyalty to their first association, in spite of moving to a different area and perhaps much closer to another chapel.' Welsh chapels in London therefore are often village chapels without a local, delimited parish. The London Welsh School has also successfully created a village-school atmosphere, without a surrounding village. Traditional societies and more recent social networks alike, therefore, draw their members from all parts of the city. They are also made up of Welsh people from all parts of Wales. Francis (1924) felt that this fact had helped create a nationwide unity amongst the Welsh in London:

> London's best gift to the Welsh has, perhaps, always been its power of wielding Northmen [sic] and Southerners into one solid race. No other English city has this unifying influence to the same degree . . . A mystic unity is achieved that eludes us in the rivalry of the towns of North and South [Wales]. Here, under some strange impulse of cohesion we realise that the whole is greater than the part . . . This much at least the London Welshmen [sic] have achieved – they do not damn one another *geographically*. (1924, 92–3)

While the people that I selected for my study may not be representative of the Welsh in London as a whole, their stories highlight many important issues of identity, community and belonging. For those research participants who had left Wales during the 1930s and the first decades of the post-war era, a common theme that ran through their narratives was a sense of need of the Welsh community in London when they arrived in the city. Nearly all of them had come from a culture where attending chapel and other organized community events was a major aspect of their lives, and when they arrived in London it was important for them to maintain these cultural traditions:

> And I think I told you – there was no question that the first thing you would look for on a Sunday was a Welsh chapel . . . Because you knew, what else would you do on a Sunday for God's sake, you know? It's going

to be quiet, and there will be nothing to do. Well of course there is plenty
to do in London, but you look for a Welsh chapel partly because you
always went to chapel on a Sunday, and I'd gone right through my
university life in Cardiff, and secondly I associated chapel with a place to
meet people socially. (Angharad, early sixties – migrated to London in
the 1950s)

Chapel was part of our lives . . . I'm not saying you were frogmarched,
but you haven't got much choice between the ages of five and fifteen . . .
It becomes part of your life and when you move away to a different part
of the country, I think the first thing you do is to have a sort of anchorage. Keeping this similar sort of pattern to one's life. It's less of a shock.
(Alun, early forties – moved to London in the 1980s)

Tecwyn – a man in his fifties who had moved to London with his wife
in the 1980s told me that: 'the first thing that we did after we came to
London, was search for a chapel, so that we would have some
company' (trans.). Edward (who had come to London as a young
man in the 1950s) explained how he had naturally 'gravitated'
towards a Welsh chapel when he arrived in London. And Frank (a
retired man who had come to London in the 1950s) also echoed these
sentiments: 'you had been brought up with a religious background in
Wales, and then the first thing that you did when you moved to
London was to find a Welsh chapel' (trans.).

Matthew, in his early sixties, had been born in London, and spent
some time in Wales before coming back to the metropolis as a young
man. He described how the chapel and the London Welsh Centre
helped to provide him with a sense of stability and anchorage, echo-
ing Alun's comments:

I found that the establishment of a London Welsh Club and church, and
of course the choir as far as I was concerned for many years, was a very
stabilizing factor . . . when I first came out of the army I was very very
unsettled, and I found it a great – comfort – I suppose comfort is the
word – to have these organizations which sort of planted your feet again
in the same as you came from. You know, from Wales. I mean for many
years my only language has been Welsh, and then coming up to London
it all changed. But you know, you still have this longing, don't you – this
belonging, if you like, and those three things, they certainly sort of
anchored me, you know?

In explaining why people experienced such a need for a Welsh
community, both the reasons for leaving home, and the circumstances

in which individuals found themselves in the city are crucial. Respondents who had arrived in London during the 1930s and into the post-war years often left Wales because of economic hardship, rather than a particular desire to come to the city. Not only did they sometimes suffer from feelings of loneliness and isolation, but they were frequently unable to return home at regular intervals because of the poor transport links with many parts of Wales. As Hannerz (1990) suggests, such migrants often base their lives around ethnic communities, rather than engaging more fully with the new culture that surrounds them:

> The exile . . . shifted directly from one territorial culture to another, is often no real cosmopolitan . . . for his [sic] involvement with a culture away from his homeland is something that has been forced upon him. At best, life in another country is home plus safety, or home plus freedom, but often it is not home at all. He is surrounded by foreign culture but does not immerse himself in it . . . Most ordinary labour migrants do not become cosmopolitans either. For them going away may be, ideally, home plus higher income; often the involvement with another culture is not a fringe benefit but a necessary cost, to be kept as low as possible. A surrogate home is again created with the help of compatriots, in whose circle one is encapsulated. (1990, 242–3)

While generations of Welsh migrants have been highly integrated into the economic life of London, they have often based their social and cultural lives within the Welsh community rather than looking towards the other attractions that London could offer (Jones 1985). Pooley's (1983) study of Welsh life in mid-nineteenth-century Liverpool suggests that a similar situation may have existed in other major migration destinations:

> It is . . . relevant to assess the extent to which the Welsh in Liverpool, although economically well integrated into urban life, sought to preserve elements of their own distinctive Welsh culture . . . It is clear that although well assimilated into the economic structure of the towns in north-west England, the Welsh managed to live in two culture worlds, maintaining their links with rural Wales whilst at the same time being accepted by the host society. (1983, 298–302)

Membership of institutions such as chapels and the London Welsh Centre gave newly arrived migrants a sense of stability and familiarity at a time when they would otherwise have been isolated from

Welsh culture. For many research participants (young and old), the concern to find other people who share a similar cultural and linguistic identity was expressed very clearly in the interviews conducted. Gwawr, a woman in her thirties who had been living in London for approximately ten years, explained that:

> What young Welsh people want to do, and the not so young people I would say . . . they just want to meet in groups, have a good chat with people who are from a similar background and probably speak the same language and have the same view of the world and have the same sense of humour.

She went on to express her own reasons for searching out other Welsh people in London:

> It was quite an interesting process, because for the first two years that I was in London, I did not make any Welsh connections whatsoever . . . Then I . . . decided I really had to do something about my social life and where I was going to be most socially comfortable was finding people with the same background as me, the same cultural background. So that is how I started getting involved.

People who speak the same language also come from the same cultural background, and might share a similar set of experiences or views. Again, as Hannerz (1990, 248) argues, 'trust tends to be a matter of shared perspectives'. Eleri, in her late thirties, had moved from north Wales to London in the late 1980s, and expressed such sentiments very strongly:

> *Eleri*   SWS [Social, Welsh and Sexy] has grown and grown. It is another opportunity to socialize and meet other Welsh people who speak Welsh or not (as the case may be).
>
> *JS*   What exactly is the attraction – the language, people who come from the same place?
>
> *Eleri*   Yes, people from the same kind of background as me I think. I feel that I'm Welsh, and . . . I feel more comfortable in the company of Welsh people, and in particular Welsh speakers . . . I enjoy being with Welsh people and I try to create a kind of Welsh island for myself and to some extent I have succeeded! (trans.)

What came across, also, was a sense in which many people valued their Welsh identities more in London than they had done in Wales, and that their collective societies made more of an effort to sustain cultural traditions than people back home in the country itself. Jane, who had moved to London at the beginning of the 1980s, explained that: 'when you are outside of Wales, it's likely that you feel more strongly about things like that than perhaps if you were still in Cardiff' (trans.). Alec, who had been a member of one of the Welsh Masonic Lodges in London for many years after coming up from Wales, echoed these comments:

JS   Do you think perhaps that the Welshness is stronger in your lodge than in some lodges in Wales?

Alec   Oh yes, I definitely think that. I say that a Welsh person outside of Wales is more of a Welsh person in his heart than a Welsh person in Wales. (trans.)

And he added later:

We don't want to forget the fact that our parents were Welsh – and that we were brought up in the Welsh language and also in the Welsh spirit – in the chapel and other things. That is important – the way we have been brought up. (trans.)

Constructing Welshness in London

Such societies therefore create collective identities primarily through drawing together people who share the same cultural background, and speak the same language, literally or more symbolically. Yet they also draw upon other senses of belonging, interweaving them with language and national identity to form powerful bonds of allegiance. Y Gymdeithas Hoywon, founded to create a social network for Welsh gay people in London, forges connections between national, linguistic and sexual identity, for instance. Equally, the Welsh chapels in London fuse religion with language to create a powerful sense of belonging. One of the Welsh ministers articulated this idea very clearly:

So when people came up to London from Wales, the first contact was the chapel in that period, and then following the war – come to chapel, and then, worship in Welsh, and Welshness was part of the knot, woven together. And that is what has kept the Welsh chapel going, that special relationship. (trans.)

Some respondents also spoke of the complex interrelationship between language and religion in their own personal reasons for attending chapel, and the role that it had played in maintaining the Welsh language in London:

Mari   The chapels were certainly a medium for keeping the Welsh language alive in London – that is true. But I have always said that keeping the Welsh language is not its main function; the faith is the important thing.

JS   Right – so the religion first, the language . . .

Mari   . . . the language second, but on the other hand, the Welsh churches have safeguarded the language as well.

JS   So perhaps in a way, language and religion have been quite difficult to separate, because you go for the religion, and without the religion it's not a chapel, but the chapels have done very important work in keeping the Welsh together.

Mari   Yes, yes. (trans.)

In one sense, therefore, Welsh societies in London draw upon multiple aspects of identity to create senses of belonging. But, in turn, Welsh life in the city is fragmented and cut across by these same phenomena of class, gender and, in particular, by generation. In recent years migration from Wales to London has taken new forms that have resulted in the emergence of a number of social networks which contrast sharply with an older generation of traditional societies.

New migration, new networks

The reasons that contemporary Welsh migrants have for leaving Wales often contrast markedly with those of previous generations of 'exiles'. Today, many Welsh people arriving in London are attracted by career opportunities rather than a more desperate sense of economic survival (Jones 2001), a situation mirroring the experience of Irish migration to Britain very closely (Gray 2000). Young Welsh people may choose to come to London, rather than leaving Wales from necessity. The city offers better chances of promotion, higher wages and an attractive lifestyle. The shifts in economic occupation also mean that the day-to-day lives of migrants have changed markedly. Communication links with Wales have improved greatly since the Second World War, and therefore regular visits home are within reach of most Welsh people living in London. Migrants who are employed in the financial and public relations sectors have more money, and a much better knowledge of the diverse leisure activities that London offers.

Their reasons for coming to London are also linked to issues of self-identity and lifestyle. Some research participants spoke of wanting to experience life in a big city, to broaden their horizons. Alice, who had moved to London in the early 1990s, explained that: 'I wanted, I [felt] a taste for life in a city, because I'd been brought up in the heart of the countryside – that was always there, that I wanted to live in a city' (trans.). For some interviewees, the anonymity of a city such as London allowed them the space to be who they wanted to be – to negotiate their self-identities on their own terms. Heulwen, for instance, who had been living in London for about five years told me that: 'I think that I can be more myself in London in a way, than I would if I had stayed home, especially back in Llanelli; I could never imagine moving back to Llanelli' (trans.).

This sentiment was expressed quite forcefully by a number of gay respondents. James, from north Wales, was in his late twenties and had lived in London for about ten years:

James   There is a lot of Welsh gay people up here. The vast majority of people I know are gay. It's because, I don't mean to shock you now, it's because they don't feel happy going home to Wales.

JS   So it is [as] if London offers them some kind of liberation maybe, the freedom to . . .

James   Especially Welsh speaking from small communities . . . you know I have got friends, very good friends who have moved back to Wales and now are thinking of moving back here, because they honestly have no . . . On that . . . Friday before when there was that bomb [in a pub in Soho], they had nobody to talk to about it. They phoned here . . . they didn't have any support. Whereas up here you do have support structures.

The whole background and migration experiences of such people therefore contrast strongly with those of well-established migrants who had come up from Wales in previous decades. Today's Welsh migrants have largely deserted the chapels and churches which were once key centres of Welsh life, and attendance of younger people at the London Welsh Centre has also declined (though the situation is complex and some activities do still attract large numbers of young people). In many ways, today's Welsh population in London is highly integrated into the dominant culture of the city. But what is striking is that although many younger respondents are not becoming involved in traditional Welsh institutions, they did express a need to meet other Welsh people that echoed closely the experiences of past generations of migrants. In short, they have perhaps become what Hannerz (1990) calls 'cosmopolitans'; part of a Welsh community, and simultaneously integrated into many aspects of London life. In the last decade, a number of new Welsh networks have been established which cater for this enduring need. Among the most important groups to have been formed is SWS which has grown to become the largest Welsh society in London. Of particular significance also are the Noson o Hwyl, organized by the Welsh Language Society, and Gwl@d (although Gwl@d is not specifically London-based, as stated earlier). All of them embody strong contrasts with traditional Welsh societies. And most are best conceptualized as networks (as opposed to 'societies') that link Welsh people across London in new ways, rather than being focused around central institutions.

New geographies

Traditional Welsh societies in London have acted as key centres, drawing together multiple activities under one roof, and within one organization. They are frequently focused around a central building, such as the chapel, or the London Welsh Centre, for instance. The decline of such traditional institutions and the emergence of a new breed of networks are bringing about a de-centring of Welsh life in London, and a renegotiation of the relationship between society and space. Again, the experience of the Welsh as an ethnic group in the city echoes strongly that of the Irish. Gray (2000, 71) describes 'an expansion of the points of reference for the Irish in London and a de-centring of the Catholic Church as the main focus for the Irish community', for instance. New London Welsh social networks often operate without a permanent, central base and are highly mobile, moving around the metropolis. Their main activity consists of informal social evenings, and these are frequently held in pubs and clubs scattered across the city. The link between societies and particular localities is therefore being weakened. As Hannerz (1990) suggests:

Cultures are by definition linked primarily to interactions and social relationships, and only indirectly and without logical necessity to particular areas in physical space. The less social relationships are confined within territorial boundaries, the less so is also culture: and in our time especially, we can contrast in gross terms those cultures which are territorially defined (in terms of nations, regions and localities) with those which are carried as collective structures of meaning by networks more extended in space, transnational or even global. This contrast, too – but not it alone – suggests that cultures, rather than being easily separated from one another as the hard-edged pieces in a mosaic, tend to overlap and mingle. (1990, 239)

As well as making extensive use of pubs and clubs, groups like Gwl@d and SWS also use e-mail and the Internet. Whilst the harnessing of cyberspace might be seen as having a deterritorializing effect, it simultaneously creates new centres that bring Welsh people together, thereby maintaining local identities. E-mail lists, for instance, are a highly effective and rapid way of distributing information about Welsh events in London, and communicating news about members. Crucially, e-mail and the Internet are technologies that young Welsh migrants coming to London are familiar with, and often have access to in their workplace. The use of such technologies is also creating Welsh communities that stretch beyond London, and link Welsh people in the city to other 'exiles' throughout the world. Gwl@d, for instance, connects together people who are interested in Welsh rugby (wherever they may be) through its Internet site. Its social activities in London stem from a single e-mail sent to the site's chat-board, inviting Welsh people in London out for a drink on St David's Day. Increasingly, groups such as SWS and Gwl@d are developing multiple networks in cities across the world. As Clifford (1997, 250) suggests, 'decentred, lateral connections' between different parts of a diaspora may be as important as the links that are maintained with the homeland.

Running the network

As suggested above, these new networks are highly informal, with their main activity being social events rather than more formal, structured meetings. In this respect they are, to some extent, redefining Welshness in the city, in particular removing a long-standing connection between culture and religion. Whereas social activities were one aspect of the day-to-day life of the chapels, this function becomes the key imperative for groups like SWS. Traditional societies arrange meetings – services and concerts; social networks try to create a space that people can use in their own ways – a kind of social platform. The founder of SWS explained to me that:

> The only thing that I do is to hire a room and the people entertain themselves. People mingle and find partners, find flats, find friends, find all kinds of things. But I just create a platform for them to do what they want to. (trans.)

Not only are the events themselves highly informal, but the management of the groups is also often far less structured than in the case of traditional societies. Frequently the work of arranging events falls to a small number of people, rather than extensive committees. Of the Noson o Hwyl, one of the members told me that:

> The whole thing is unofficial, you know? Nobody says to me 'Right John, do this', you know? It's me and Alun who are the main part of it really, but other people just pitch in with things as well, so there we are. Just an excuse to meet up really. I appreciate the opportunity . . . to speak a bit of Welsh . . . once a month. (trans.)

SWS has a very similar structure:

> SP . . . I decided that we didn't really need a committee. It's too Welsh anyway to have a committee – people who say and don't do, you see. So I decided to do it [SWS] once every two months, and that's what happens – so we have six nights each year.
>
> JS And is there still a committee?
>
> SP No. Well there are people who I phone, there are people who are more active than others. There are people who aren't on the committee who are active; there are people on the committee who are active. But I just use whoever is fresh and ready to give their energy at the time. Because it's me who makes the decisions anyway . . . So no, I don't believe in committees any more. (trans.)

To a large degree, therefore, traditional societies with a fixed central building, and formal meetings and organizational structures, have been replaced by informal social evenings that move around the capital, organized by a network of individuals.

Dipping in and dipping out: new ways of belonging

While the way in which these social networks are managed differs strongly from more traditional societies, those who belong to such groups also use them in different ways. In discussing the experiences of European ethnic groups in the United States, Gans (1979) highlights the emergence of an ethnic identity or symbolic ethnicity in the children and grandchildren of original migrants. Importantly, Gans suggests that this identity is characterized by a shift in attachment from cultural organizations to ethnic symbols:

> Since ethnic identity needs are neither intense nor frequent in this generation . . . ethnics do not need either ethnic cultures or organizations; instead they resort to the use of ethnic symbols . . . Identity cannot exist apart from a group, and symbols are themselves a part of culture, but ethnic identity and symbolic ethnicity require very different ethnic cultures and organizations than existed among earlier generations. (1979, 1)

While Gans's theoretical framework here refers to those people born into ethnic groups, rather than original migrants, it resonates strongly with the findings of the present study. Many young Welsh people expressed a strong sense of Welsh identity, but this was often not articulated through membership of formal organizations, or a Welsh community. The kind of involvement that such people seek to have with organized Welsh life has changed significantly. As Gwawr explained,

> All of us who are in London, or the vast majority, are working in some form of profession. We are working very hard, we work extremely long hours and we do not have the leeway to schedule in formal, formalized events.

Social events arranged by the new networks typically take place once a month, and demand little commitment in between meetings. They are an occasion on which to meet other Welsh people, to socialize and to maintain a sense of Welsh identity. Many of the groups have no formal membership lists or fees, and the people attending social events change constantly as new 'members' join while others move away.

A number of respondents also described how they had joined SWS or the Noson o Hwyl when they first arrived in London, and had later developed their own network of friends from such events, lessening the need to go along to regular social evenings. Heulwen (who expressed a strengthening of her Welsh identity since arriving in London) described her own experience in this respect: 'I don't think that I have been to a Noson o Hwyl this year . . . [The] people I have met, I tend to phone them up independently [of social events], and that is [after] six years of going regularly' (trans.). She added that:

> Sometimes I feel I want to meet new people, but I have started a new job recently, so I'm meeting a lot of new people. And a lot of people that were going to the Noson o Hwyl when I started going have left. They have left London, or they don't go as regularly, and there's a new group there . . . It's not as important . . . If I wanted to meet John, or if I wanted to see Robert, or whoever, I can phone them up, and arrange to go out for a drink or something. If I wanted to go and see a film, I could go to see a film, or a band or [have] a meal – we could do that anyway. (trans.)

The involvement that such respondents seek with organized culture therefore contrasts with the experiences of older interviewees. Another aspect of this change is that younger respondents often engage much more with mainstream culture in London; they are less a part of a self-contained Welsh community. To use Hannerz's term, they are cosmopolitans, drawing both from ethnic and host cultures:

> cosmopolitanism . . . includes a stance toward diversity itself, toward the coexistence of cultures in the individual experience . . . The cosmopolitan's surrender to the alien culture implies personal autonomy vis-à-vis the culture where he [sic] originated from. He has obvious competence with regard to it, but he can choose to disengage from it. He possesses it, but it does not possess him. (1990, 239–40)

Hannerz's comments here echo Gray's (2000) exploration of contemporary Irish identities in London. What emerges strongly from the notion of the 'cosmopolitan' in the work of both authors, is a sense of self-identity being constructed through multiple places and attachments:

> Most of those who took part in my research articulated a cosmopolitan sense of identity in London which related to what they described as their exposure to and experience of diverse cultures and identities . . . Their sense of themselves as Irish therefore, had a multi-located dimension that

involved reference to both Ireland and England/London and everyday practices that involved bridging the gap between these places, both culturally and emotionally. (2000, 76)

Gwawr echoed these comments in relation to the Welsh in London:

I think maybe a big difference that I pick up from people who are a generation above me – in their fifties and sixties – is that they did see themselves as a community. Maybe they were less engaged in London culture and more engaged in Welsh culture and I think that the balance has shifted in that most younger Welsh people in London now have a spread of friends and a spread of social life and they do not orientate themselves always back to London Welsh people or Welsh people.

Many younger respondents described how taking part in social evenings formed one aspect of their lives, set within a wider range of activities, rather than being an overarching diary of events. Kate, who had attended SWS on several occasions, felt that this might indicate a sense of abandonment of their Welsh culture between meetings: 'I mean all those people will walk out of SWS and probably not think about it until the next month and they probably have very anglicized lifestyles.' For such people, therefore, a sense of belonging to a Welsh community has shifted significantly. A kind of deinstitutionalization has occurred whereby many Welsh people do not define their Welshness primarily through membership of formal organizations. And secondly, Welsh 'exiles' in London are increasingly living identities that are multiply located, and not bounded by a sense of an overarching Welsh community.

Conclusion

In my own research, issues of self-identity were important in defining both the relationships that I negotiated as a researcher and the theoretical focus of the project itself. For many of the Welsh people I interviewed who were living in London, membership of societies or networks is important in allowing them to maintain their cultural traditions and negotiate their self-identities. Despite the differences in experiences between generations of Welsh migrants, the need to meet others who share a similar identity, and who speak 'the same language', is an enduring one. For established migrants who came to London in the 1930s and the early post-war decades, membership of the Welsh community was often a natural step, and one taken out of a feeling of necessity. Far away from home, Welsh societies offered stability and familiarity, lessening feelings of isolation and loneliness. Such migrants' lives often revolved around the Welsh community, which provided them with an overarching diary of events.

In recent years, both the nature of collective Welsh life in London, and the ways in which individuals buy into it, have changed. New social networks are redefining the nature of community and the construction of what Welshness might mean away from home. Decentred and mobile, such networks move around the city, rather than taking place within a fixed central building. Often footloose, and frequently operating as much in cyberspace as on the ground, in some ways they loosen the attachment between particular societies and local territories. Many of them are part of wider networks that connect Welsh 'exiles' in major cities around the world. Yet equally, Internet and e-mail technologies play a part in binding Welsh people in London together, sustaining more local identities. Many of the more recent migrants interviewed expressed a very strong sense of Welsh identity. But this identity is not worked out primarily through membership of a separate, all-encompassing Welsh community. New social networks allow people to continue to meet other 'exiles', but on a very different basis. For migrants who are highly integrated into and involved with London life, new Welsh networks can be dipped into as a strategic resource. Such changes in the nature of Welsh life suggest a redefinition of community into more flexible forms. And they point also to the ways in which our identities are constantly negotiated through attachments to multiple positions and places.

This chapter is based upon Ph.D. research funded by the University of Wales Swansea and the Economic and Social Research Council. I would like to thank both sponsors for their support. Thanks are also due to Charlotte Davies, Stephanie Jones and Pyrs Gruffudd for their helpful comments and advice. I am indebted to all of the research participants in London who shared their experiences with me.

References

Atkins, P. J. (1977). 'London's intra-urban milk supply – circa 1790–1914', *Transactions of the Institute of British Geographers*, 2, 383–99.

Atkinson, P. and Hammersley, M. (1995). *Ethnography: Principles in Practice* (London: Routledge and Kegan Paul).

Bartholomew, K. (1991). 'Women migrants in mind – leaving Wales in the mid-nineteenth century', in C. G. Pooley and I. D. Whyte (eds.), *Migrants, Emigrants and Immigrants: A Social History* (London: Routledge).

Becken, P. and Jones, S. (1985). *Dragon in Exile: The Centenary History of the London Welsh RFC* (London: Springwood).

Beddoe, D. (1988). 'Women between the wars', in T. Herbert and G. E. Jones (eds.), *Wales Between the Wars* (Cardiff: University of Wales Press), pp. 129–60.

Clifford, J. (1997). *Routes: Travel and Translation in the Late Twentieth Century* (London: Harvard University Press).

Clwyd, H. (1987). *Buwch ar y Lein: Detholiad o Ddyddiaduron Llundain 1957–1964* (Cardiff: Honno).

David, T. (1991). 'The rise and fall of the London Welsh', *Planet*, 85, 56–62.

Ellis, T. I. (1971). *Crwydro Llundain* (Swansea: Christopher Davies).

England, K. V. L. (1994). 'Getting personal: reflexivity, positionality, and feminist research', *Professional Geographer*, 46, 1.

Evans, M. (1988). 'Participant observation – the researcher as research tool', in J. Eyles and D. Smith (eds.), *Qualitative Research Methods in Human Geography* (London: Polity).

Francis, J. O. (1924). *The Legend of the Welsh and Other Papers* (Cardiff and London: Education Publishing Company).

Francis-Jones, G. (1984). *Cows, Cardis and Cockneys* (Borth: Gwyneth Francis-Jones).

Gans, H. (1979). 'Symbolic ethnicity: the future of ethnic groups and cultures in America', *Ethnic and Racial Studies*, 2, 1–21.

Goffman, E. (1969). *The Presentation of Self in Everyday Life* (London: Penguin).

Gray, B. (2000). 'From "ethnicity" to "diaspora": 1980s emigration and "multicultural" London', in A. Bielenburg (ed.), *The Irish Diaspora* (Harlow: Pearson Education).

Griffiths, R. (2001). 'The Lord's song in a strange land', in E. Jones (ed.), *The Welsh in London 1500–2000* (Cardiff: University of Wales Press).

Hannerz, U. (1990). 'Cosmopolitanism and locals in world culture', *Theory, Culture and Society*, 7, 237–51.

Heald, T. (1983). *Networks* (London: Hodder and Stoughton).

Jackson, P. (1983). 'Principles and problems of participant observation', *Geografiska Annaler*, Series B, 65, 39–46.

Jones, E. (1981). 'The Welsh in London in the seventeenth and eighteenth centuries', *Welsh History Review*, 10, 4, 461–79.

—— (1985). 'The Welsh in London in the nineteenth century', *Cambria*, 12, 1, 149–69.

—— (1996). 'The Welsh in London (part 2)', *Yr Enfys*, Winter 1996–7, 4–6.

—— (ed.) (2001). *The Welsh in London 1500–2000* (Cardiff: University of Wales Press).

Jones, M. (1946). *They Passed Through: A Brief Narrative of the Work of the Welsh Services Club, 1941–1946* (Conway: R.E Jones and Brothers).

Katz, C. (1992). 'All the world is staged: intellectuals and the projects of ethnography', *Environment and Planning D: Society and Space*, 10, 495–510.

—— (1994). 'Playing the field: questions of fieldwork in geography', *Professional Geographer*, 46, 1, 67–72.

Knowles, A. K. (1997). *Calvinists Incorporated: Welsh Immigrants on Ohio's Industrial Frontier* (Chicago: University of Chicago Press).

Linehan, D. (1998). 'An archaeology of dereliction – poetics and policy in the governing of depressed industrial districts in inter-war England and Wales', (unpublished manuscript).

Morgan, P. and Thomas, D. (1984). *Wales: The Shaping of a Nation* (Newton Abbot: David and Charles).

Owen, A. D. K. (1937). 'The social consequences of industrial transference', *Sociological Review*, 24, 4, 331–54.

Owen, M. (1989). *Tros y Bont: Hanes Eglwys Falmouth Road, Llundain* (London: Eglwys Jewin).

Owen, W. T. (ed.) (1989). *Capel Elfed* (London: Eglwys y Tabernacl, Kings Cross).

Philo, C. (1995). 'Animals, geography and the city: notes on inclusions and exclusions', *Environment and Planning D: Society and Space*, 13, 6, 655–82.

Pooley, C. (1983). 'Welsh migration to England in the mid-nineteenth century', *Journal of Historical Geography*, 9, 3, 287–306.

Smith, D. (1993). *Aneurin Bevan and the World of South Wales* (Cardiff: University of Wales Press).

Smith, S. (1988). 'Constructing local knowledges – the analysis of self in everyday life', in J. Eyles and D. Smith (eds.), *Qualitative Research Methods in Human Geography* (London: Polity).

Walter, B. (1997). 'Contemporary Irish settlement in London – women's voices, men's worlds', in J. Mac Loughlin (ed.), *Location and Dislocation in Contemporary British Society* (Cork: Cork University Press).

—— (1999). 'Inside and outside the pale: diaspora experiences of Irish Women', in P. Boyle and K. Halfacree (eds.), *Migration and Gender in the Developed World* (London: Routledge).

Whyte, W. F. (1995). *Street Corner Society* (London and Chicago: University of Chicago Press).

Williams-Davies, J. (1978). '"Merched y Gerddi" – mudwyr tymhorol o Geredigion', *Cylchgrawn Cymdeithas Hynafiaethwyr Ceredigion*, 8, 3, 291–303.

Internet sites

SWS – www.swsuk.com

Gwl@d – www.gwladrugby.com

10 Conclusions: reflecting on Welsh communities

Charlotte Aull Davies and Stephanie Jones

Community: theoretical deficiencies, empirical vitality

We began this volume by considering the deficiencies in the concept of community as a theoretical construct. Theorizing about community has long been closely linked to Tönnies's (1955) *Gemeinschaft/ Gesellschaft* distinction between the kinds of social relationships prevailing in pre-industrial societies (personal, lifelong, multifaceted) and those found in industrial societies (impersonal, transient, single-purpose). Many classic community studies, while purporting to test this hypothesis, were in effect simply reproducing examples of it, with minimal critical examination of its applicability on the ground. Researchers in industrial societies sought, and found, community in those areas believed to have been left behind by the processes of industrialization – for example, in the rural peripheries of state societies. Subsequently they were rather more surprised to discover community in some industrial working-class areas and other urban neighbourhoods. But they were not surprised by the nature of these communities. Working from within this Tönnies-inspired theoretical paradigm meant accepting assumptions of community boundedness and integrity, as well as homogeneity and stability. Any characteristics to the contrary were interpreted as signs of community breakdown, regarded as inevitable in any case, since influences from outside – that is, from the surrounding industrial society – were bound to be destabilizing and to undermine community. Communities by definition were clearly-bounded social systems that were hegemonic over some specified locality and its inhabitants.

Given this perspective, community studies could not provide much in the way of analytical generalization. The prospect of learning more about the social processes at work in communities was essentially foreclosed by a theoretical perspective that presupposed such processes would operate to maintain them as homogeneous, integrated and comparatively harmonious social units. Statistical generalization – even in the unlikely event that a society was shown to be composed of a multitude of essentially similar communal units – was uninformative about macro-level social processes and hence unable to provide any enlightenment about the nature of this larger society. In essence, the concept of community was not theoretically useful because it gave virtually no scope for effective criticism or the development of any understanding of social processes beyond Tönnies's original conception. Community studies, to the extent that they operated within this paradigm, could do little more than produce examples of the continued existence of communities, that is, localities with *Gemeinschaft*-type relationships, along with reports of the degree to which they were being threatened or undermined by the forces of industrialization that surrounded them. Communities were viewed as temporarily successful survivors from a previous social order destined eventually to be overcome. This perception by social researchers both echoed and reinforced the concern frequently voiced by other commentators on the nature of modern society, who bemoaned the loss of close supportive communities that were believed to characterize a previous age. In fact it is possible to find examples in Western social thought expressing such concerns virtually from biblical times onwards (Wellman 1999, 3–6).

It is not at all surprising, therefore, that the concept of community has been severely criticized as an essentially uninformative theoretical concept. Either a given collectivity in a specified locality can be said to exhibit the kinds of social relationships that constitute community, in which case there is little beyond the descriptive that can be said about them, or, to the degree that they deviate from these ideal relationships, they are exhibiting community breakdown whose ultimate cause is to be found in the pressures from an external modern industrial society or, more recently, from forces of globalization (cf. Robins 1991). Given the serious weaknesses of the theoretical perspective to which it is tied, the resilience of the concept of community is quite remarkable and is mainly due to the mass of empirical evidence of its importance to ordinary people.

> Wherever they have looked, researchers have found thriving communities. This is so well documented that there is no longer any scholarly need to demonstrate that community ties exist everywhere, although the alarmed public, politicians, and pundits need to be constantly reassured

and re-educated. But there is a pressing need to understand what kinds of community flourish, what communities do – and do not do – for people, and how communities operate in different social systems. (Wellman 1999, 2)

Thus in spite of the critique which meant that the concept of community was out of favour with social theorists for decades, the concept continued to be significant and useful for much social research. Certainly researchers working in disciplinary traditions – anthropology being prominent among them – which emphasize real people's lives, research 'on the ground' and the perspectives of research subjects, have continued to pay heed to the communities to which people say they belong, at least to frame their research, even if the nature of such communities is not always their primary focus.

Policy makers have also utilized the concept of community in a sometimes cynical recognition of its positive connotations for most people. Indeed, one of the major weaknesses of 'care in the community' has been its uncritical assumption of the classical concept of community as pre-existing in a given locality, whether rural village or urban neighbourhood, and encompassing all those within that locality in a set of mutually supportive social relationships. Under this assumption, the major provisions necessary to ensure care for individuals requiring it were ensuring that those who were already in a community could remain there, and establishing small (usually residential) units in order to place others in communities, so that they too could benefit from community social ties while also making use of local resources and services. Much of the critique of care in the community has been based upon exposing this naive version of the nature of community. In particular, critics have pointed to internal divisions that mean the burden of care is not shared but falls on a few individuals (e.g. Glendinning 1983), usually women (Dalley 1988; Brown and Smith 1989). Furthermore, the nature of belonging to communities is always problematic, implying criteria for exclusion as well as inclusion, and those most in need of community support may be least well equipped to ensure their own acceptance and full participation (Davies 1998, 121). Nevertheless much really useful research, far from discarding the concept of community care, has problematized it. Wenger (1991), for example, examined the reasons why community seems to exist, in the sense of providing back-up care, for some and not for others. In the process she uncovered, and began to account for differences in personal networks which were seen to be a fundamental component of communities and essential to the analysis of their effectiveness as loci for care provision.

Characterizing communities

This approach to community, when interpreted more broadly, is the one that we advocate and have adopted in this volume. Community is not a theoretically pure concept; and we make no attempt to provide an integrated definition of it. However, even though it is not possible to specify the types of collectivities that may be seen as, or see themselves as, constituting communities, we recognize that it is an idea with empirical meanings for our informants and one which influences their social relationships and social actions.

> Community ties may be structured around links between people with common residence, common interests, common attachments or some other shared experience generating a sense of belonging. In each case competing definitions of 'community' are constructed, yet while the numerous meanings of 'community' are contested . . . there is no doubt that the communities of which we are members play a significant role in shaping our social identities and patterns of action. (Crow and Allan 1994, 1)

Thus, characterizations of communities such as those offered in this volume need to concern themselves with two broad aspects of community: the kinds of social networks that make them up, whether widely dispersed, open personal networks or more densely overlapping and bounded networks; and the symbolic constructions that also constitute communities (Cohen 1985), linking them to ideas of belonging and to personal identities.

These two aspects vary in their relative significance in different communities and have to be investigated empirically, and this has been the approach of the contributors to this volume. In the chapters in Section 1, in which the community is readily associated with a particular locality, the networks tend to be comparatively dense and interlocking. But contributors report indications of internal differentiation and even schisms: between men and women (Jones); between incomers and locals (James); and even within a single family (O'Neill). At the same time, they explore the meanings of community – the ways in which it is constructed – in these localities. Jones discusses a re-creation of community in spite of economic factors that have virtually totally destroyed its material basis for integration. James, in contrast, shows how an ideal of community, based more on external perceptions than socio-economic reality, is used as a kind of cultural capital to control access to networks and institutions. Murphy's community was essentially called into existence as an effective media representation of a disparate collectivity facing a common legal battle for their homes. And O'Neill reports on a community whose perception of its own dissolution far exceeds the reality. The contributors to Section 2 consider communities based on more dispersed networks and look at issues of belonging and personal identity. Philpin provides an example of a rural village in which the personal networks of traditional healers serve as a powerful medium for incorporation (or reincorporation) of individuals into the community. Furthermore, participation in these healing practices (in the sense of knowledge and acceptance of them) forms an important cultural component of the symbolic construction that defines this community, one that clearly can be used to differentiate as well as to incorporate. In contrast, the farming community in west Wales, which might be assumed to be based primarily in interlocking personal networks, is shown by Hutson to be deeply influenced and currently seriously undermined by the constructions of it originating from outside. In particular, the personal identities of farmers appear to be compromised by the external cultural critique of the purpose and meaning of farming. Williams, in contrast, finds that the personal identities of vegetarians and 'alternatives' in a west Wales village are closely tied to their participation in a critiqué of the food-consumption practices prevailing in the wider society. At the same time, their own food beliefs and eating habits are much more variable than is commonly assumed, as are their links – through both social networks and cultural congruencies – to the locality-based community of Newport. Segrott's chapter documents the transformation of a Welsh immigrant community in London from one that was organized spatially around several localities to one that exists in cyberspace, dependent on new communication technologies for the maintenance of its networks. Clearly, this research suggests a new direction for the study of communities and demonstrates that they can be facilitated as well as weakened by globalizing forces and technologies (cf. du Gay 1997).

Future directions

This volume has investigated empirically varied manifestations and meanings of community in Wales, with all contributions being based on recent ethnographic research. It encompasses many of the significant axes found in Welsh society and addresses a range of contemporary issues. Thus individual chapters concentrate on communities in rural Wales, in the Valleys, and in urban and suburban areas. Three contributors are concerned with migration: of these three, two discuss the effects of incomers on small Welsh communities, one taking this as her main focus, the other considering it peripherally; and the third looks at Welsh immigrants to London. Two other contributors consider the crises in the farming community and in the socially and economically deprived communities of former centres of heavy industry. Nevertheless, since one of the purposes of this volume – and of Anthropology Wales in whose annual conferences most of these papers were first discussed – is to encourage the anthropological and/or ethnographic study of Welsh society and culture, we want particularly to draw attention in our conclusions to areas and issues that are not included here and that we believe should be identified for future research of this nature.

Perhaps the most obvious gap is in the geographical coverage of Wales. Most of the research presented in this volume was conducted in south or west Wales, with two exceptions, a contribution from mid-Wales and one from London. Clearly, work in the north and east would provide significant new insights and a fuller picture of the range of Welsh communities. In addition, the insights resulting from Segrott's research argue strongly for further ethnographic work on the Welsh diaspora, the Welsh-American community, for example (cf. Jones 1993 for a historical treatment of this community). Another omission, and a very important area for future research, is that of Wales's ethnic minority communities. Aside from some of the publications of Charlotte Williams (e.g. 1995), based mainly on her own autobiographical observations, we know of no recent published ethnographic work in these communities. However, there is at least one project currently under way in Swansea, a re-study based on the Rosser and Harris (1965) study of family and social change, which incorporates substantial ethnographic research in four Swansea communities, one of which was selected primarily because of its large ethnic population (Charles 2000).

One failing common to community studies and ethnographic research more generally has been a tendency to focus on collectivities which are more peripheral, less powerful, further down the social hierarchy, rather than to 'research up'. One reason for this is the comparative difficulty of obtaining access to social and political elites, especially for purposes of long-term and in-depth ethnographic research. Nevertheless, this is an area that is ripe for such research in Wales and elsewhere. Keeping in mind possible comparisons with the Welsh immigrant community in London, research among the Welsh-speaking community of Cardiff, many of whom have moved to the capital from rural north and west Wales to take up positions in the media and the Welsh bureaucracy, is long overdue and potentially very valuable. Certainly this collectivity is widely remarked upon and speculated about in the media and elsewhere, and it would be a benefit to public debate if such speculation could be informed by empirically based analysis. Another network-based community, overlapping but by no means coterminous with Cardiff's Welsh-speaking community, is that composed of the higher-grade civil servants in the Welsh bureaucracy centred on the Welsh Office and, more recently, the National Assembly. Very little is known of this professional community, certainly not from an ethnographic perspective – its composition; the interrelationships, both formal and informal, through which it functions; its internal culture; and how it perceives its relationship with the Welsh polity. A recent anthropological study of the European Union – Cris Shore's (2000) *Building Europe: The Cultural Politics of European Integration* – is based on extensive ethnographic research among European Commission civil servants in Brussels and provides both a stimulus and a model for a similar study in Cardiff.

Shore's main focus in this research is to discover how this European elite is attempting to solve the problem of legitimacy stemming from 'the fact that the "European public", or *demos*, barely exists as a recognisable category, and hardly at all as a subjective or *self-recognising* body' (2000, 19). Clearly this question bears close resemblance to the question of the historical development of national consciousness and the creation of national communities, for which the anthropological perspective of Anderson (1983) in developing the concept of nations as imagined communities has provided one of the most influential theoretical metaphors for the study of national identity in recent decades. Many of the same issues, albeit on an

altered scale and in a different context, of the creation of a national
consciousness and a self-recognizing civic community in Wales,
which Shore addresses for the EU, are relevant for processes
currently under way with regard to the National Assembly for Wales.
There is some research addressing these issues, expressed mainly in
terms of assessing the success or otherwise of the Assembly's professed
goal of inclusivity (e.g. Chaney et al. 2000; Chaney and Fevre 2001).
However, very little is available that approaches the issue from the
perspective of cultural politics, or utilizes ethnographic research
based on an empirical approach to the question of community to
explore how (or whether) a Welsh national community is currently
being re-imagined, and what role the National Assembly and the
emerging bureaucratic elite may be playing in this process.

Such a study of this metaphorical or imagined community, looking
at the two aspects of social networks and symbolic constructions that
have been pursued for other communities in this volume, would
surely make an important contribution to the emerging body of
social analysis in and on Welsh society. And the study of community
at all levels, when the concept is appropriately problematized and
empirically investigated, offers great potential for future research.

References

Anderson, B. (1983) *Imagined Communities* (London: Verso).
Brown, H. and Smith, H. (1989) 'Whose "ordinary" life is it anyway?',
  Disability, Handicap and Society, 4, 2, 105–19.
Chaney, P., Hall, T. and Dicks, B. (2000) 'Inclusive governance? The case of
  "minority" and voluntary sector groups and the National Assembly for
  Wales', *Contemporary Wales*, 13, 203–29.
Chaney, P. and Fevre, R. (2001) 'Ron Davies and the cult of "inclusiveness":
  devolution and participation in Wales', *Contemporary Wales*, 14,
  21–49.
Charles, N. (2000) 'Social change, family formation and kin relationships'
  (R000238454, unpublished research proposal, funded by the ESRC).
Cohen, A. P. (1985). *The Symbolic Construction of Community* (London:
  Routledge).
Crow, G. and Allan, G. (1994). *Community Life: An Introduction to Local
  Social Relations* (New York: Harvester Wheatsheaf).
Dalley, G. (1988) *Ideologies of Caring: Rethinking Community and
  Collectivism* (Basingstoke: Macmillan).

Davies, C. A. (1998) 'Caring communities or effective networks? Community care and people with learning difficulties in south Wales', in I. R. Edgar and A. Russell (eds.), *The Anthropology of Welfare* (London: Routledge).

du Gay, P. (ed.) (1997) *Production of Culture/Cultures of Production* (London: Sage/Open University).

Glendinning, C. (1983) *Unshared Care: Parents and Their Disabled Children* (London: Routledge and Kegan Paul).

Jones, W. D. (1993) *Wales in America: Scranton and the Welsh, 1860–1920* (Cardiff: University of Wales Press).

Robins, K. (1991) 'Tradition and translation: national culture in its global context', in J. Corner and S. Harvey (eds.), *Enterprise and Heritage: Crosscurrents of National Culture* (London: Routledge).

Rosser, C. and Harris, C. (1965). *The Family and Social Change: A Study of Family and Kinship in a South Wales Town* (London: Routledge and Kegan Paul).

Shore, C. (2000) *Building Europe: The Cultural Politics of European Integration* (London: Routledge).

Tönnies, F. (1955 [1887]). *Community and Association* (London: Routledge and Kegan Paul).

Wellman, B. (1999). 'The network community: an introduction', in B. Wellman (ed.), *Networks in the Global Village: Life in Contemporary Communities* (Boulder, Colorado: Westview), pp. 1–47.

Wenger, G. C. (1991) 'A network typology: from theory to practice', *Journal of Ageing Studies*, 5, 2, 147–62.

Williams, C. (1995) 'Race and racism: some reflections on the Welsh context', *Contemporary Wales*, 8, 113–31.

Personal Names Index

Subject Index